Goodbye

Wifes and

Daughters

University of Nebraska Press | Lincoln and London

Susan Kushner Resnick

Goodbye
Wifes and
Daughters

Library of Congress Cataloging-in-Publication Data
Resnick, Susan Kushner.
Goodbye wifes and daughters / Susan Kushner
Resnick.
p. cm.   Includes bibliographical references.
ISBN 978-0-8032-1784-3 (cloth : alk. paper)
1. Bearcreek (Mont.)—History—20th century.
2. Bearcreek (Mont.)—Social conditions—20th
century. 3. Coal mine accidents—Montana—
Bearcreek—History—20th century. 4. Coal mine
accidents—Social aspects—Montana—Bearcreek
—History—20th century. 5. Coal miners—
Montana—Bearcreek—History—20th century.
6. Wives—Montana—Bearcreek—Biography.
7. Women—Montana—Bearcreek—Biography.
8. Disasters—Psychological aspects—Case studies.
9. Bearcreek (Mont.)—Biography. 10. Coal
mines and mining—Montana—Safety measures—
History—20th century. I. Title.
F739.B36R7 2010   978.6'652032—dc22
2009030035

Set in Monotype Bulmer by Kim Essman.
Designed by A. Shahan.

To David, the best husband a writer could have.

Once in the 40s

We were alone one night on a long
road in Montana. This was in winter, a big
night, far to the stars. We had hitched,
my wife and I, and left our ride at
a crossing to go on. Tired and cold — but
brave — we trudged along. This, we said,
was our life, watched over, allowed to go
where we wanted. We said we'd come back some time
when we got rich. We'd leave the others and find
a night like this, whatever we had to give,
and no matter how far, to be so happy again.

WILLIAM STAFFORD

Contents

Acknowledgments

Why is the author's family always thanked at the end of the acknowledgments? Not this time. I thank David, Carrie, and Max for everything they did to make this book possible: observing that "someone should write a book about that," as we waited for our steaks at the Bearcreek Saloon; picking actors and actresses to star in the movie; and allowing me, without complaint, to abandon my mothering post so I could gather this story. I love you three more than anyone in the world.

For helping to bring this book to the public, I thank my agent, Wendy Strothman, who saw the women's story as I did and believed in its worth; my editor, Heather Lundine, who won me over when she told me that the story made her cry; Rhonda Winchell, who often kept me from crying; copyeditor Jonathan Lawrence, who taught me to think with more precision; and Leslie Rubinkowski, who contributed wisdom and support on writing and fashion.

The friends and families of the miners were astonishingly welcoming and forthcoming with their painful stories. I am especially indebted to Bob Wakenshaw, for giving me all the facts I needed, but more importantly, for giving me his friendship; to Wayne Freeman, for being bold enough to explore the mine buildings with me and for escorting me up the Beartooth Highway; to Denny Becker, for urging me to pay attention to the abandoned mine buildings and poignant cemetery when I drove through Bearcreek; to Dan Gainer and Burt Douthit of the Olcott Funeral Chapel, for giving me so many leads; to Bob Oxner, for being calm enough to keep me from panicking inside the Bull Mountain mine; to Jim Beadle, for providing copies of all the official pre- and post-disaster reports; to Karen Bjork, archivist extraordinaire of the Montana Historical Society, for being able to find anything that still exists; to Oakla Oleinik, for bringing her father back to life for me; and to Jeff McNeish, for answering so many questions, confirming so many theories, and generously sharing so much information. Your great-grandfather would be proud of you. Finally, for opening your wounded hearts and lovely homes to me, I thank Thelma Mourich Bischoff, Virginia Sommerville Casey, Gil Sommerville, Marlene Sudar Reed, and Doris Anderson Spaulding.

Also, thanks to the following people, several of whom have passed on since I interviewed them: Jonna Adams, Nathan Adams, Mari Aguirre, Andy Anderson, Linda Anderson, Evelyn Bateman, Louis Barovich, Mike Barovich, Joe Basone, Sally Becker, Jane Laird Biestek, Louise Van Black, Marlene Freeman Bradford, Melody E. Bragg of the National Mine Health and Safety Academy, James Brophy, Luba Barovich Brown, Alec Cameron, Margaret Meiklejohn Cameron, Gary Cline, Phyllis Cortner, Lynn and Pits DeArmond, John DeMichiei, Frank and LuDon Deville, Pearl Deville, Olga Marinchek DiPasquale, Linda Dutcher, Tom Ennes, Scott Faulkner, Carol Feist, Tom Flaherty, Winnie Freeman, Rita Gibson of the State Law Library of Montana, Sam Giovetti, Art Halpin, Peggy Hatfield, Jim Herbal, Marilyn Muller Hobbs, Mrs. Henry Hodnik, Leo Hodnik, Josie Germanetti Horton, Bill Houtonen, Pete Jovanovich, Norma Besinque Johnson, Leo Jordan, Lewis Jordan, Dorothy Lindsay Jorgenson, Ray Kotar, Joe Lester of the National Weather Service (Billings, Montana), Leslie Linn, Clem Lodge, John Mance, Katrina Wilson Martin of the State Law Library of Montana, Magi Malone, Jody Martinez of the *Ukiah Daily Journal*, John Maxwell, Robert Mc-

Donald, Marlene Mourich Matranga, Jessie Cameron Mourich, Lou Mourich, Sam Mourich, Jane McKee, Jack McNeish, Bob Moran, John Muller, Ray Mus, Vince Mus, Mike Naglich, Don Nordstrom, Jerry Nordstrom, Jane O'Donnell, Jennie Starkovich Pasek, Dale Pelo, Marvin Pelo, Frank and Linda Planichek, George Plank, John Plank, Jim Quigel of the Historical Collections and Labor Archives at Penn State University, Bonnie Ransdell, Marion Reid, Mary Reid, Paul Reid, Willard Reid, Dorothy Williams Repac, Kevin Richardson, James Saastamoinen, Josephine Meyer Schwartz, Wilma Shupak, Mary Smith, Charles Thom, Glenn Tjeltveit, Jeanne Wakenshaw, Betty Waters, and Julie Yanchisin.

Introduction

Bearcreek, Montana, used to be wild. In the 1920s, when it was still new, there were eleven saloons. Eleven saloons and not one church. It was a town of brothels and fistfights and rollicking parties to celebrate brides brought over from the old country. The miners worked and drank and worked some more, surviving on the miles of coal spread under the mountains. Some called it a coal camp, but it was different from the others. Montana Coal and Iron, the firm that owned the area's largest mine, didn't rule the community—there was no company store that the miners were forced to patronize, no company-owned houses they had to live in. The residents of Bearcreek were free to shop and sleep where they wanted. There were two hotels, rows of profitable businesses, a hospital, and a bank. People said it was a little slice of utopia, this village that sprouted up in the middle of vast natural beauty.

Bearcreek is wild today, too, but in a different way. Now, the sagebrush grows tall on hillsides once congested with streets and houses, the places where the miners held those parties and the shopkeepers laid out their shoes and skillets. Horses wander through hollowed-out mine buildings that have disintegrated in the decades since the tragedy that cut off the town's blood supply. During its glory days, almost two thousand people lived in Bearcreek. On Election Day in 2005, thirty-three voters reelected the mayor, a man named Pits who also happens to own the only saloon still in business. One saloon, with pig races that give tourists and travel writers a reason to come to town, but still, after all these years, no church. No hotels or hospital or bank, either, and the closest store is a little quilt shop. It's technically located in Washoe, a twenty-one-resident village up the road from Bearcreek that was established enough, until the 1950s, to have its own grammar school and post office. But now Washoe blurs into Bearcreek and its tenuous hold on an identity. The cemetery on the hill is arguably Bearcreek's most populated spot.

The people who remain and those who speak fondly of the Bearcreek they once knew refuse to call it a ghost town. But almost all of them will admit this: Bearcreek was killed, as surely as if it had been flattened by an earthquake or burned by a wildfire. Cause of death: the worst coal mine disaster in Montana's history. The 1943 disaster killed 75 men, leaving 58 widows and 125 fatherless children. Since that day, there have only been three underground coal mine disasters in the United States that have killed more men. But none of those destroyed a community. By the time the disaster struck, Bearcreek had segued from Wild West rowdy to Norman Rockwell wholesome. Fewer people lived there, but it had become the quintessential all-American hometown. After the disaster, it was broken and nearly empty. Utopia? Never again.

The first time I heard about Bearcreek, I didn't even know its name. A gray-bearded former river guide who owned a bed-and-breakfast in Wyoming gave me one piece of advice about visiting Montana. On a particular road, he told me, there's an abandoned coal mine. *Make sure you stop and look at it*, he urged. *And on the other side of the road, there's a cemetery with photos of the miners embedded in some of the gravestones. Very moving.*

It sounded interesting, though I was actually dreading the trip from his nurturing hideaway in the Grand Tetons to Montana. I just wanted to skip the whole state completely.

I'd come West from my New England home in 2005 with fresh loss dominating my life. A good friend who'd never smoked had died way too young from lung cancer. An even younger neighbor had died in his sleep while on a business trip. And most traumatic of all, my mother had died, suddenly and unexpectedly, at sixty-nine. She'd had a fairly rare lung disease called pulmonary fibrosis, but it hadn't curbed her life until she fainted one day, landed in the hospital the next, then suffocated to death less than a week later. She didn't suffer, a nurse told me, because she lost consciousness before she stopped breathing. Just like the Bearcreek miners as they lay on the ground in the mine and faded out. *They didn't suffer*, people still say, *they just went to sleep*.

Three months after my mother died, I flew across the country with my family for a long-planned national parks vacation. I didn't want to go. I wanted to stay home, staring and sighing until I felt better. I tried to cut the trip short and cancel the Montana leg. The Grand Tetons and Yellowstone National Park seemed doable; Montana—so foreign to someone who grew up in Rhode Island—seemed overwhelming.

The only reason we'd added Montana to the itinerary was to drive the Beartooth Highway, a gorgeous sixty-eight-mile road of hairpin turns that climbs through the mountains leading from Yellowstone to southeastern Montana. Charles Kuralt, who hosted the TV show *On the Road*, christened the highway the most scenic drive in America. But before we took the trip, we learned that for the first time in its sixty-nine-year history, the highway had been closed for the summer due to mudslides. Well, I thought, now there really was no point in hitting Montana. I looked into canceling hotel reservations and changing plane flights, but with all the fees and phone calls required, those chores became paralyzing as well. I gave in to Montana.

We found an alternate route from Yellowstone and landed in Red Lodge, the town at the end of the Beartooth Highway. Also a former mining town, Red Lodge has fared much better than Bearcreek. Because of the highway, it's been a tourist destination for decades. Its main drag consists of upscale restaurants and gift shops filled with the kind of treasures you only buy on vacation: chokecherry lip gloss, cowboy cookbooks, whistles carved from antlers. These bobble markets share sidewalk space with a few biker bars, some real estate offices, and a thrillingly comprehensive penny candy arcade. A few minutes outside downtown, there's a wild animal sanctuary where injured or abandoned wolves, mountain lions, and other normally fierce beasts heal and live in peace. Our kids played with a baby bobcat that lived in the director's office. It was one of the highlights of our vacation, and the most exciting activity we found in Red Lodge.

We asked the waitress at our hotel's restaurant for advice on how to keep busy. She told us there was only one choice.

"Pig racing," she declared.

Pig racing? I really wasn't in New England anymore.

She directed us to the Bearcreek Saloon, the restaurant-bar-pig-racing establishment down the road from Red Lodge and from those abandoned mine buildings the o vner of the bed-and-breakfast had told us about. The saloon, which serves the best steak I've ever tasted, gets crowded, especially when the racing begins. Patrons can place two-dollar bids on any segment of a twenty-five-square grid. Five squares are then randomly selected and assigned to each of the story-book-cute pigs lined up in the starting chutes of the track behind the saloon. The pigs wear colored vests and appear to be smiling. Once the gate is opened, they run around a tiny track toward the finish line and their reward: a pile of pigweed. Mayor Pits, who wears a big cowboy hat and bellows commentary into a microphone with a voice like an auctioneer, declares the winner. The crowd hanging over the track cheers. Whoever bet on the winning pig gets twenty-five dollars cash. The rest of the money goes into a scholarship fund awarded yearly to local college students.

The decor inside the saloon is simple: dark wood, floral table-cloths, and framed copies of the newspaper articles from the week of the mine disaster. The stories hang over nearly every table. The *Billings Gazette* front page nailed just inches from my face told how the Bearcreek women had held themselves together as their lives dissolved.

"Unbounding faith and hope—the indestructible courage and stamina of women the world over since time began is manifest by those who waited for word of husbands, sons, fathers and brothers trapped in winding passageways of the Smith mine at Bearcreek," began the story written by a woman reporter clearly in awe of her subjects. As was I. My most normal of losses hurt an awful lot. I couldn't imagine how those women had endured the loss of everything. They had lived everyone's worst nightmare, losing not only someone they loved but the neighbors, families, homes, and livelihoods that had rooted them.

That night, I began interviewing the people of Bearcreek. The folks sitting at the bar—the friendly mayor's wife, the gentleman in the white cowboy hat who'd been an infant when the disaster happened, the quilt shop owner who served as town historian—told me what they knew and gave me the names of other people to contact. Before flying home, I visited the cemetery. Stark and virtually unadorned, with dry weeds and haphazard clusters of graves, it reflects the raw simplicity of loss. I also picked up the only volume that existed on the disaster, a forty-page pamphlet published by the local historical society.

Back East, as they say Out West, I started making calls. Almost everyone I reached agreed to an interview, despite the facts that I was a complete stranger and that I was threatening to irritate their most delicate scar tissue. It was as if they had been waiting sixty-odd years for someone to just ask them what happened.

I was driven to tell their story by four forces: fascination at how the surviving women managed to continue getting dressed every morning after facing all that loss; the need to honor their heroics by sharing their story with the world outside their tiny neighborhood; anger at those who had let the disaster happen; and hope that someday history will stop repeating itself. The Smith Mine disaster isn't just a sad story. It's also a cautionary tale. What happened in 1943 is still happening in coal mines today: owners violate safety rules, the government looks away, and sweet men die.

Fewer American miners die today than sixty years ago, but the numbers aren't consistently declining. More coal miners died in 2006 than had in the previous eleven years. And the causes of those deaths haven't changed. A gas explosion trapped and killed twelve men in West Virginia's Sago mine that year, an event made even more painful when family members were mistakenly told that all the miners had survived. In 2007 six miners and three rescuers died in Utah's Crandall Canyon mine, a tragedy blamed on unsafe mining practices and a possibly corrupt mine owner. There's no reason to believe that the United States is immune to another major mine catastrophe like those that are still quite common in Chinese and Russian coal mines.

"In a perfect world, employers would sufficiently value their workers that they would do everything they can to ensure their safety," Cecil E. Roberts, current president of the United Mine Workers of America, wrote in 2007.

The UMWA is fighting for that perfection, but its leaders need to stay tenacious. Despite new safety legislation inspired by recent disasters, many laws are never actually enforced. Violators are fined, but the fines aren't always collected. Men who make a better living as underground coal miners than they might in other manual jobs don't always feel entitled to demand safe conditions or union protection, though it's more than reasonable to expect life *and* money from a job.

Nobody ever took responsibility for the Bearcreek disaster, and the families didn't get any compensation for their pain. All those people died, and even more grieved, but it was as if they didn't matter. That sense outraged me more than anything else. All people matter. I hope this story will be a reminder of how much.

Goodbye

Wifes and

Daughters

Prologue: *The Centennial*

If you look at a map of Montana, the western border shows the profile of a sad old man. His bottom lip pouts and his craggy nose faces down in disappointment. If you imagine the south-central part of the state as the man's jaw, Bearcreek is located close to the base of his throat, the spot where one's hand automatically goes in times of shock and sorrow. You'd think the folks who once called this their home wouldn't want to come back to a place that slammed them so hard with those two emotions. The day before the tragedy that changed everything, Bearcreek was a jolly all-American town of coal-mining families just trying to get through the war. They carried ration books to the market and drove only as far as their gas points allowed. But they still had fun, with movies in the winter, fishing in the summer, and dances year-round. The day after the mine exploded, Bearcreek's heart was broken. And through all the decades that followed, the fracture never fully fused. So, why come back? Their hometown has been dying for more years than it thrived. They've managed to move on with their lives. But none of these facts kept them away from the town's Centennial Celebration in 2006. Hundreds of visitors showed up. That's how wonderful this place once was.

Bearcreek's children have gotten together every few years for decades. These reunions, with their dinner dances and printed programs, are evidence of how powerful tragedy can be. It can tear families apart, but it can also keep communities together, no matter how far their members scatter. Maybe these people stage so many elaborate reunions—five between 1989 and 2006—because only those who waited those nine long days for survivors and then wept together through so many funerals truly understand the depth of this loss. Or maybe because they're determined not to forget the catastrophe that most of the world overlooked. It was wartime. Bad things were happening everywhere. The deaths of some anonymous coal miners and the demise of a tiny town barely registered.

Thelma Mourich Jovanovich Bischoff headed down early to help serve the pancake breakfast. Sunbeams were just starting to pick their way through dense, gray clouds. Thelma, who lives five miles away in the tourist town of Red Lodge with her cat and, sometimes, her grandson, was on the planning committee for the celebration. A bubbly woman who's still flirtatious in her eighties, Thelma wears jeans and drives through blizzards. She's always game for a party, even if it means showing up at dawn.

She was up pretty early—for a teenager—the morning of the explosion, too, on account of an ex-beau who'd surprised her with a visit the day before. He'd messed up her plans for that night's high school dance, not to mention infuriating her steady boyfriend. Thelma must have thought that was her only problem as she walked up the hill to her grandmother's house, where the surprise visitor was staying. Then emergency sirens started ringing, and Mrs. Mourich instinctively knew that the mines weren't screeching because a man had snapped his leg or fallen on the tracks.

"This is the big one," Thelma's grandmother told her.

For years the older woman had been worrying about what could happen in that mine, where her husband had once worked and her three sons still did. But maybe she'd developed protective calluses from all the tragedy she'd known already. Thelma, whose dad managed the mine's electrical system, was only sixteen. She had no idea how hard grief could hit.

Virginia Sommerville Casey still cries when she talks about the winter of 1943. Maybe that's why she stayed at the celebration for just a few minutes. She'd put on a dressy brown blouse and walked to the party from her Bearcreek house. She's a tall woman who as a teenager was as beautiful as a movie star. Now, though she's still the type of woman whom people would call *handsome*, she hides her big blue eyes behind tinted glasses. Virginia is warm and welcoming, the type of woman who nurtures visitors with hot coffee and impromptu meals, but she's shy, too. So when she couldn't find any of her old friends among the crowd jamming Bearcreek's main drag, she walked back home. Maybe she just didn't need any more reminders of the worst day of her life, when her run as a contented young wife and mother stopped short.

Many of the people Virginia had grown up with were in the old stone bank building, a tiny structure that serves as town hall these days. The Centennial planning committee had laid out artifacts from Bearcreek's heyday on long tables. People squeezed past each other to see keepsakes that had survived decades in attics. Among them: schedules from the days when a train ran through town; tin signs advertising Smith Mine coal as offering *More Heat Per Dollar*; grade school group shots, circa 1938, with scrubbed and combed miners' kids smiling in front of the mountains; an album of obituaries summing up the lives of those whose trajectories had shifted abruptly after the mine disaster; union membership lists; photos from prom nights; and an Army uniform from World War II.

After looking at the mementos, people began to claim spots for watching a parade. A handful of older folks climbed onto a flatbed trailer decorated with a long Bearcreek Bearcats banner, settled into plastic patio chairs, and held onto signs proclaiming their high school graduating classes. When the parade began, they waved those signs—1940! 1949!—as the crowd cheered. If it hadn't been so hot, some of them might have tried to squeeze into the letterman sweaters they'd brought from home.

Wayne Freeman sat in a folding chair watching the parade. He waved to his cousin on the alumni float, happy to see someone he recognized. Wayne, who had just turned seventy, was six when the mine exploded. His grandfather was the superintendent of the mine, and his great-uncle held onto its purse strings. A federal inspector had chronicled pages of safety violations months before the explosion. After the explosion, kids sometimes shot dirty looks at Wayne, and adults sometimes cursed his family out loud for what they may or may not have done to cause the disaster.

Wayne spent part of the celebration trying to sell copies of a fictionalized version of the mine disaster that he'd written and recorded on tape. In his story, the union leaders are the bad guys and his family's culpability isn't mentioned. Revisionist history, of course, but that's what he heard at his dinner table. He also saw the effect the disaster had on his relatives. Several of the men in his family committed suicide or went insane after the explosion. They couldn't bear the pain, Wayne says.

One of the Centennial's afternoon activities, in addition to the three-legged races and other vintage games meant to replicate the old Labor Day picnics, was a walking tour of Bearcreek's few remaining streets. The tour leader pointed out landmarks. *This is where the doctor's house was*, she said, *that's where the high school stood*. Doris Anderson Spaulding walked with the small group. Until she was thirteen, when the mine disaster pierced her family, she called this area home. She still knows the streets by heart, so she couldn't help raising her hand to correct the leader.

"No," she said in a soft voice, when the woman announced who had lived on a particular corner, "they weren't the first family in that house."

Doris didn't mean to be contrary—she's too well-bred for that—but what she seemed to be saying was this: you aren't seeing everything.

And that message could have applied to the entire day. The laughter and balloons and country music bands didn't represent the Bearcreek she'd left decades earlier. Maybe before the disaster the town had been light and frivolous, and once in a while after, but this joviality was an aberration. Like the sun pushing its way through the morning clouds, the joy felt forced. Just driving through this town, bracketed as it is by crumbling mine buildings on one side and a desolate cemetery on the other, makes the chest tighten. This big party, Doris could have been saying, doesn't make up for anything that happened.

Before the walking tour ended, she bowed out to sit in a cool car. The weather in Montana is apparently as unpredictable as it is in New England. All summer it had been unexpectedly hot—as it was on the day of the explosion.

That February morning it was so mild that men went outside without wearing coats. By nightfall, as rescuers tried to get into the mine to save their comrades and as women stood outside waiting for news, the temperature had fallen to below freezing and a blizzard was brewing. The weather on the day of the Centennial was strangely similar. When the sun dropped away in the afternoon, the warmth abruptly vanished. A cutting wind blew the smoke from the evening's pig roast all the way across the main road, so that those who had been there in 1943 might have been reminded of the smoke pouring from the mouth of the mine.

Bob Wakenshaw had seen that smoke. He smelled it and breathed it, too, as he peered into the mine entrance waiting for his father and both grandfathers to walk out. But as the day grew colder, his mother, Mary, sent him to a neighbor's house to wait. There was no need for an eleven-year-old boy to shiver like the rest of them, she decided, even though she wouldn't leave the mine for sixty-two hours, and then only for a nap.

As night fell on the 2006 Centennial of his birthplace, Bob stood at the hillside cemetery. The townspeople had worked hard to identify all the graves and raise money to build a new shelter where people could read the directory, or just sit and remember. Bob had come the previous day to put flowers on his family's graves. They're clustered together on the left side of hill: a stone for the triplet babies who would have been his big brothers, if they'd lived past their first day; markers for his sister and mother and grandmother, who lived full lives despite all the sorrow they bore; monuments to his father and one of his grandfathers, whose life stories take far less time to tell.

A minister wearing jeans and a black vest conducted a service to rededicate the cemetery. He read from Ecclesiastes and imagined what the buried folks would say if they could speak.

"As we sat at the bottom of the mine that day we thought of our families and wished them well," he said, quoting conjured-up coal miners. "It's good to see they made it through the tragedy."

He made it sound easy, getting on the other side of a tragedy, but Bob knew better. He stood close to his wife and children and grandchildren, but even their love couldn't purge his grief. The temperature kept dropping, and most people hugged their body heat into themselves. Bob took off his jacket and put it on a shivering woman's shoulders. He bowed his head and prayed. The evening sky, now deep blue and gray, looked like a bruise.

1 The Romance

She should have thrown salt over her shoulder. Knocked wood. Spit onto her fingertips. Anything to fight back the evil spirits. Instead, Mary Wakenshaw practically invited them into her house.

"Dear Bud," she wrote to her husband. "I'm glad I'm a coal miner's wife and thankful for it."

She was comparing herself to the women she saw all around her on a California military base in 1943. Those wives—the unlucky ones—were hugging and kissing their men for what they knew could be the last time. The soldiers' wives had come from all over the country to say their good-byes before the men crossed the ocean to fight for the best American values: Democracy, with all of its fair play and justice; and Capitalism, which paved the way for anyone to realize his dreams of wealth and freedom. Those wives were making a noble sacrifice. Still, it wasn't easy to say good-bye.

"Really," Mary wrote, describing the sad scene, "it's pathetic to see them grasp the few minutes of happiness they can."

She was on a road trip with her daughter, Fannie, a tall girl with broad shoulders and a confident smile. Fannie had come to the base to marry her high school sweetheart before he shipped off. She adored the young man so much that she'd pasted the butt from the last Camel cigarette he'd smoked before leaving home six months earlier in her scrapbook. Now, finally, she'd get to be his wife. Mary, Fannie, and the boy's parents and brother had traveled fifty-four hours by train from their homes in the Montana mining town of Bearcreek. They drove two hours to the Billings, Montana, train depot, boarded an overnight that took them past snow and mountains and more snow before stopping in damp Portland, Oregon, where they switched to another sleeper that would bring them to California. The trains were crowded and dusty, with overpriced coffee and lousy cheese sandwiches for sale. Mary's hands were always dirty. Fannie slept with her head on her mother's shoulder, but Mary couldn't find herself a comfortable position. Instead of resting, she wrote letters to Bud, sometimes twice a day.

"I pinned the balance of my money in a rag and in my girdle, so hope it's safe enuf," she wrote.

She told him about the soldiers who mobbed the train platforms, and the pair escorting a prisoner of war. Though the country had been at war for more than a year, and it had touched Mary in the form of ration books and tire drives, this was her first up close look at it.

"Bud, you couldn't believe in a million years what war is like till you see it out here," she wrote in one of the letters. "I mean soldiers, huge barracks built in the hills and soldiers, soldiers everywhere. It's a beautiful day out. I hope it stays nice."

The train swayed and her pen jumped. She had to pause when she lost her daylight to the eclipse of a tunnel, but she never broke her connection with Bud. She was only thirty-eight, but they were coming up on their twentieth wedding anniversary. They'd buried three children, raised one to adulthood, and seemed to be doing a decent job with their boy, Bobby, who was about to turn twelve. He was a good kid, though sometimes prone to typical preadolescent shenanigans. In December, a boy at school had called him a Jap, probably the most vile insult to spit at a kid in those times, so Bobby slugged him. The teacher banned Bobby from the annual Christmas pageant, so he had to endure the humiliation of watching from the audience right next to his mother. But if that was their son's worst crime, Mary and Bud could consider themselves lucky.

They were lucky in love, too. They'd reached that stage in their marriage during which so many couples—even those who've held on to respect and affection—become more business partners than romantic ones. But Mary and Bud seemed to have preserved the tender parts of their relationship. She asked often, in her letters, if he missed her. And she signed every one of them with a plea for his safety: *Take care of yourself.*

Because she knew that her family was making a sacrifice, too. Bud was a coal miner working more hours than ever because of the war. Coal fueled those trains that took the soldiers and their wives all over the county. It powered the factories where the girl riveters worked, as-sembling bombers and ships for the war. The very coal her husband cleared from under the Bearcreek hills went directly to the Army and Navy. Mining as much coal as possible was considered a patriotic duty. Bud's mine ran twenty-four hours a day, six days a week.

Unlike the soldiers' wives, who were new at this game, Mary sent her husband into danger every day. But when the possibility of death hovers for most of your life, as it had for Mary—first she worried for years about her coal-mining father, who'd already had his head smashed by falling rock in the mine, and now Bud—it didn't feel as scary anymore. It became normal, and almost unnoticeable. Maybe, in order to get up every morning and watch a man go into the earth, you need to numb yourself a bit.

While Mary took in America's landscape that February, Bud spent his time immersed in its internal riches. Every working day he walked into a cave full of coal and blew things up. He was a shooter at the Smith Mine, one of the crew who drilled holes into the walls, stuffed explosives in those cavities, set them aflame, and ran for cover. The coal tumbled off the mine's walls, filling the air with dust. When it cleared, hours later, other crews rolled in machines for collecting the coal and loaded it onto open boxcars. The cars brought the black hunks of profit out of the mine to the tipple, where it was cleaned and sorted, loaded onto railroad trains, sold to big companies and little homeowners, and, finally, burned for fuel.

Unlike shaft miners, who climb into a little cage and then drop down to the coal bed as if they're taking an elevator from the penthouse to the lobby, the Smith men rode straight into the mountain to harvest their coal. Once they were inside, a hoist lowered the cars they rode in, called mantrips, to the main tunnel, which sloped down gradually and led to a honeycomb of smaller paths and rooms. There they worked and ate and became best friends. The men divided into crews based on skill—shooters, trackmen, timbermen—and, sometimes, language. It wouldn't do anyone any good for an Englishman to be paired with a Montenegrin if they couldn't communicate. For one thing, they wouldn't get as much work done. And, of secondary importance to some, they wouldn't be able to protect each other if they couldn't shout warnings using the same urgent words.

It was dark and airy in the mine, with parts of the black walls as shiny as patent leather. It was never too hot or too cold, since the temperature stayed about fifty-seven degrees year-round. The men especially appreciated their temperature-controlled workplace when it was frigid or sweltering outside. And when they saw their fathers stooped and bowlegged from decades of crawling and crouching in other mines, they appreciated the height of the Smith. The ceilings were luxuriously high—high enough for Bud, who was six-foot-two, to stand up straight.

Bud had been working in the mine for eighteen years, but he aimed higher. He already had a second job as the Bearcreek constable, but he dreamed of becoming sheriff of Carbon County. He ran for the job in 1942 on the Democratic ticket. He came up with a campaign slogan and had it printed on business cards: "Pledges Efficiency and Economy," people read when he passed them out. He rigged a poster advertising his candidacy to the top of his maroon Ford to remind anyone he passed on the road of his hopes. His chances looked pretty good, until he got lied to. The sitting sheriff had promised Bud that he wouldn't run again. Then, maybe because he saw how popular Bud was becoming, he changed his mind and entered the race at the last minute. The county seat was home to a large Finnish population, and the incumbent was a Finn. He won the election, and Bud stayed at the mine. His life would have turned out quite differently if he'd left mining for a clean uniform and an office in the courthouse.

Mary would have rested easier if he'd won the election, too. Though Bud was earning more money now because he was working so many shifts, the paychecks were never enough to compensate for the danger. He'd already been hurt once, back in the twenties, while trying to link two coal cars. When he stepped between the cars to insert the pin that would hold them together, one car rolled. Chomping together like a nutcracker, the cars trapped and crushed his left leg. Bone snapped in two places. His buddies threw down their tools and rushed him to the hospital. The doctors examined the wound and talked about amputating Bud's leg below the knee. For some reason, they decided to wait and see if it would heal instead. They set it in a wooden trough weighed down with a bucket of sand, and he stayed still until the bones fused. When he could finally walk without crutches, he swayed a bit, because the injured leg had healed shorter and at a different angle than the healthy one. His gait reminded Bobby of John Wayne.

So many things could hurt a man underground. Falling rocks, fire, blasting powder. Even breathing was dangerous.

"Man, the air was foul today," Bud had said more than once at the dinner table.

He and his union brothers didn't push for cleaner air, though. It was wartime, and getting the coal out was the priority. How would it look if they beefed about their conditions when the kids in the armed forces were suffering so much more for the country? At least coal miners got to come home to lovely women like Mary every night.

Mary was a seventeen-year-old housewife when they met, though she'd never been married. She cooked and cleaned while her younger brother attended high school and her father mined coal. It wasn't the life her mother had planned for her.

She'd been born in Czechoslovakia in 1905 and toddled onto American soil three years later. Her parents settled in northern New Jersey, where the smokestacks clouded out the sun. Her father worked on the docks and her mother took in ironing and cleaned houses, when she could breathe. When her asthma got too severe, she took herself to the doctor. He predicted she'd die if she stayed in New Jersey. Go West, he said, where the air is still clear and dry.

Mary had been a city kid, shooting marbles on the sidewalks, jumping rope double Dutch, and following the neighborhood organ grinder and his monkey around. The wild west was nothing like home. She was ten when her family got off a train in southern Montana and began to homestead 320 acres adjacent to an uncle's land. Mary and her brother, Godfrey, went to school in town during the year, but in the summer they worked harder than children should to keep the farm going. They planted wheat and fence posts, hauled springwater for miles, burned sagebrush, and killed rattlesnakes. A rattler attacked Mary once and she remained unconscious for several days, only to awaken to see her mother working on her funeral shroud.

Besides running the ranch, their father worked at the local coal mine. Their mother stewed cottontail rabbits for dinner in their one-room house. Their land was in Crow Indian country, and Mary and Godfrey befriended an old Indian who herded sheep near their ranch. He let them ride his pony and view the world up close through his field glasses. Their mother trimmed the man's hair and gave him eggs to take home.

At one time in her childhood, Mary's life actually intersected with Bud's. She and Godfrey always passed a big rock on their way to school. Their father had told them a legend about an old man who had stopped at the rock to rest during a February blizzard back in 1905 and had frozen to death. That summer, when the snow finally melted, a rancher found his body. He was lying with his legs crossed and his hands on his chest, as if he were just napping, and he still wore the coat, vest, striped pants, and fine shoes he'd tied on the day he died. The rancher and the local coroner found a watch, a pair of glasses, and seventy-five cents in silver in his pocket. They settled him into a box and buried him by the rock. A few months later, Bud's father, Adam, heard about the mysterious corpse. He hadn't seen his own father in a while, but since the old man tended to move a lot, he hadn't been too worried. Now he contacted the coroner and helped him dig up the body. Sure enough, there lay his father, Thomas Wakenshaw.

It was a story Mary's mother would have appreciated, but by the time Mary found out about the coincidence, her mother was long gone. She died when she was thirty-eight, shortly after her children had left the house for a trip into town. Mary, who was fifteen, was heading back home from her errand when she saw her father on a horse in the distance. He was riding toward her, and she could tell by how urgently he rode and how stiffly he sat in the saddle that she didn't have a mother anymore. He was rushing to town to get the undertaker.

After the funeral, Mary's father sold the farm and moved his teenagers to Bearcreek, where he'd be closer to the mine and where Mary would be able to find a future.

And there he was, sitting in the stands at a baseball game.

Bud Wakenshaw was nineteen when he glanced over at the girl he'd spend the rest of his life with. She'd grown up to be a petite brunette with twinkling eyes, high cheekbones, and a narrow but perfectly shaped smile. He had a job in the mine, as his father did, and spent his free time working at his parents' ranch. He'd grown up around the ranch, the beloved only child of a happy couple.

His mother, Mag, had suffered more than one miscarriage and had given up on trying to bring a live baby into the world by herself. She and her husband, Adam, decided to adopt. But they were firm on one requirement: they wanted a girl. They arranged to meet two nuns from a Helena children's home at a nearby train station and adopt a newborn girl from them. The nuns stepped off the train, one holding a boy and one holding a girl. Mag insisted on taking the girl, but the nuns said she was already spoken for. Bud's parents were about to leave, childless once again, when one of the nuns pulled a classic trick. *Hold the baby while I use the bathroom,* she asked Bud's mother, and handed her the boy. Mag cradled that baby, looked into his soft eyes, and gave in to fate. By the time the nun returned, Mag realized she couldn't let go.

They named the baby Robert, but everyone called him Bud. He grew into a quiet man who was strong in spirit and body, the perfect balance to Mary, who was as delicate as she was vivacious. They got married seven months after they met, at the Pollard Hotel, which was and still is the fanciest establishment in Carbon County. Visitors see the same broad center staircase when they walk through the main entrance, and look out at the street through the same tall, arched windows as the young couple did. Their wedding day coincided with Easter Sunday and April Fool's Day of 1923, so people believing in signs could have predicted that the marriage would be either a miracle or a joke. Bud wore a fine suit with a silk tie and combed his thick auburn hair back off his forehead. Mary teased and curled her bob, then styled it so one perfect S-shaped curl fell onto her forehead. She stepped into a dress with a bodice made of two layers of lace. After the kisses and cake, Bud and Mary honeymooned at his parents' ranch, then moved into a hilltop house in Bearcreek. It had cold running water and an outhouse. Three months later, Mary was expecting.

It must have been so exciting, knitting booties and daydreaming about the baby who would be born right around their first wedding anniversary. By summer, Mary would be proudly pushing a pram all over town.

But the pain started too early. She was only seven months along and the contractions wouldn't stop. The doctor was helpless; all he could do was catch the premature baby she delivered. It was a boy. Then two other boys, children she hadn't even begun to dream about, descended into the world. The triplets were perfectly formed, with all their fingers and toes and tiny noses, but they were much too small to survive. She named one baby after Bud, one after her father and one after his father. Robert, Frank, and Adam lived for an hour and a half.

Her father built them a coffin that wasn't much bigger than a cigar box. A friend draped silk handkerchiefs on top of the babies, and a horse-drawn sled pulled them through the snow from the house to the Bearcreek cemetery. Mary and Bud said their prayers over a small, white gravestone shaped like a pyramid. It was carved with the words no mother should ever have to see: Wakenshaw Babies.

Whenever things got bad, Mary told herself to *keep pushing*. So she pushed through her grief. A year later, Fannie was born. The little girl developed scarlatina and rheumatic fever as a child, but survived. Six years after that, Bobby arrived. Life settled down. Bud and Mary hosted potluck dinners, dressed up for dances, and attended all the school events, where Mary talked to everyone. She went to ladies' club meetings and he went to union meetings. They camped by mountain lakes with other mining families in the summer. He played Santa Claus almost every December, passing out candy and fruit, courtesy of the union, to kids in the center of town.

Two weeks after her trip to California, Mary was home in Bearcreek waiting for a basketball game to begin. It was a Friday in February, and she was happy to be back to her routine. Fannie had gotten married, kissed her husband good-bye like all those other young wives, and returned to business college in Billings, though she was spending the weekend at her parents' house. Bobby, who'd stayed with his grandparents while his mother was away, was back in the nest, too. And she didn't have to remind Bud to take care of himself anymore; she was there to do it for him.

It was the last normal day of Mary's life.

None of her children played on the Bearcreek High School basketball team, but that didn't matter. Everyone in town went to the games, just as the adults attended the high school dances long after they'd graduated. And Mary had been rooting for the squad since she was a teenager and her brother played on the town's first official team. The Bearcats had gotten better and better every season, filling the high school with more and more trophies and banners. In 1939 they won the biggest contest of all, the state Class B championship. The whole town had celebrated with a big banquet. Since then, though, the team had gone downhill. This year they'd posted more losses than wins.

Mary, Bud, and Bobby sat in the bleachers. It was an unofficial game, but important just the same. The referee stood in the center of the court and held up the ball. The players froze in their positions until he blew the whistle. Then they exploded up the basketball court, intent on giving their fans the happy ending they deserved.

After the game, Mary and her family headed home. On the way, Bobby would have tried to catch a glimpse of the slag heap by the mine buildings. The pile of coal waste was always burning, so it glowed, like magic, when the wind blew through it. He was surrounded by majestic mountains and the endless Montana sky, but the smoldering mound delighted him.

Inside their narrow rectangle of a house, Mary and Bobby got ready for bed. Bud prepared for his next job. As town constable, he needed to make his nightly rounds. There hadn't been any serious crime in Bearcreek since early in the century, when one guy killed another at the pool hall, and, later, when a boardinghouse resident shot his roommate to death for annoying him and stealing his liquor. These days the constable just broke up brawls or found drunks a safe place to sober up.

As Bud got ready to leave, Bobby took a prized box of candy out of his dresser drawer. Walnettos, chewy squares of caramel dotted with walnuts, were they boy's favorite sweet. He broke the package in two and offered half to his father. He probably wouldn't have shared his stash with many people, but he adored Bud. At eleven, he was still young enough to worship the man who took him sledding and surprised him with gifts. One morning, Bobby woke up to see a Popeye lamp in his room. Bud didn't drink, but he went to the local saloons to play pitch and poker. When he won, he'd spend his take on punch cards, which were like lottery tickets that paid out in prizes: sometimes candy, sometimes a rifle, sometimes a sailor man leaning on a lamppost.

Now Bobby wanted to pay back that generosity with Walnettos.

"Not right now," Bud told him, as he grabbed his blackjack, a small but deadly weapon made of leather and weights. "I'll have one later."

Then he hurried out the door.

His dad got home from rounds very late and went to the mine very early, so later would mean tomorrow after his shift. That was okay, though. Bobby would save his dad's Walnettos until he saw him again.

The next morning, February 27, 1943, Mary placed a three-minute egg in its cup and presented it to her father-in-law. Adam Wakenshaw, who lived close enough to the family to join them for every meal, had been eating the same breakfast since he was a boy in England. And, of course, he always ate it the same way: cracking off the top of the shell with a spoon, then scooping out the yolk. Adam had a lot of long-standing habits. He almost always wore a dress suit. And he'd been mining coal for most of his life. At seventy-two, he was the oldest miner at the Smith Mine.

It was no place for an old man, but Mary's sixty-five-year-old father, who lived with them, was also breathing in coal dust all day. With all the younger men fighting the war, the retirees had been called back. And they weren't allowed to quit unless they found a replacement, which was almost impossible. *Soldiers on the home front*, one politician would later call them. Bud wasn't old enough to retire, but if the country hadn't been at war he'd probably be farming instead. He'd already made a deal for a parcel of land; he just had to wait for peace to cultivate it.

On this morning, as Mary served all three of them their eggs and bacon, they were actually excited to get to work. After working at the same mine for eighteen years, today was the first time they were all scheduled for the same shift.

While the men ate, Mary packed their sandwiches and poured fresh water into the bottom compartments of their cylindrical tin lunch pails. Outside her kitchen window, she could see the sun on the foothills. It was going to be a warm day, the kind that melts the snow just enough so it sparkles. A perfect day for welcoming spring.

That's just what Mary had planned. Once the men left and the kids rolled out of bed, she was going to drive to the train station in Red Lodge and pick up a shipment of chicks that were on their way from Billings. After Bud's leg had been crushed in the mine all those years ago, he'd used his workers' compensation money to buy some Anaconda chickens. He'd been raising them in a big chicken coop out back ever since, and he'd just gotten word that his fluffy new babies had arrived. Mary's big chore of the day was to bring them home. She'd do some shopping in town, too, and before she knew it, it would be time to feed these men again.

Their shift ended at four. They would be hungry for a hearty dinner.

2   The Inspection

Gerald Arnold had never seen such a dangerous mine.

In November 1942, the federal mine inspector had left his office in Salt Lake City, Utah, and made his way to Montana. It took him almost a whole day to get there. Not bad when you consider he was traveling to a different world.

Bearcreek had one main drag with all the usual business establishments. Arnold drove by Little Joe's confectionery, Erma's hotel, and a barbershop on one side of the street. On the other he passed a market, whose owner let miners' wives shop on credit during strikes or slowdowns so that nobody went hungry. At the end of the strip sat the First and Last Chance Saloon, so named because depending on which way you entered town, it was either your first or last opportunity to alter your mind-set. Up in the foothills, a giant white B practically glowed through the muted sagebrush. The letter, shaped from layers of boulders, stayed so bright because the high school students regularly whitewashed it with brooms.

Roads like doodles wound up and down and around the hillsides, tiny houses seeming to dangle from the slopes. Arnold had been in many mining camps, so the architecture was familiar: unpainted boxes with four rooms and sometimes a porch. Indoor toilets were a luxury.

Bearcreek was incorporated in 1906, and less than a generation later more than a thousand people called it home, all of them living on coal. The area wasn't even five miles long, but by the 1920s four major mines operated in the Bearcreek valley. Many of the men whacking coal out of the earth in those days had taken trains and boats and more trains from France and Yugoslavia, Italy and Scotland, all so they could transfer their skills from the old country to the new. They supported enough saloons and brothels to keep all the itchy miners satisfied. Drunken fistfighting was the unofficial town sport.

The fun stopped with the Great Depression. Mines closed completely or cut production. Without enough work, men moved on, taking their rage and bad manners with them. Those who stayed settled down, importing wives from their European villages or falling for the smart girls who came to town to teach. They struggled, building highways when the mines weren't hiring and living off fish from the mountain lakes.

Bearcreek was the kind of place that wouldn't have gotten a second look if it hadn't been settled amid such beauty. The town rested at the base of the Beartooth Mountains. Some of the peaks in the range were jagged, especially the one shaped like a bear's tooth, but near Bearcreek the mountains were soft and rounded, undulating and hypnotic to look at.

Arnold, a tall, thin man with an angular face and a receding hairline, wasn't concerned with the scenery as he chugged into town. He was entering Bearcreek to perform a long-overdue inspection on the Smith Mine, the largest and most modern coal mine in the area, maybe even the whole state. It should have been done more than a year earlier, after Congress passed legislation requiring coal mine inspections. But the man who was supposed to cover Montana was an Army Reserve officer, and he'd been called up before he could perform any inspections. The next man the Bureau of Mines assigned to inspect Montana hadn't taken the mandatory training class. But with the war on and so many men gone, the bureau couldn't be too picky. The higher-ups decided to send the untrained inspector to Bearcreek anyway, as long as Arnold went along to teach him on the job.

At forty-six years old, Arnold was something of a mining authority, despite having come to the business relatively late. While many boys began mine work long before they needed to shave, Arnold was already twenty-five when he got his first mining job. Despite having only an eighth grade education, he jumped right into a foreman's position. He'd also had jobs supervising mines in Colorado and inspecting them for an insurance company. He'd trained as a civil engineer, and discovered a new formula for tracking injured miners. He married the daughter of a Colorado mine owner in 1922, and they'd had a baby girl two years later. She was a young woman now, smart and beautiful and dreaming about a career in journalism.

The couple had moved to Utah, and Arnold had started working for the Bureau of Mines a year earlier. His wife called him Gerry—no one else would have dared—though he liked to refer to himself as "G.O." in formal situations. Other family members called him "Gerald." His wife was home now, waiting patiently as he traveled around the country trying to keep men safe.

Arnold and his underling pulled into the parking lot in front of the Smith Mine, leaving the car among the scratched and dusty Fords and Chevys from the 1930s. Detroit wasn't producing new models these days, but come peacetime, the miners who saved their war earnings would probably be able to upgrade. The mine was now churning out an average of eighteen hundred tons of black diamonds every twenty-four hours. About three hundred souls in the region were surviving on coal. Some more than surviving.

W. R. Freeman greeted Arnold and offered the men a seat in his office, a small room in a low-ceilinged building down the road from the processing plant.

Freeman, the mine superintendent, was the face of Montana Coal and Iron. He was sixty-six years old, with a full head of gray hair and an imposing build. He looked like a well-preserved quarterback, with his handsome face and thick neck. His regal posture was somewhat intimidating. He'd certainly come a long way from the twelve-year-old with grimy hands he'd been when he started mining. Though he still spoke like a Brit from his days growing up in a Lancashire County mining village, now he wore a suit and made quite a nice living. He owned one of the biggest houses in the region, with three bedrooms and an open porch, but he didn't even live there year-round. Every winter, he and his wife spent several months in Long Beach, California.

W. R. Freeman wasn't the richest man running the mine. That would be his youngest brother, James, the general manager. James was one of the mining company's largest bondholders. He ruled from an office in Billings, and lived in an impressive house in the big city. But he kept a custom-built beauty of a home near the mine, too. Among the two-story house's many amenities: a fenced lawn and garden, wood-paneled walls, a butler's pantry, two bathrooms, and three bedrooms. There was a guesthouse out back. And if that wasn't enough space for entertaining, he owned two cabins in the area. He drove a snazzy Nash Ambassador.

James had the doughy face and potbelly of a prosperous man. But while he was certainly rich, he reportedly wasn't showy or stingy with his family. On Friday nights he would often drive his sister and her grandsons to the Red Lodge movie theater, drop them off, and then return to drive them home. He welcomed the extended family to his cabins for get-togethers. And he was always snapping pictures of the relatives. Later, he would develop them in his own darkroom.

But that all happened when he was in town. Usually, he stayed in Billings and left local family and business matters to W.R.

The elder brother had never entertained a federal inspector before, but he couldn't have been too worried. The government required him to let the inspectors into all the mine properties and to post their findings for public perusal. But no matter what they found, he wasn't required to fix anything. The theory behind the law was that if inspectors could show just how dangerous a mine was, miners would demand upgrades and mine owners would be inspired to make them, presumably to save face.

"The power of public opinion will be brought to bear," Arnold once explained, reading from a memo his boss wrote.

But that was all the power he could hope for. The law had no teeth. Even if Arnold discovered deadly conditions, the most he could do was inform the state inspector, who didn't have power to officially close mines either. He'd have to bring the issue before the state's Industrial Accident Board.

The Smith had won the honor of being the first coal mine in the state to be inspected because it was the gassiest. That meant more methane than normal seeped out of the coal. Methane, a natural byproduct of coal, could kill with violence or at leisure. It exploded like crazy, but it also had the power to snuff out oxygen, slowly suffocating its victims.

All mines secrete some gas. The amount depends on how much forest proceeded civilization in each particular mine's neighborhood. Coal comes from plants—ancient plants that dinosaurs lumbered through during the Cretaceous era. When the ferns and mosses died, they ended up buried and squashed and chemically altered. A few million years later, they'd turned into black seams of coal, deposited in Bearcreek through the folding and tilting of the Beartooth Plateau. But as the plants turned to coal, they released methane gas, which hid in the seams. The methane escapes when the coal moves.

Freeman and Arnold visited for a while. After discussing some logistics of the inspection—where they'd start, who would lead them around—they put on their hats and coats for a walk through the compound. Freeman walked Arnold into the machine shop and around the little building where they stocked the explosives. The inspector began taking notes.

Motors not grounded, explosives stored too close to highway and dwelling. No warning signs.

He walked across the trestle, the high railroad bridge that ran from the mouth of the mine to the processing buildings. The track looked okay, but there were gaps in the floor. When he looked down, he could see the road far below. He walked into the tipple, kicking up coal dust as he stepped. The building was made of wood covered by corrugated sheet metal—a fire hazard. If the building became engulfed, the coal dust would blow, too. It should have been swept out long ago.

Tipple not cleaned often.

Arnold stood for a moment and watched the men sorting the coal. One worker climbed over moving gears to get to his workstation. Another ducked under a buzzing machine to reach a part he needed to grease. As hard as he looked, Arnold didn't spot any guards covering gears or blades. Over and over again he made a note of it.

Guards needed at all points.

He knew the men could hurt themselves on exposed machine parts, but few of the men who worked in the coal-processing areas bothered with protective clothing. From head to toe, they were vulnerable. Hardly any of them, Arnold noted with dismay, wore safety caps or shoes.

The next morning, Arnold rode into the mine on the mantrip with the miners. A mantrip is similar to the open train cars that carry the coal, except it has benches on which the men cram together for transport into the mine. Before the ride stopped, a man jumped off. Arnold made yet another note. Jumping off a moving vehicle could get you killed.

But that was the least of these guys' problems. He'd already learned, by reading the record books, that there was way too much gas in this mine. Methane was being reported daily.

As soon as he started walking through the tunnels, he could see why. To harvest coal, men burrow into the earth, building paths and rooms. Depicted in pen and ink, the mine looks a bit like a centipede, with its long central corridor forming the body and all the tunnels spiking out of it appearing like legs. Each limb had multiple rooms cut into it, so a more detailed map would resemble a honeycomb. Miners create entire subterranean worlds, really, where they eat and piss and tell cute stories about kids or dirty ones about women. To keep the walls and ceilings from collapsing on their heads, they wedge timber beams among the coal. To keep the methane-laced air from killing them, they must make the tunnels as wide and clear as possible.

That wasn't happening in the Smith Mine. The passageway through which the fresh air from outside made its way to the deepest part of the mine was too narrow. In some places it was blocked by fallen rock, which impeded the air flow. Doors along the path led to passageways and rooms that were being mined. If the doors stayed closed, the air would flow unimpeded to its final destination. But if men left the doors open or the doors leaked—both common occurrences—some of the air would drift into the rooms instead of going straight to where it was needed most. The east side of the mine was getting much less clean air than the west. Arnold wasn't sure how much less, but he collected air samples to send to a lab in Pittsburgh. He'd include the results in his final inspection report.

He held up his safety lamp to test for gas. It was his only investigative tool and certainly not a precise one. The safety lamp looked like a lantern, with a wick that told stories. When it detected gas, the flame changed shape and turned blue. Enough gas—and not enough oxygen—and it blew itself out. As he traveled through the mine, Arnold's flame danced, announcing traces of gas in some places, explosive amounts in others.

But the miners usually did little or nothing when they found excess gas. The foreman should have been insisting that they shut down the power and stop working until enough fresh air flowed in. Instead, the Smith men usually kept working despite the safety lamp's warning. Their main remedy was to "brush" the gas out. This archaic method consisted of nothing more than swishing the air around. They'd hang a piece of canvas, called brattice cloth, to direct the flow of air to or away from the coal face where the gas had been discovered. Sometimes, they'd just whip a coat or piece of canvas in the air, as if they were shooing away flies. Or they'd drive the coal car up and down the track a few times until the gas dissipated.

At least twice during the previous two years, men had detected and cleared gas using one of these ineffective techniques, only to have miners ignite gas and start fires in the same spots shortly afterward. This proved either that the gas was never sufficiently cleared or that it accumulated again very quickly. In either case, no one told Arnold of the incidents.

Then there was the dust problem. It was all out of proportion. Coal dust, created by all the things these men were doing—drilling, cutting, blasting—can spontaneously combust. A mining lab had already analyzed a sample from the Bearcreek coalfield a couple of years earlier. Using a mathematical formula, researchers came up with a figure of .438 to describe the ratio of "volatile to total combustible matter" in the coal. The scientists knew that dust from coal with a ratio of .12 was explosive. The Smith coal, nearly four times more explosive than that, was considered *highly* explosive.

With gas around, coal dust is even more dangerous. The best way to cut the risk is to smother the dust with pulverized rock. Special machines could distribute the so-called rock dust, but this could also be done by hand. Spread some rock dust around a gassy mine and you may have saved many lives. That was common knowledge, at least in other parts of the country. The Bureau of Mines recommended rock-dusting for all mines, but Montana law didn't require it.

The state was also lax on mixing gas with fire. To light their way through the mine, most of the men in the Smith hooked old-fashioned carbide lamps onto their caps. They called the canisters filled with liquid accelerant "open lights" because the flame was right there at the front of the lamp, turning the men into walking candles. Closed lights ran on batteries, with glass covering lightbulbs.

Everyone knew closed lights were the way to go if you wanted to live until quitting time. More than fifteen years earlier, the Mine Inspectors Institute of America had put this reality in writing. Their report blamed open lights for 70 percent of the mining explosion deaths in the United States. Most of the Pennsylvania coal miners and all of the Utah coal miners had stopped using them. The institute had wanted them prohibited nationwide by 1926, and the Bureau of Mines sent notices to mine operators all over the country recommending against them long before that.

"An open light and gas constitute a vicious hazard," the bureau officials wrote. "While if there be coal dust present in the vicinity the consequences are multiplied many times."

Management at the Smith must have missed the memo, or ignored it. As Arnold looked around, he saw far too many open lights. Yet the Smith Mine certainly wasn't backward in other practices. The mine was considered one of the most advanced in the state, having been "mechanized" in 1927, meaning the miners used machines instead of mules and picks to get the coal.

At least the men handling explosives wore closed lights. Arnold watched a team of them get ready to blow the coal down. One would drill while another tapped on the roof with a pick to make sure it wasn't about to fall on them. Then, the shot-firers packed cartridges filled with black pellet powder, coal dust, and fuses into the holes, and lit them.

This was wrong in so many ways. Black powder burned intensely and wasn't considered safe anymore. The men should have tested for gas before blasting. They shouldn't have used a match. And they probably shouldn't have been blasting at all at that point in the shift. By law, blasting was to be done at the end of shifts when nearly all the workers had left, except in a few special areas.

Arnold found even more hazards: too many explosives hanging around underground; a live wire nailed to a wet post; spilled oil. But even those infractions weren't the worst. In the dark of the mine, Arnold spotted a tiny orange light. As he got closer, he saw that it was attached to a man, who brought it to his mouth and inhaled. These miners, surrounded by gas and coal dust and explosives, were smoking cigarettes.

After inspecting the mine for more than a week, Arnold called a meeting. Crowded into one of the small mine offices were the Freeman brothers, one of their sons, their assistant manager, three foremen, and the chief electrician. Arnold took the floor.

There is simply too much gas in this mine, he told them. Further, they would have to get rid of everything that could ignite it, especially the cigarettes and the open lights. They'd have to start searching the men to make sure they weren't sneaking in cigarettes. And they'd have to order closed lights for every miner. Sure, that might take some time, given all the war-related red tape, so while they waited, the foremen would have to examine every place men wearing fire on their foreheads worked, several times a day, to make sure the rooms were gas free. The foremen would have to start carrying safety lamps with them constantly, and signing daily gas reports, to prove that someone in charge was paying attention to the fluctuations.

James Freeman didn't like what he was hearing. This guy made it sound as if his mine was a disaster waiting to happen.

"If I thought the mine was in as dangerous a condition as you picture it, I would close down tomorrow," he said.

"The mine is exactly as dangerous as we have told you," Arnold shot back.

Then he paused and added what the mine officials wanted to hear.

"The mine can be operated with reasonable safety provided certain precautions are taken," Arnold explained.

That meant they had to eliminate as many hazards as they could, as quickly as possible, he reiterated.

Arnold continued with his list. Ventilation needed to be increased dramatically. When that happened, though, the mine would dry out. More coal dust would build up, making it even more vital to tame it with rock dust.

The mine operators grumbled some more about how they'd never be able to get the men to quit smoking, and how hard it would be to make so many changes during wartime. But in the end, they at least acted as they should have, agreeing to nearly everything Arnold had suggested.

To keep them honest, he sent his preliminary inspection report to the state mine inspector and asked him to make sure the company was working on the improvements. He also sent a copy to Tony Boyle, the district president of the United Mine Workers of America. And, of course, he reminded the mine operators that the report had to be posted at the mine for all the workers to see. Who knew? Maybe the power of public opinion *would* be brought to bear.

3   The Teenagers

It's hard to think about boys when you're trying to write a newspaper article. So for a few minutes at least, as Thelma Mourich sat at her typewriter in journalism class, she was forced to concentrate on leads and spelling instead of the many males who brought out the natural flirt in her. Thelma was blond with sultry blue eyes and a party-girl personality. Once cast as the Queen of Hearts in the Bearcreek grade school play, she never seemed to give up the part.

In November 1942, Thelma was a junior in high school and a columnist for *The Bear Facts*, the school newspaper that came out every other week. The twelve-page, mimeographed paper wasn't just something for kids to stuff into their notebooks or step on in the school hallways, as they may have done at other schools. *The Bear Facts*, which cost fifty cents a year (fifteen cents more if you had it sent to the post office instead of dropped at your doorstep), was the publication of record for Bearcreek and Washoe. Sure, the people in the two villages could drive over the hill to Red Lodge to buy a weekly put out by professionals, or they could subscribe to the *Billings Gazette*. But there was only one news organ that ran all the important dirt from their pocket of the world—who drove a car into a pedestrian on Main

Street, who visited city relatives for the weekend, or who got his leg amputated after an accident at the Smith Mine.

That victim would have been a boy with the unfortunate name of Robert Vagina.

Thelma and her friends might have smirked when they typed up that one, but they probably cringed, too. Every miner's kid knows how hazardous his or her dad's job is, how he could walk out of the house on two legs one morning and return with just one if a machine jammed or a ceiling caved in. And nearly every kid on the staff of *The Bear Facts* was a miner's kid.

The story about Vagina ran in the October 16 issue of the paper. He'd worked on a picking table, where boys separated worthless pieces of rock from valuable coal. The stones went to the rock dump. The pickers eventually moved on to more important jobs. Miners worked their way up the ladder, just like lawyers and doctors, getting the scut jobs first then earning promotions to more glamorous and lucrative positions. If Vagina hadn't lost his leg, he might have made it all the way to foreman.

The fifteen-year-old was sorting through fistfuls of coal when his foot got caught in a chain. He was dragged with his leg jammed into the workings of the picking table until two men cut him out with a torch. They grabbed his torn body and carried him to a car, no doubt trailing blood all the way to the parking lot. It took about fifteen minutes to get to the former whorehouse that now served as the county hospital. The surgeon eyeballed the wound, drugged the boy to sleep, and sawed off his leg. A few blood transfusions later, he was ready to rethink his career path.

This was the kind of mishap Inspector Arnold probably would have wanted to know about as he scrutinized the mine that fall, but no one from the company mentioned it. They probably didn't see the need to point out hazards he might have missed. He'd given them enough to work on already.

Thelma's father, Frank, had been in the room when the inspector told the mine bigwigs all that was wrong with their operation. As head electrician for the mine, Frank had been invited to hear what needed to be done, and might have been asked to explain why certain problems existed. He emerged from the superintendent's office with a to-do list that practically added up to a part-time job. His tasks, aimed at preventing electrocution and fire, included redesigning the whole electrical system, insulating wires, building protective platforms, and posting "High Voltage" signs throughout the mine, among other things.

Frank Mourich had been working in coal mines since he was thirteen. He'd been born in Austria in 1901 and set eyes on the Statue of Liberty when he was three. His father, Jacob, was such a talented carpenter that a czar had reportedly ordered furniture from him. His mother, Ursula, brought eight babies into the world and would outlive all but one of them. A few of her children died in the old country. One swallowed a match and another jumped off a haystack onto a pitchfork. Her daughter Annie was thirty when they found her frozen body in the snow two miles from her Bearcreek house. She was wearing a nightgown. It would be decades before anyone said aloud that Annie's husband had probably killed her.

Jacob and Ursula came to Montana so he could work his carpentry magic at the mines. He built the trestle that supported the trains as they transported coal to the picking table, and men to the dark mine tunnels.

Frank was their eldest of three sons. He was twenty-three when he married a small woman with a pixie cut and a memorable laugh. She delivered their first baby the next year. Frank Jr. was one when Thelma came along.

Thelma was always close to her big brother. He was a high achiever, as so many firstborns are. Not only was he the president of the senior class and one of the star Bearcat basketball players, but he was brainy, too. As a senior, he and a few other boys took a correspondence course in aeronautics from the University of Montana. Frankie wrote a *Bear Facts* article about the class, calling the scholars "future war eagles" who were getting ready to replace downed flyers overseas. He was keyed up about going to war, and quite patriotic. In one editorial he described all the ways coal contributed to the war effort: coal products were used to make piston rings, waterproof jeep covers, and TNT for bombs, he reported.

"It makes one feel kind of proud to live in a town like ours," the young writer concluded.

But at home, he was just a regular big brother. The family ate dinner at 4:30 or 5:00, after Frank got home from the mine. But the kids couldn't just enjoy their spaghetti and sweetly describe their days. No, Frankie had to throw peas onto Thelma's plate every so often. Their dad might have chewed harder and squeezed his fork and knife in his fists, but he didn't yell. He just got up and left the table.

Frank could be stern—Thelma stayed out of trouble at school because she was afraid of getting him angry—but he was affectionate, too. He hugged Thelma's mother every morning before he left for work and every afternoon when he returned. And he knew how to have fun.

In the summer, when the mines were closed more than they were open, he packed up the family for fishing trips on East Rosebud Lake. It was a picture-perfect spot, with mountains and wildflowers rising up around the water. Other mining families usually joined them. They spent the days courting trout and the nights frying them over open fires. After the kids fell asleep in their tents or, when they were little, in the backseats of the cars, their parents must have sat around smoking and talking and listening for bears.

Thelma wasn't crazy about camping. She'd rather be sitting in velvet seats and peering at the stars in a movie theater. Frank drove his family to Red Lodge twice a week to see a picture. He changed out of his overalls and put on a button-down shirt and trousers for the occasion, bought candy for the kids before the show, and let Gene Autry or Humphrey Bogart help him forget about the mine and the war. While he spent his days making safety improvements that fall and winter, he had the choice of seeing *Priorities on Parade* or *Secrets of the Underground*, both shown at the Roman Theatre for eleven cents a ticket. When the curtains flapped together over the screen, the Mouriches always headed up a block to the Busy Bee Café for hamburgers.

On the off chance that there wasn't a decent movie to see, the Mourich family popped in on the grandparents for some homemade sauerkraut and sausages, washed down with a little homemade wine. Or they'd just visit with Frank's brother and his wife, who lived next door. Frank's father had built both of their houses and given them to the young men as wedding presents. The homes were pretty fancy by Bearcreek standards. Thelma's had a big front porch, three bedrooms, and an indoor bathroom that Frank installed himself. Other families were still using outhouses and taking sponge baths with boiled water. There was a kitchen big enough for a table but small enough to close off and darken when Frank wanted to process photos. The radio sat in the parlor, playing news for Frank and sappy music for Thelma.

The Mouriches even had a telephone—a rarity in Bearcreek—in case the guys at the mine needed to reach Frank in a hurry. Thelma and her best friend, Louise, put that telephone to good use. For a while, the grocery store was the only other place in town with a phone. They crank-called the store with the Prince-Albert-in-a-can gag. When jokes failed to fill the hours between school and supper, the girls moved on to contraband. Louise stole cigarettes from her aunt so she and Thelma could experiment. They sparked a match and sucked in the bitter fumes. Thelma choked and gave up. Louise got the hang of it and developed a habit, which wasn't much of a surprise. Smoking sort of went with her wild image. Louise would grow up to be a bachelorette and a career girl, who was known to dance on the tops of bars.

If she wasn't making mischief with a girlfriend, Thelma was probably with her boyfriend, Eli Jovanovich. Her parents weren't so fond of Eli, not because he was a bad kid, but because they thought Thelma was too young to be dating. Their worries came a few years late.

Thelma was fresh out of grade school when Eli first noticed her.

They got to talking, and the next thing she knew he'd asked her to the winter ball. He was president of the junior class, an office that came with the honor of leading the grand march into the ball—with his date. The girls in the junior class were horrified. A freshman girl in the grand march, instead of them? The nerve!

But Thelma was in love. Eli was kind and handsome, with a cleft chin and dark, wavy hair. From that ball until now they'd been an official couple: going to the movies, doubling with Frankie and his girl, and making out in cars parked on top of the coalfield. By the fall of 1942, Eli had graduated and Thelma was a junior herself.

She and her friends put the newspaper together in a second-floor classroom filled with typewriters. Their adviser, who was also the high school principal and superintendent of all the Bearcreek schools, was a stern-looking grown-up with round glasses and a handkerchief folded just so in the pocket of his suit coat. He occasionally contributed firm snippets, such as "A bond a day will keep the Japs away," that ran in block letters at the bottom of the editorial column. He pushed the kids hard enough that the paper consistently earned high honors from the National Scholastic Press Association.

When they weren't writing war commentary and accident reports, or covering elementary school events such as the eighth grade history class's creation of a Bearcreek map or the little kids' perfect spelling scores, the news staff was designing and assembling the paper. The production staff stenciled in artwork or cranked the mimeograph machine or posted papers to more than fifty local boys serving overseas. Other kids sold advertising. One of the biggest ads, of course, was for "Superwashed Smith Coal—Montana's Best Fuel." But JC Penney ran an ad, too: rayon prom dresses for $3.98 and rayon hose for 79 cents. And Natali's Café in Red Lodge bought space, too. The restaurant promoted its "raviolo [sic] and steak dinners," but was really known as one of the best places around to go for a dance and a drink.

Deadline pressure can make even the most seasoned journalist a bit punchy, and Thelma and her friends certainly weren't immune to shenanigans. The elegant brick school building had long, rectangular windows, plenty big enough to toss a typewriter out of, which Leo Hodnik was rumored to have done.

Leo wasn't at school anymore. He'd dropped out after junior year and was working at a chrome mine. No doubt at least one senior was a bit subdued without him. Sports editor Melvin Anderson had been goofing around with Leo since they were little boys.

A regular play day for them involved climbing to the rimrocks above their neighborhood, Leo's dog trailing behind. They'd settle onto a good ledge, maybe dangle their skinny legs in the air, and then, as the big brown-and-black dog listened, Leo would play the harmonica and Melvin would sing. Or they'd find some other boys and play a game they called shinny. It was like hockey, without the ice. They made sticks out of the curved roots of chokecherry trees and used busted-up milk cans as pucks. Sometimes someone's body got in the way of someone else's stick and a fight commenced. Melvin and his brother, Elmer, were always getting into spats. When their frequent fights got heated, Mrs. Anderson would call them in the house—to calm them down or punish them, for she was the disciplinarian in that family—until they got spit back out again to continue playing with Leo.

Elmer was two years older than Melvin. He was a sensible, shy boy who'd survived polio at age two. Melvin's little sister, Doris, was in eighth grade. She had a wicked crush on one of her teachers, doodled "To Hell with Hitler" on the cover of her binder, and liked to listen to *Fred Waring and His Pennsylvanians* on the radio, which was fine unless she changed her dad's 9:00 news program to hear it. Her fairly tranquil father grew annoyed when she pulled that one, but he never got angry enough to take her over his knee. Doris was Daddy's pet and always avoided spankings. Unlike Melvin.

He'd been an imp since his earliest days, a blue-eyed brunette with curls as unruly as his spirit. His mother kept trying to plaster his hair down, but it kept rising up again. By high school, he was tall and handsome. Though not tall by basketball standards—he stood five foot ten—he served as the Bearcats' starting guard just the same. He was vice-president of his high school class and had performed in all the school plays. Maybe he aspired to be a star like Wallace Beery, whose "toughness and rudeness" he admired, according to a profile of Melvin in *The Bear Facts*. Or maybe acting would bring him closer to starlets like Betty Grable, whose pipes and legs made him swoon. Melvin was smart enough to go into any field he wanted—he'd scored a B in the college aeronautics class—but he wasn't the most attentive student. He tried to escape bookkeeping class via the window one day but got caught when he fell into a puddle of water on the gym roof below him. And he skipped school enough times to prompt the principal to visit the house for a little talk.

Seeing that man at the door must have made Melvin's father furious and embarrassed, but he couldn't have been shocked. Emil Anderson had been called wild in his day, too. And being a cutup certainly wasn't unusual in Bearcreek. Coal miners were known for their practical jokes and hard drinking, and Melvin came from a long line of them. His family tree could be used to trace the evolution of coal mining in the United States. His grandfather, who started mining in Finland and fathered eighteen children, brought his skills across the ocean in search of a better life, only to be blacklisted for talking about forming a union. Two of his uncles had died in nearby non-unionized mines. Now his dad was an officer in the Smith union. And Melvin's older brother had gone even farther. He'd traded coveralls for a tie when he took a job with the Bureau of Mines after high school.

Melvin had been best man when his brother got married at the end of October. Their wedding was small: just a few people in Rev. Rhodes's parlor in Red Lodge. Elmer stood next to his bride, a coal miner's daughter who'd graduated from Bearcreek High with him. Jane Laird, of *The Bear Facts* advertising staff, was the maid of honor. Melvin's girlfriend stood behind him, quite possibly dreaming she'd be the next new Mrs. Anderson. She and Melvin were apparently at peace that week, though they had a somewhat tumultuous relationship. Their favorite song, according to *The Bear Facts*, was "Sweethearts or Strangers," whose lyrics chronicled an on-again, off-again love affair. By January, they would be off once more.

The newlyweds celebrated with a party at the Andersons' house, then on a honeymoon in Billings. The bride's mother threw a blow-out of a wedding shower at a big hall near the mine when they got back. Seventy-six women showed up. They tested their cleverness with a quiz game and their coordination with a ring toss. Melvin's mother took first place.

The Bear Facts covered the shower, of course. All sorts of parties made it into print. Thelma had written an article about the soiree the sophomores threw for the freshman to welcome them to high school. The annual initiation was a little wacky. Besides a jitterbug contest and a duo's rendition of "You Are My Sunshine," there was a mock wedding ceremony, some yodeling, a tap dance solo, and a game that required students to roll peppered eggs across the floor with their noses.

The junior prom that November was certainly more dignified. The kids decorated the gym in red, white, and blue before heading home to put on ties and dresses. The stylish girls would show off their fig-ures with shoulder pads and cinched waists, knee-length skirts, and liquid makeup on their legs instead of stockings.

The Welch Brothers band drove all the way from Wyoming to sup-ply the tunes. The class hired them for fifty dollars and, luckily, they'd scheduled the dance to be held a few days before gas rationing began, or they wouldn't have gotten them at all. Thelma danced with Eli, and everyone drank pop and ate candy and threw confetti on each other. The girls who didn't have dates complained about all the boys who were in the service or who had quit school to work in the mines instead of being on the dance floor where they belonged.

Parents came to the dance, too. It was a shame to leave a good band and an open dance floor to the kids. That junior prom was an important night for some of those older couples, though they didn't know it at the time. Some of them may have been holding each other and swaying to love songs for the very last time.

4 The Union

Tony Boyle was a murderer.

But not yet.

The worst that could be said about Boyle in 1942—and certainly was said, by many—was that he was obnoxious. Egotistical. Slick. Ambitious.

The district president of the United Mine Workers of America would someday be the top man of the entire union, and all of his actions seemed designed to get him there. Which wasn't a bad thing for the miners of Montana.

On a Tuesday in December, not too long after the high school girls had tucked their prom dresses into their closets and Inspector Arnold had returned to his Salt Lake City desk, Boyle stood before a room full of union representatives and mine officials. Members of the latter group belonged to the Montana Coal Operators Association, a lobbying group whose main purpose was to keep mining concerns flush. Boyle had arranged the meeting to discuss Arnold's safety recommendations, which he wanted to turn into law.

Boyle was short and pointy-looking with small blue eyes. The way he slicked back his hair made him look even more ratlike. He wore double-breasted suits and fedoras that appeared to have come from

Al Capone's closet. He looked older than his forty-one years and spoke more eloquently than many who had, like him, finished just eight years of school. But, for all of his flourish and big words, his speeches still sounded like he was reading from a bad script. His role: eloquent savior of the working man.

He came from a coal-mining family, as most of those working men did. He was born in a cabin at a Montana coal camp, and claimed that his father died of consumption in his arms. He followed his elders into the mines when he was fourteen, but he soon left to work for a railroad. Then he mined copper, got an electrician's card, and went back to the coal mines. Despite his bad temper, he managed to win union elections, becoming district president in 1940. He had a red-haired wife and a twelve-year-old daughter who was known for her perfect curls and superior attitude.

Boyle's job was to protect the men he called "these people who work in the bowels of this earth." It could be frustrating work. A year earlier he had tried to prevent miners from accidentally blowing up their co-workers by pushing for a legislative bill that would have banned blasting during shifts. He'd almost succeeded.

He convinced Montana state representatives to support the "no blasting" bill, and two state reps from Carbon County were among those who introduced it. When it came up for discussion, Boyle and a union board member drove to the domed state capitol in Helena and addressed members of the House committee on mines and mining. Quoting from a study he'd made, Boyle explained how explosive forces or subsequently falling coal could kill men during blasting. Though Montana mining laws on the books stipulated that blasting should be done at the end of shifts in most cases, Boyle must have wanted to tighten those regulations. The chairman, whose cousin had died under the exact circumstances Boyle had described, especially liked the idea. Once he said he was in favor of the bill, the rest of the committee agreed that it should pass. Boyle left the meeting satisfied that he had done some good.

But the bill never made it out of committee. The Montana Coal

Operators Association, with representatives from all of the state's mines, had the money and influence to change politicians' minds. And that's what they did with this bill. They managed to arrange a second hearing on the bill, during which one of the bill's sponsors—a Carbon County representative—completely reversed himself and claimed that miners in his district didn't want the blasting on shift to stop. Despite Boyle's arguments to the contrary, based on meetings he'd had with miners, all but one of the committee members voted to kill the bill they had so recently praised.

Boyle had also tried that year to get the legislature to amend a bill regarding state mine inspectors' powers. The amendment, which would have allowed inspectors to shut down dangerous mines, "met with dastardly defeat," Boyle said.

Maybe Boyle's latest attempt would be more successful. Now it wasn't just his word, but the word of a federal mine inspector insisting that the mines weren't safe. Montana mining codes had barely changed since 1911. Miners were still laboring under laws designed during the days when mules hauled coal. Coal mines had been mechanized for a long time, but the regulations had not caught up.

Before he left Montana, Arnold had met with Boyle to talk about all the problems he'd found in the Smith Mine. Boyle then called the union's executive board together. They discussed Arnold's recommendations and decided to approach the coal operators with a plan. Perhaps they could all work together.

Boyle began his presentation. His voice sounded like a snarl, but the words were genuine. He still wanted to get a law on the books that would give state inspectors more power, he told those assembled. He talked about Arnold's report. And he asked the mine owners to back him on a bill requiring stricter safety regulations. Boyle hoped to bring such a bill to state representatives when they reconvened after Christmas.

One of the union representatives read his motion.

"The executive board of District 27 desires to be on record as agreeing to recommendations made by Federal Coal Mine Inspectors and moves this joint board that the recommendations made by said inspectors be enacted into the state mining laws on the session of the Legislature convening January, 1943."

The men sitting around the conference table discussed the motion and some of Arnold's points. The mine operators, including a representative from Montana Coal and Iron, which owned the Smith Mine, maintained that they didn't see any need for new laws based on the inspection of one mine. Who knew, they rationalized, if the inspectors would require things like rock-dusting and a smoking ban in the other mines. Wouldn't it be better to wait until the feds had checked out all the mines? They also objected to requiring safer blasting powder because it cut down on profits. The so-called permissible explosives resulted in too much small coal that they couldn't sell, they claimed. Their customers wanted big, lump coal.

When it was time to vote on whether to jointly propose the bill, the union members supported Boyle's idea. The mine owners practically laughed him out of the room.

"The Montana Coal Operators Association feels in voting as it did that it was in no position to vote otherwise as the motion is too indefinite and at this time the association has no definite idea what the recommendations, if any, will be for the coal industry in Montana as a whole," they wrote in a statement. "It is, however, willing to cooperate to the fullest possible extent with the Federal and State coal mining inspectors."

In other words, they had no interest in supporting Boyle's efforts to make the mines safer. He had probably been crazy to expect that they would. But Boyle, arrogant and self-important, wasn't the type to doubt himself.

Mary Wakenshaw, who was so grateful to be a coal miner's wife, knew how rough union work could be. And not just for the men wearing ties.

When the Bearcreek workers set out to form a union, they knew that everything from blacklisting to death had befallen other American miners who'd tried to organize. They knew the sad epilogues: the nineteen miners killed and fifty wounded after a peaceful march for rights in Pennsylvania, 1897; the dozen striking miners' wives and children burned to death in Colorado, 1914; the famous shootout between miners and company heavies in Matewan, West Virginia, 1920. Though the National Industrial Recovery Act, which granted workers the right to form unions and bargain collectively with their employers, had passed in 1933, it was still daunting to fight The Man.

Mary's husband, Bud, helped birth the local, though not without a literal fight. One night years earlier, he was driving home after a union organizing meeting with three of his friends. Suddenly, a car pulled up beside theirs and forced them off the dark, winding road. The three thugs from back East who were in the car must have thought they'd taught the miners a lesson, maybe scared them out of organizing. They obviously didn't know men from Bearcreek: strong from years of taming coal, tough from years of hunger and struggle. Bud and his friends burst out of the car, grabbed the strangers, and pounded on them until they were subdued and bloody. Then, for good measure, they tipped their car over before driving away. The union they'd been organizing blossomed.

Bud was strong, but he didn't use his force indiscriminately. Only when necessary, like the time he was making his constable rounds and came upon two miners fighting. They both pulled pocketknives, so Bud grabbed them each by the collar, banged their heads together, and escorted them to the jailhouse. Or the day some religious fanatics came to the house and began playing records they hoped to sell. Bud threw the phonograph and the man using it out the door.

But he was a gentle man, too, one of those proverbial quiet but effective leaders. Which may be why he'd been elected president of Local 858 in 1939.

The miners met every other week in the union hall. Sometimes the men brought their kids, who ran around in other parts of the building while the dads discussed their important and secretive business. At the beginning of every meeting, the union warden asked for the password, which, presumably, everyone in attendance knew. Then they'd get down to the issues of the month. Sometimes they'd vote to waive dues for members who couldn't afford them. Other times they took up collections to help out members who were too sick to earn a living. Or they talked about the Labor Day picnic.

That picnic was the event of the year. The day began with long speeches by union officials, but once they'd finished, everyone let loose. One of Melvin Anderson's aunts usually won the women's contest to see who could pound the most nails into railroad ties. His sister, Doris, usually placed in the top three in the footrace, winning a cash prize of one, two, or three dollars. Someone always won a ham, and there were prizes for the largest family to march in the parade and for the gluttons who ate the most watermelon, pies, or crackers. The day ended with a baseball game. People looked forward to the picnic all year, so they were particularly disappointed when the union had voted to cancel it the previous September. Yet another of their simple pleasures gone. They decided to put the money toward war bonds instead.

Still, Bud and his union brothers had plenty of other issues to cover at their meetings. Management often tried to dance around their contract. At one meeting they reviewed a report from Tony Boyle himself, who'd been to the mine to fight with Superintendent W. R. Freeman about overtime pay for the machine operators.

"The overtime section of our joint agreement has been abused by the men and the management of the Montana Coal and Iron Company," Boyle wrote in the report. "It is abused at present."

Boyle and his officers had managed to negotiate a living wage for the Bearcreek men. Bud earned about $240 a month, Melvin's father got around $260, and electrician Frank Mourich took home about $336. Mine superintendent W. R. Freeman, for all of his pressures, didn't make much more than the head electrician, just about $375 a month. His brother James, however, earned at least $1,000 a month, sometimes double that. And he certainly wasn't doing any dangerous work.

Surely, union leaders also pushed for a safer workplace, but fair wages and hours seemed to take most of their energy. Years later, a Princeton University professor would write in a book about coal mining that despite impassioned speeches about mine safety, union officials seldom fought hard enough for safety before Congress or when haggling over contracts.

About the same time Boyle tried, but failed, to get the mine operators to back new safety legislation, Inspector Arnold sent the Freemans a letter. It told a frightening story. The results of the air analyses taken during the inspection showed high gas levels in the mine—enough gas, he wrote, to "require serious consideration of the ventilation system." "An immediate improvement is needed in the interest of safety," the letter stated. "I trust that you will take steps to improve the situation and warn mine officials of the hazards involved."

A Montana Coal and Iron secretary typed a reply to Arnold. In it, James Freeman assured Arnold that his men were already upgrading ventilation and that they weren't finding much gas in the mine anymore.

"Our fire bosses report merely traces of methane in just a few places," the letter said.

Dr. John Oleinik would have disagreed. Recently, the local physician had been treating more and more miners with symptoms of gas inhalation. They came to his two-story clinic with headaches and weakness that couldn't be explained by anything else. Oleinik, a small but fit man with sad-looking eyes and a long nose, loved his patients. He was a fervent liberal who believed in workers' rights and equality for all. Raised in Carbon County by a woman who made her husband quit mining because it was too dangerous and a man who toiled on a farm to send all three of his children to college, Oleinik had learned to act on his beliefs. He once tossed a beefy cowboy from a renowned local rodeo family over a bar because he was bullying someone in the saloon. And at the University of North Dakota School of Medicine he befriended several Jewish students and grew furious as he witnessed the anti-Semitism they endured. When his friends dropped out of North Dakota and transferred to the University of Nebraska medical school, he joined them. After graduating, he came back to Bearcreek to practice medicine, helping countless miners' families. He delivered Mary and Bud's only surviving son, Bobby. Then, when the little boy got older, he took out his tonsils and wrapped his hands in bandages after he fell and burned them on smoldering grass. The doctor once ran to Thelma Mourich's house after her mother called the office wailing, "He's dying! He's dying." The "he" in question turned out to be the family dog. Oleinik had also faced the gruesome chore of sawing off Robert Vagina's leg when it got caught in the Smith Mine's picking table.

Because Oleinik was as curious as he was compassionate, he began to wonder just how bad the mine's air was. His patients seemed sicker than ever that winter, so he guessed that the air was getting worse. As Freeman dictated letters denying any gas problem, the doctor decided to analyze blood samples from eighteen miners to prove his suspicion. The crimson drops were laced with an average of 27.5 percent carbon monoxide—some containing as much as 37 percent—enough to cause headaches, nausea, vomiting, and loss of judgment. He'd taken the blood samples at least two hours after the men had left the mine, so the carbon monoxide concentration was undoubtedly higher while they were underground. Fifty percent carbon monoxide would make a man pass out; 70 percent would kill him.

Oleinik had tested his own blood, too. One day five or six years earlier, between checking throats and listening for fetal heartbeats, he took a ride down to the mine and spent more than four hours underground—about half a shift. Before emerging, he stuck a syringe in his arm and drew a blood sample. Back at the office, he did his analyses and saw that his blood contained 18 percent carbon monoxide.

He had tested himself in an attempt to help one of his patients, a Smith miner who had suffered from carbon monoxide poisoning and couldn't work anymore. He was trying to get compensation from the Industrial Accident Board. Oleinik testified about the carbon monoxide levels found in his and the patient's bloodstreams, but the miner didn't get a penny. The board claimed that there wasn't any carbon monoxide in the Smith Mine at all. The man appealed the case to the Montana Supreme Court but still won nothing. He died of the poisoning eighteen months later.

Oleinik continued to encourage sick men to demand compensation for their illnesses or to stay out of the mines. They refused. They'd sit in his examining room, rolling their sleeves down and buttoning their cuffs as they agreed to think about his advice. But he knew they wouldn't take it. Even with union protection, the men worried that they'd get fired for complaining.

Despite dismissing Arnold's written warning about the gas, James Freeman followed through on some of his recommendations. He instructed his foremen to start carrying safety lamps and checking for gas where the men worked. He told men to start fixing the leaky doors, building boxes for the explosives, upgrading the electrical systems, and clearing some of the junk that impeded the air flow. And he even launched a new project. To increase ventilation, he ordered his men to drive another air shaft to the surface. Once it was cut through, all kinds of fresh breezes would flow through the mine and the miners' lungs.

But he wasn't so sure about some of the other suggestions. Rock-dusting? That was an expensive proposition. The new equipment would cost a fortune. So, despite the coal dust that literally piled up inside the mine, inches thick on the rails, Freeman overruled the suggestion. He had no problem authorizing his employees to order enough closed lamps for every man to use. What he may not have known was how much time would pass between the decision to order the lamps and the actual placing of the order. At least the company would be able to charge the miners for the new closed lights when they arrived. They'd have to rent them, with the cost of their safety coming out of their paychecks.

Because of the war, ordering supplies wasn't a straightforward process. The clerks in the mine office first had to write to the company that made the lamps and to the Bureau of Mines asking for a priority rating. The War Production Board issued these ratings, based on importance, to ensure that things like garden hoses weren't being manufactured before guns.

A representative from the lamp company would eventually call the mine office in late January to discuss the order, though a mine manager wouldn't order 183 potentially lifesaving lights until February 8. It would take almost eight weeks for them to arrive in Bearcreek. By then it was too late.

5 The Mice

Frank Mourich had been extremely busy since the inspection in November. It was up to him to address all the electrical problems Arnold had ticked off. With men still wearing carbide lamps, there was no room for stray sparks or downed wires.

Mourich didn't take safety lightly. His father-in-law had developed pneumonia after being severely gassed in the Smith Mine a few years earlier. Around the same time, Mourich himself had sucked in a dangerous dose of carbon monoxide while in the mine. That spring day, a cluster of miners smelled smoke and called Mourich to investigate. Together, in a move that one of the men would later admit was foolish, they headed straight toward the smell until they found a fire. But before they could put out the fire and return to work, they started to succumb. One of the older men stumbled. Mourich, surely beginning to feel impaired himself, must have realized that they were inhaling carbon monoxide. He led the man toward fresh air and ordered the others to evacuate, too. By the time they wove their way to the exit, Mourich and the old man were about to topple over. It took oxygen and time, but they eventually healed enough to go back to work. The fire took eight days to extinguish.

But even now, despite all that the miners were supposedly doing to make the Smith Mine safer, Mourich knew the air still wasn't right. His friends complained of killer headaches.

And he'd seen the mice.

They ran out of the mine when their tiny brains signaled a life-threatening oxygen deficit. It was the modern equivalent of the canary test. A generation earlier, miners carried the little birds into the mine along with their candles and shovels. If a canary's fragile system became saturated with carbon monoxide and the bird collapsed, the men knew they'd be next and they ran out. They'd clear the air and bring down another bird. If that one lived, the humans could work safely. If it died, they cleared the air again and retested with another canary. Now the mice gave the same warning. Thelma's father mentioned it over dinner one night.

"It's the strangest thing," he said to his family. "I keep seeing mice leaving the mine."

Other miners noticed it, too. One man would tear bread from his sandwich to scatter for the mice, as if they were his pets. They usually gobbled the scraps up, but for a few days that February he noticed that the bread just sat there. The customers had vacated the premises.

No one heeded the rodents' warnings, though. The men all continued to punch in for their shifts. Overtime was overtime, after all.

Which is part of the reason Mourich was at work on that Saturday morning, February 27. It was also partly because of his daughter Thelma's summer romance. People came to Yellowstone National Park to see the geysers spurt their smelly water and to snap pictures of the biggest waterfalls they'd ever seen. They also came for some pampering. Mother Nature and her geologic quirks took care of the first part. Hospitality experts handled the second. No doubt there were some professionals who fried eggs and scrubbed toilets for the tourists, but a good number of the summer jobs went to kids, and many of the kids came from Bearcreek.

Every year, a fellow who grew up in Carbon County would put on his version of a job fair for the local teens. He'd ask them their age and what they wanted to do and whether they had any experience stripping beds or busing tables. Thelma was fourteen when she had her first interview, but she looked older. She told the recruiter she was sixteen, and he hired her to work at the Canyon Hotel. She somehow convinced her parents to let her go into the wilderness and mop up for strangers.

The Canyon, which could sleep more than six hundred visitors, was said to be a mile around. It had a giant lounge with a high ceiling supported by plain, angular beams. It could have been mistaken for an airplane hangar if not for the grand staircase and art deco lamps. Chairs and desks were scattered here and there for solitary letter writing or flirty chats over cocktails. The waiters, of course, wore bow ties.

Thelma shared a mess of a room in the staff dormitory. She was great at making up guest rooms—as fast and thorough as any of the other maids. But when it came to her own quarters, she was too busy. Thelma and her roommate emptied their overflowing trash can and made their beds once, but only because they were tricked into it. The Canyon's formidable head housekeeper didn't like the girls, so when she left a note on their door saying they had better clean their mess before any frolicking would commence, they got nervous. What if she fired them and ruined the rest of the summer? Their room looked perfect when they left that night, much to the amusement of Thelma's aunt, a fellow employee, who had written the note.

Usually, though, as soon as work let out, Thelma washed her face, combed her hair, and went looking for excitement. Sometimes it was down to the dance hall. Other times, she and her friends stuck out their dainty thumbs and caught rides to different parties around the park.

On one of those nights in Yellowstone, at one of those parties, she found a boy with a Hollywood name: Del Stark. She and her steady boyfriend, Eli, had an agreement, sort of a "what happens in Yellowstone, stays in Yellowstone" kind of thing. So, Thelma cozied up to

Del until the end of the summer of 1942, when they kissed good-bye. She didn't expect to see him again. He had other ideas.

On the last normal day of Thelma's life, she came home from school and got ready to go to yet another dance with Eli. This time it was the annual junior class party, a bash proceeded by an exhibition basketball game and followed by a late-evening lunch. Thelma always looked great, but even a natural beauty had to work at it. She was probably fussing with her curls or choosing a lipstick color when her secret past showed up on the doorstep. She pulled open the door and smiled through her shock at Del.

She invited him in, of course. He'd probably been expecting to take her to dinner or a movie, some place where they could get close again. But she told him she had plans that night. Some girls would have shown him to the door and thanked him for the visit. Not Thelma. Del had used his gas rations to drive all the way from Billings—close to seventy miles!—to surprise her, and she couldn't send him away. She didn't want to leave him in the living room to twiddle his thumbs with her parents all evening, either. So she came up with a plan. She would bring both boyfriends to the dance, and hope Eli would someday forgive her.

With that decision made, it was easy to figure out what to do with Del for the rest of the weekend. He could sleep at her grandparents' house up the road. And Thelma would spend Saturday with him. Her parents were going to Billings to buy her mother a fur coat with the bonus money her father had been earning.

Not so fast, her father decided. *We're not leaving them alone all day Saturday to do who knows what.*

The fur could wait. Thelma's mother would stay home to supervise the teenagers, and Frank would put in a shift at the mine the next morning. He might as well go in, he told his wife. Overtime was overtime.

Frank reported to the washhouse at about eight that Saturday morning. He pulled off his street clothes and hung them in his metal locker, took out his blackened overalls, and stepped into them. Everyone around him did the same. There was Bud Wakenshaw with his father and father-in-law. Frank's brother, who repaired machines underground, was on the shift too, and so was his good buddy Emil Anderson.

Emil was Melvin Anderson's father. His official job was greaser and repairer, but he could really do anything in the mine. And everywhere else. He was a small man, about five foot seven and 140 pounds on a fat day, with gold wire-rimmed glasses and an extremely wide smile. He looked more like an accountant than a coal miner. He was gregarious and kind and always busy—practically the definition of a Renaissance man. Though he'd quit school after eighth grade to start mining, he certainly wasn't ignorant. He ordered books and studied them until he taught himself to be an electrician. He read *The Billings Gazette* every day and sport magazines like *Outdoor Life* every month. He helped his sons with their high school math homework even though he'd never formally learned it himself. But he wasn't just brainy. He built bedrooms onto his family's house and loved to flyfish. He made fantastic flies, too. He ordered feathers and a particular type of thread from a mail-order catalog and spent winter evenings tying them, then sold them for a dollar a dozen to the other miners. But his greatest love, besides his wife and kids, was music.

Every day after work, Emil practiced his trumpet for half an hour. Every Saturday night in the summer he played in the Red Lodge Band, which put on street concerts outside the fancy Pollard Hotel and played marches during the annual the Fourth of July rodeo. Those concerts must have seemed a long way off on that February morning, but they'd come soon enough.

Emil and Frank and seventy-five other men clocked in for the underground shift that day. After changing their clothes, they lined up to get their headlamps. Each lamp was identified with two brass ID tags. Whenever a man took a lamp from its hook, he left one tag behind on the wooden shelf and took the other with him into the mine, either tucking it into his pocket or hooking it onto his lunch pail. That way, the bosses could keep track of who had which lamp, and who was in the mine on each shift.

They grabbed their helmets and lunch pails, walked to the trestle, and squeezed onto the mantrip. They passed the sign reminding them not to miss a shift if they wanted America to win the war. They passed the dog, a cocker spaniel named Brownie who waited every day outside the mine for his master to come off shift and reward his loyalty with half of a sandwich. They rumbled over the tracks, across the highway, and into the mouth of the mine. The coal above their heads held fossils of leaves, reminders of the life that had existed on this spot millions of years earlier. Daylight vanished. Only a handful of the men would ever see it again.

6 The Notebook

Margaret Meiklejohn looked out a window in her four-room house to see if her father was heading up the road yet. Such surveillance was part of her daily routine when he spent the middle of the night in the mine: she'd wake early in her quiet bedroom, make her way to the kitchen, and prepare for breakfast. It was this twenty-four-year-old only daughter's job to nourish and care for her father. She'd time her cooking so the meal would be ready when he walked through the door, which meant putting the coffee pot on as soon as she saw him approaching the house.

The miners never worked the same shift all year-round. Often they'd work days for two weeks, then nights for two weeks, then back to days again. On February 27, Jack Meiklejohn, a fifty-four-year-old with bright white hair, worked an odd shift that overlapped night and day. He clocked in sometime after midnight, then left in the morning, after the day shift had started. He was a fire boss, a fairly prestigious position, one of the men who inspected the mine for gas, then cleared it out if necessary.

Margaret cracked the eggs and stirred the oatmeal for her father's breakfast. Sometimes she fried ham with the eggs. Sometimes, just the porridge, a staple for a man who'd grown up in damp Scotland.

She hoped her father would have an appetite this morning. The day before, he'd walked into the house looking green. The carbon monoxide that permeated so much of the mine's atmosphere made him weak and nauseated.

"Someday that place is gonna fly sky high," he said. "It's so full of gas."

Margaret hated to hear him talk like that. She hated that he worked in the mine, period. He'd gotten badly burned in a mine fire three years earlier and had spent plenty of time, wrapped like a mummy, in a local hospital. She'd begged him to quit, but he told her he couldn't. He'd been mining for more than thirty years. It was all he knew.

Margaret, a solid girl with a broad face and a pug nose, had good reason to worry about her father. He was her whole family. One weekend when Margaret was thirteen, she and her parents had taken a fishing trip with some other mining families. On Sunday morning, Margaret's mother sat at a gas camp stove flipping pancakes for breakfast. Margaret stood nearby. Suddenly, the stove exploded. Flames covered her mother's body. Margaret's father ran to her with a blanket to smother the flames, and she jumped into the river to ease her pain. But neither rescue attempt saved her. Three weeks later, on another Sunday morning at breakfast time, she died in a hospital bed. She was forty-four. For the rest of her life, Margaret would loathe fire.

"Fire and me don't agree with each other," she'd say when she was an old woman.

Maybe her mother knew she'd die young, because she taught Margaret a lifetime's worth of housekeeping lessons before that fire killed her. Margaret was just a young teenager when she began cooking and cleaning for her father. Their house was small and certainly not luxurious. It got so cold in the winter that her father would shut off the water when he and Margaret left for work and school so the pipes wouldn't freeze. Still, the pair built a nice life together. Jack took Margaret out for fancy dinners at hotels, and taught her to drive. He fished for trout while she sat on the riverbanks embroidering. She adored him.

It would be bittersweet, then, in a few weeks when Margaret would marry a young mine worker named John Cameron. She was six years past high school graduation, more than old enough to get married. Still, after the small March wedding, it wouldn't be just Dad and her anymore. Their small family would be divided once again.

Jack Meiklejohn was having a rough winter. Since the first of the year, he'd been arguing with his fellow fire bosses about the gas in the mine. All of them moved from room to room holding safety lamps over their heads, trying to detect methane before the other miners got to work. If they noticed the lamp's flame growing, they knew there was some gas in the area. If the flame went out, there was probably an explosive amount. They guessed about gas levels using a crude method of estimating how far from the coal face, or wall, they found the gas. When they decided there were only "trace" amounts of methane, they'd usually clear the gas by hanging a flap of brattice cloth in a particular way so it would change the air flow. But when they couldn't deny that a toxic amount of gas was present, the fire bosses would "deadline" that part of the mine, posting a sign that the area was off-limits. Miners were forbidden to work in deadlined areas. One man had been fired recently for breaking that rule.

Meiklejohn often discovered more gas than the other fire bosses. He'd told Margaret and a good friend about this discrepancy.

"They think I'm finding gas where they say there is none," he said.

It seemed to be a matter of conscience. If there was only a little bit of gas, Meiklejohn felt comfortable brushing it out and not reporting it. But when he knew there was too much gas for brushing to make a big enough difference, he was compelled to report it. The other two fire bosses weren't as concerned about his findings. They may have been reluctant to deadline too many rooms because that would limit coal production. Or indicate a serious problem in the mine.

Normally, the fire bosses recorded the high gas levels and deadlined sections on a board that hung outside the mine entry; this way, when a shift started the miners would know what lay ahead. Later, they would write the same details in a log kept in the mine office. But Meiklejohn decided to keep a third record of his findings. He began carrying a little black notebook, which Margaret had bought for him, whenever he went into the mine. He'd write what he found in the notebook, whether his colleagues agreed or not.

Meiklejohn must have filled several pages with ominous notes that last week in February. On Tuesday, a shooter wearing an open flame ignited a cloud of gas and started a fire. On the same day, a miner noticed more smoke than usual hanging in the air after the day-shift workers had finished shooting, leading him to conclude that less fresh air was circulating to clear the smoke. The next day, some men reported a horrible odor coming from one part of the mine, and two days after that, a motorman noticed more coal dust than usual in the same area.

Dr. Oleinik continued to prove that the mine was indeed gassy. In the middle of the week, a miner came to his office complaining of the lethargy and pain of carbon monoxide poisoning. A blood test showed that the miner, who was planning to retire from mining at the end of the week, had at least 20 percent more carbon monoxide in his system than normal. Many of the other miners probably did, too, though some managed to avoid the danger. Just that week, one crew had refused to work a particular area of the mine because they knew it contained a perilously high amount of gas.

The men working the night shift on the twenty-sixth had worried more about dust than about gas. At about eight o'clock, workers were battling a fire. It seems a cave-in had caused a live wire to fall on a sec-tion of track and ignite. It took about two hours for them to put the fire out, and a foot or so of track was ruined. The incident churned up even more coal dust than usual, though much of it had settled by the time Meiklejohn started his shift. He came on during the dark early morning, and spent hours inspecting rooms, taking notes, and clearing patches of gas. The night before, he had found gas in four-teen places, mainly on the southeast side of the mine. He'd record tonight's gas findings in the office record log before heading home. The sun rose. His shift would be done soon, and then he'd be at his kitchen table, eating Margaret's hot breakfast.

Once Margaret got married, Jack Meiklejohn would most likely become a grandfather. It would be nice to add to their tiny family. He'd been one of thirteen kids, growing up in a naturally boisterous household. Having only one child himself must have been a drastic change, and since his wife died, the days and nights had been even more quiet. Maybe Margaret would fill his house with noise again. She was already getting some mothering practice by taking care of a neighbor's baby. Virginia Sommerville had a one-year-old girl named Connie. Sometimes, when Virginia got too exhausted or was practically buried in dirty diapers, Margaret would take the baby over to her house and play with her there. Virginia certainly needed a break. She was just a kid herself. She would have been a junior at the high school with Thelma Mourich, if she hadn't dropped out after eighth grade and gotten married so young.

Some blamed her husband, Gil, saying at twenty he should have known better than to get involved with a girl just out of grade school. But Virginia was hard to resist.

If you go by all the old photos, she was the most beautiful girl in town. Tall and blond with big round blue eyes, she was as stunning as any calendar girl. Gil, with his chiseled cheekbones and blond curls, wasn't too bad either. He was already working at the coal mine when he first saw Virginia delivering copies of *The Billings Gazette*. She was a lanky girl with a grimy bag slung over her shoulder, trudging up and down the coulees, but he couldn't miss her beauty. He waited for her every day, first saying hi, then chatting a little longer, then, finally, asking her out to the movies. She said yes. She was fourteen and lived at home with her father and older sister. Her mother had died the year before. Something about heart and kidney trouble.

Later, Virginia would wonder if it was her mother's death that had led her to Gil. Maybe she was looking for someone special to love, she'd say. And even if that hadn't been a factor, surely her mother would have talked some sense into her when the relationship started to get serious.

The movie date went well. So did the nights spent dancing. Then Virginia graduated from grammar school and started doing the things high school girls do. Gil drove her into the hills above Bearcreek, parked the car, and took her into his arms. One day as they snuggled in that gray Chevy, he asked her to be his wife.

They couldn't very well wed in Carbon County—someone would definitely recognize them and tell her father. So they headed north to Stillwater County and lied about their age. On the day they got married, Gil was twenty and Virginia was fifteen. He wiggled a dime-store ring on her finger.

When they told everyone the news, Gil's mother took over the social hall and threw Virginia a lavish bridal shower. The Sommervilles seemed to be related to just about everyone in town, through blood or marriage, so a big crowd welcomed her to the family. The guests brought beautiful gifts, not that the newlyweds had the room or need for any of them. The couple moved in with his parents, settling in a little bedroom off the kitchen.

The baby arrived the next winter. The little girl looked blue the first time Gil saw her, and for two days he thought she was dead and that the doctors were keeping the truth secret because they were afraid to tell Virginia. Virginia was so weak after the delivery that she couldn't lift her head to wash her face in a basin, never mind hold the baby. Maybe the doctors just wanted her to recover before breaking the tragic news, Gil thought.

But mother and baby Connie ended up being just fine. And now, a year later, Virginia spent her days in love: with her daughter and husband, with her domestic life, with her future.

She and Gil had just rented an apartment five miles over the hill in Red Lodge. The town was famous for its location and for its Old West history. When Yellowstone tourists stopped in town after their ear-popping drive over the Beartooth Highway, they walked the same streets as many western legends. Buffalo Bill Cody, when taking breaks from his Wild West show, used to relax at the Pollard Hotel. Calamity Jane, carrying tobacco and refusing to ride sidesaddle, often showed up in town, causing the proper women to shake their heads in disapproval. Liver Eatin' Johnston was the town's first constable and lived in a cabin that still sits on the outskirts of town. The Sundance Kid was arrested for trying to rob a Red Lodge bank, but escaped before he could face the consequences. And Ernest Hemingway, a former bouncer at a Red Lodge brothel, honored the town by mentioning it in *For Whom the Bell Tolls*.

And now Red Lodge would be Virginia's home, too. For the first time in her married life she wouldn't be sharing a kitchen with her mother-in-law. It wasn't that she disliked her. Mrs. Sommerville, besides being so welcoming to Virginia, shared some of her skills with the girl. She'd been a baker's apprentice in Scotland and was known for her pastries. She taught Virginia how to bake currant cake, a favorite among the Scottish families. She'd shown her exactly how to roll out the stiff dough and when to add the sweet fruit. She was like a second mother to Virginia. But that didn't mean the girl wanted to stay with her forever.

"It's hard living with another woman," Virginia said.

She wanted her own place, where she could decorate the baby's room and plan the meals herself and listen to her radio soap opera, *Pepper Young's Family*, as loudly as she pleased. She wanted to comb Connie's hair and dress her in frilly pink outfits without the supervision of a more experienced mother. At first, Gil wasn't too thrilled with the idea of moving. He knew his parents needed him around to give them rides and help with the chores. His father, whose legs had been bowed by decades of mining and whose foot had been crushed by a runaway coal car, couldn't do everything himself anymore. Besides, Gil didn't see any reason to move.

But Virginia's request got louder. She fussed and yelled and jumped up and down. The young couple argued. She wanted an apartment in Red Lodge. He wanted to stay at his childhood home in Bearcreek. Finally, he gave in.

"Okay, go ahead," he said, surrendering.

She started to look for a place immediately. It was cold walking down Red Lodge's icy sidewalks, and slippery in some spots, but she was on a mission. Eventually, she found the perfect place off the main drag, down a handful of stairs from street level. A few rooms in the basement that they could actually afford. It might be hard to get the baby carriage down those steps, but otherwise it was just right.

"I'll take it," she told the owner.

Soon she'd be living on a city street, not in the middle of sage-brush and snakes. Once they settled into their basement apartment and the snow melted, Virginia would be able to bundle the baby up and walk from the market to the post office to the dress shop whenever she wanted. But she wouldn't waste too much money on herself. She was saving all she could for Connie's future. So far she had sixty-five dollars.

Virginia hadn't moved into the apartment yet, so her neighbor Margaret still had time to spend with baby Connie. Maybe that morning, after her father ate breakfast, she'd go visit her young friends. Though it was a Saturday, Gil wouldn't be home. He was working the day shift at the Smith Mine.

Gil stood by a conveyor belt and watched as the coal rolled past him. His job was to classify the chunks of coal into various categories: nuts, lumps, even fancy lumps, all going to different uses. The mine's big clients, such as the Great Western Sugar Company and the Ideal Cement Plant, depended on Smith coal to run their factories. The company wouldn't be able to hang on to big clients like those if it shipped the wrong grade of coal. Gil's job was important, but it wasn't as lucrative as the underground work his father and older brother did. Someday, though, he'd get promoted. Maybe he'd even be a fire boss, like Jack Meiklejohn.

Meiklejohn met up with one of the other fire bosses to discuss which rooms still needed inspecting. He told his colleague that he'd finish the rooms, marking them with his initials and the date when he did. If he deadlined any of them, he'd make a note on the board at the entrance. But he didn't get that far. A little after nine in the morning, Meiklejohn started to leave the mine. Before he could get out, coal dust detonated and fires flared throughout the mine. One of them probably erupted in front of him. He headed back to where he'd been working. Though he was burned, he kept going, fighting against his pain and the potent gas. As he rushed past a string of coal cars, he began to falter. Later, the rescuers would find his handprints running down the side of the coal car he used to steady himself.

7 The Explosion

Mary Wakenshaw hustled her kids into the Ford. The men were gone, the kitchen was clean, and she needed Bobby and Fannie to help pick up the chicks that were waiting at the Red Lodge train depot. First, though, she had to navigate the packed gravel roads that coiled through the mountains and into the next town. The hill between the communities was so steep that drivers hung water bags from their hood ornaments—even in the wintertime—in case they needed to pull over and cool down their engines. But the five-mile drive could be tough even before the big ascent. Just to get to the steep hill, Mary had to back the car out of her driveway, steer it up one hill and down another, pull onto the main road, turn left onto a coulee lined with houses, and exit out the horseshoe bend.

That's where she was when she spotted the smoke.

It was coming from the mine entrance, an opening that could look as innocuous as a garage doorway or as frightening as a howling mouth, depending on your expectations. Mary and her kids looked toward the sky and saw two men running across the trestle toward the mine. Nobody *ran* across the trestle unless something was very wrong.

With her heart pounding, Mary put the car in gear and turned around. She knew everyone who lived along the coulee and could have knocked on almost any nearby door. But, probably at Fannie's urging, she chose to stop in front of the home of the girl's new in-laws, the Thoms.

Mary jumped from the car as Mrs. Thom strolled out of the house to greet her.

"What's going on at the mine?" Mary asked. She had no time for pleasantries or coffee. She just wanted an answer.

Mrs. Thom couldn't give her one. She had no idea there was even a problem at the mine. Mary would have to uncover the story for herself. She slid back onto the car's bench seat, drove down the road, and parked as close as she could to the mine entrance. She wouldn't leave for sixty-two hours.

Bud Wakenshaw was as deep in the mine as a man could get. It snaked under Mount Maurice for three miles, and he was in the furthest working room with two other men: a sixty-eight-year-old driller and a thirty-three-year-old shooter. His crew had been on the job, drilling their holes and loading their explosive powder, for about an hour when the mine went dark.

"*What the f——?*" one of them surely cursed.

Bud wasn't one to panic. Just as he kept his anger in check when he clanged knife-wielding drunks together, he also bore his fear and sorrow privately. Bobby had seen him cry only once, after Bud's beloved dog had died. Spot, a black and white English setter who always accompanied Bud on his pheasant hunting trips, was murdered during a rash of neighborhood dog poisonings. Bobby watched as Bud walked away from the house carrying the dog's body and a shovel. There were tears on his father's cheeks. Bud buried the dog and never spoke about his grief. But he also sold all but one of his guns and never hunted again.

So, when something went awry that morning in the mine, he probably kept his cool. After all, the lights had gone off before.

Frank Mourich probably felt a bit more aggravated. He was in the machine shop not far from Bud and his crew, rehabilitating broken parts of mining and electrical equipment. He and a machine repairer had been sitting at a work table when the power cut off. All the lights rigged throughout the mine had died. The men might have been able to find their way out of the shop by the light of their headlamps. But they weren't doing terribly dangerous work, so they could have taken their helmets off. If that was the case, they would have had to feel their way out of the shop. Their eyes would never acclimate to the dark. In a lightless coal mine, there's nothing for the pupils to adjust to. They would have been stranded in the ultimate blackout, with no moon or stars or far-off streetlamps to tease their pupils.

Mourich also knew it wasn't unusual for the lights to go out, since most of the electricity flowed through one main circuit. Power failures happened once in a while, and the men knew the routine: stop work, move to the main passageway, and wait for the electricity to return.

Crews all over the mine threw down their tools and headed out of the rooms where they had been working. Some, like Virginia Sommerville's father and brother-in-law, grabbed their coats and lunch pails, knowing they could be in for a long wait. Others sat against the cool wall of the main tunnel, some of them probably grateful to have a break so early in the shift.

Not surprisingly, they didn't all follow the standard procedure. Some decided to find out what had happened. They aimed forward, toward the exits. They had no idea there had been an explosion.

Somewhere in the mine, one of those open headlamps, those flames that turned the men into walking torches, had collided with a band of methane gas. The man wearing the flame had been instantly ignited, his clothes, hair, and skin burning off his bones. The force of the explosion blew nearby men off their feet and into walls. They toppled from motorcar seats. One miner shot straight up, splattered against the ceiling, and crashed down onto a pile of coal.

The initial explosion churned up the coal dust that had been collecting on every surface of the mine. It coated the walls like flour on a breadboard and piled up on the ground like tiny sand dunes. Instants after the first blast, the dust particles caught fire. Once a speck of coal dust flares up, the flame spreads as if someone has lit a line of gas on the ground. More men blew apart. Timbers that had kept the ceiling from falling on their heads went flying, crashing into bodies and machinery. The wind blew tools and machine parts and lunch pails through the air, rendering them lethal.

Some men, thinking they could outrun the explosion, sprinted for fresh air. A switchman, who must have mistaken the loud noise for a runaway car that hadn't been hooked up properly, ran to catch it. But he caught a lungful of carbon monoxide first and collapsed against a wall. Others fell as they walked, their legs wilting under them.

The carbon monoxide, created by the burning methane, spread throughout the mine, writhing through tunnels, rooms, and bloodstreams. The light, odorless gas was brutal and sly, an enemy that knocked men down before they could see it coming. As they sucked it in, it displaced the oxygen in their blood, gradually suffocating them. They could go from drowsy to dead in minutes, depending on their location in the mine, how concentrated the gas was where they fell, and the condition of their bodies. Carbon monoxide, also called white damp by miners, is so dangerous because it's lighter than air and absorbed by the blood more readily than oxygen. Without oxygen, tissues and organs die, the heart beats in crazy patterns, blood pressure drops, and the brain can swell, killing brain cells by squeezing them to death. Some carbon monoxide victims just doze off. Others have seizures and fall into comas before dying.

Emil Anderson knew this. After the lights went out, he knew that the gas would be coming for him and that his only hope was to hide from it in a pocket of fresh air. He and his crew scrambled to the end of the passageway where they had been loading coal. There they found a room that hadn't filled with poison yet. They began to grab the debris around them and pile it over the doorway. Stuff that moments earlier would have been considered junk—empty explosive boxes, pieces of timber, knocked-about lunch pails—now served as invaluable lifesaving props. They frantically stretched brattice cloth and piled wood and coal and metal over the room's entrance in an attempt to make it airtight. The crew of five included a sixty-one-year-old widower and a twenty-eight-year-old with a toddler at home. There was another young father and middle-aged married man. Emil, with Melvin and Doris still depending on him for their futures, headed the biggest family.

Help had to arrive eventually. If they could just capture and detain the pure air, they'd be able to wait it out. Other men had done it. A generation earlier, a fire had trapped hundreds of copper miners underground in Butte, Montana. Twenty-nine of them barricaded themselves in a tunnel and erected a "bulkhead" to keep out the gas. They stacked up everything from timbers to dirt to underwear. They used a shirt to plug the only exposed hole, yanking it out when they needed to judge how close either gas or aid were. They lived in the cave for thirty-six hours, nearly running out of oxygen, before they tore down the walls they'd built. Then they walked or crawled out of that mine. Twenty-five of them survived.

Rescue techniques had surely improved since that disaster in 1917, so it was reasonable for the Bearcreek men to assume they'd be found much earlier than the Butte men.

Emil and his comrades might have done a better job of sheltering themselves if they'd been trained properly. The Smith men hadn't sat through a mine rescue training since 1930. A federal first-aid instructor, whose course may have included rescue techniques, was supposed to come to the mine in 1942, at James Freeman's request. But the training never happened. The instructor wasn't free to travel to Bearcreek until after February 20, 1943—a week before the explosion. But instead of scheduling the class then, Freeman instructed his staff to put it off even longer. In a February 9 telegram, Freeman suggested waiting until school got out in June, "when busses will be available and men not so busy."

Almost all of the men on the shift had been working the third seam, or level, of the mine. Men in the third seam loaded coal onto cars which were then pulled by electric locomotives to an intersection, or "parting." At the parting, a hoist took the cars up to the second seam, from which they were hauled to the coal preparation plant.

A small crew of men worked in the second seam. These men had the greatest chance of escape.

Ignac Marinchek, a stocky but handsome man who smoked a pipe and had held his baby grandson exactly one time, had been laying track in the second seam. He heard the explosion and ran to the closest door. He knew if he got through it, he'd be safe. First, though, he had to clear the garbage piled in front of the exit. As Marinchek scraped the trash out of his way, he began to feel faint. It got harder to breathe, harder to move his arms to unblock the doorway. Fresh air waited on the other side of it. If he could just get there, or even collapse into the door and suck some of that oxygen from under it, he might be okay. But if he fell backwards, onto the pile he'd just cleared, he'd be even further from salvation. He must have known he was about to lose consciousness. He might have prayed for an angel to nudge him forward. But no one heeded his prayers. When at last Marinchek passed out, he fell backwards, away from the air.

A few feet away, a wiry thirty-four-year-old named Willard Reid had been pumping water out of the mine when the power failed. Though it wasn't a complicated job, it was vital. The Smith Mine was flanked by underground streams and rivers just looking for a chance to let loose and flood the tunnels. The pumpmen worked to keep the mine dry, but the miners still worried about the water. Some were sure that if they died in the Smith, it would be from drowning.

When the lights didn't flicker back on, Reid knew there was trouble. Almost immediately, he heard what sounded like a freight train roaring toward him and felt unbearable pressure in his ears. He shut down his pumps, ran for the main tunnel, and threw himself to the ground. Debris was blowing from the third seam as if a twister were coming through. The pressurized air tossed him on the tracks, shredding his jacket and bruising his body. Even after the gust stopped, Reid stayed down. He knew the wind would return, blasting even stronger the second time. He held still for what felt like half an hour before the second rush came.

Then, silence.

When Reid finally stood up, he spotted Eli Houtonen, who spent his days as a rope rider, escorting cars into and out of the mine shafts. He, too, was heading toward the exit, but he'd grown confused. Reid tried to guide him. The door was only seventy-five feet away. They were almost out. Then Houtonen fell.

"Get up!" Reid yelled. "Come on!"

Reid, one of the best baseball players in town, was strong and persistent. He kicked his friend and wrestled him to his feet. He started to drag him, but Houtonen buckled again. Reid tried to pull him up a second time, but it was futile. Houtonen was dead weight, unconscious, though his heart continued to pump.

Reid kept running toward the door. Then he felt himself falling, a long, steep tumble. His last thought was to land facedown, so he'd be closer to whatever clean air remained. He sank to the ground as he ran, his headlamp still glowing.

A dimpled redhead named Alec Hawthorne, whose son was working deep in the mine, had been operating the hoist that brought coal from the third seam to the second when the power went off. He instantly felt the most intense wind he had ever experienced come up the slope, bringing airborne sticks and rocks with it. As he was getting bombarded, he ran to the closest telephone and dialed the office at the surface of the mine.

"There's something seriously wrong down here," he yelled into the receiver. "I'm getting the hell out."

The man who answered the phone couldn't understand Hawthorne. Not knowing about the explosion, he thought he'd just picked up a bad phone line. He told Hawthorne to hold on for a second while he walked to a different office to try another one.

As Hawthorne tried to flee to safety, he passed out, his body folded in half over a railing. When the man from the office grabbed the other phone extension and tried talking to him again, nobody answered.

8 The Panic

Everybody would remember the weather.

It was the kind of warm winter morning that reminds you how wonderful spring feels, the kind that gets you thinking about planting peas and putting the top down. At first, that shirtsleeves weather was the only memorable thing about the day. The people of Carbon County were doing the usual small-town Saturday chores. They were lining up at the post office to collect their mail. They were driving into town to do some grocery shopping. They were finding out that their lives were about the change forever.

At least that's what happened to Frankie Mourich, the older brother of Thelma and the son of Frank, the mine's electrician. He dressed early that morning and headed down the hill to the Bearcreek post office. It was a tiny but important place, where people caught up with their neighbors and with the outside world, particularly when the postmaster slid a Sears and Roebuck catalog into every family's box. On this morning, one of the envelopes in the Mourich pile came from the U.S. government. It was Frankie's draft notice. He was to report to the Navy, which wanted him for the Air Corps.

Frankie was pumped. This—defending his country—was the dream of many an American boy. And he'd been preparing for a while, with his aeronautics course and the ra-ra editorials he'd written. So, naturally, he was full of smiles and energy after he opened the letter. When he finished sharing his news with people at the post office, who must have offered congratulations and good-luck wishes and silent prayers that he come back alive, he headed to the Union Market, which was owned by the father of one of his buddies. He co-owned a bar, too, from which his son sneaked beers for the gang. It should have been a great day for Frankie Mourich, a day as bright as the sky. But instead of celebrating at the market, he learned about the mine trouble.

His sister, Thelma, already knew.

She'd gotten up and prettied herself, then headed for her grandmother's house to greet Del Stark, one of her two dates from the dance the night before. Despite her hopes that all three of them could have fun together, it hadn't been the most pleasant evening. Her boyfriend, Eli, was predictably angry to be part of a threesome. But Thelma, being the optimistic girl that she was, intended to make the best of the situation. She'd spend the day with Del, as planned, and worry about Eli later. It would all work out.

After visiting with her grandmother for a few minutes, she and Del headed out. As they walked away from the house, the wailing began. It came from the mine, a normal noise gone crazy. When a shift began or ended, the whistle sound was brief and blunt. Now, it went on and on without pause. Everyone within earshot knew this signaled some kind of emergency. A man may have gotten hurt, or a gas fire sparked. Either way, the miners would clear out and take the rest of the day off.

Thelma hurried to her house to tell her mother. She met her in the street, right by the spot where the miners always gave the kids Christmas candy.

"This is it," her mother said. "I know it."

"No, no," Thelma said. "Everything is going to be alright."

Her father couldn't be the injured man—he was too experienced to make a careless mistake. Her mother was just overreacting, as mothers so often do. Everything *would* be alright, Thelma was sure.

"Not this time," her mother said.

Thelma had two uncles. One was working in the mine with her father. The other, Lubes, was asleep.

Lubes, the baby of the family, worked outside the mine because his older brothers thought it was too dangerous for him underground. He had put in a shift the night before and had just gone to bed when his little boy woke him up. The boy had been playing outside, where some older kids explained what the long whistle meant. He knew his dad would want to know. Lubes, awakening to hear the siren for himself, was startled at first. Then he relaxed.

"Oh, there are always explosions in the mine," he told the boy, before rolling back to sleep.

Not everyone was so cavalier. As Emil Anderson struggled to barricade himself into a pocket of clean air, his family was sitting down to breakfast. They had nothing major planned that day. Doris would play outside in the melting snow with her friends. Melvin might need some recovery time from his Friday-night activities. Their mother would wait for Emil to come home, as she had throughout their twenty-one-year marriage.

As the Andersons salted their eggs and sipped their coffee, they heard a knock on the door. It was one of Melvin's friends, oddly missing his usual energy. There was a commotion over at the mine, he told the Andersons. They'd better come. Forgetting about breakfast, they rushed over to the mine to join the crowd. Doris and her mother would wait with the other women for news. Melvin would spend the day standing on top of the mine opening, hoping for a chance to go in and help save his father.

One of Doris's close friends was at home with her mother. It was her father's thirty-ninth birthday that day, and they were getting ready to throw him a little party that evening. The girl's mother was doing something in the basement when she heard the sirens. She became so distraught that the thirteen-year-old girl had to use all her strength to drag her up the stairs and out of the house so they could walk to town to find out what had happened.

A neighbor interrupted Margaret Meiklejohn's breakfast preparations with urgent news. Something must be wrong at the mine, the neighbor said, because the town doctors had just run across the road toward the mine opening.

Margaret bolted out of her house and ran right into her fiancée's brother. He'd been looking for her, expressly to keep her away from the mine. She was to head to her future mother-in-law's house instead, he instructed. The Camerons didn't have a loved one in the mine at the moment, but they had a house very close to it. They immediately opened their doors to anyone who needed food, rest, a bathroom, or a babysitter. Margaret could help out there until her father came home.

For decades to come, the people of Bearcreek and Red Lodge would remember exactly what they were doing when they heard either the sirens or the news: the wife and son of a trapped miner who were strolling down Red Lodge's main drag when a lady doing yardwork told them; the fifteen-year-old brother of a trapped miner who was cleaning his projection booth at the movie theater when he got word; the son of a trapped miner who was grinding grain for the hogs and feeding silage to the cows at the family ranch when two of his aunts broke the news; the kid who abandoned his sled, disobeyed his older brother's order to stay put, and sneaked to the mine with his friends; the miner who stayed home for one more day after recovering from colon surgery and decided to take a walk in the foothills with his young daughter that morning. He saw the smoke from the top of a slope.

"Oh my God—the mine," he yelled as he scurried down the hill, leaving the little girl to chase behind.

"This week probably will be one of the most eventful during the war in the lives of American civilians," predicted the *Billings Gazette* the previous Sunday.

The paper's editors were correct in heralding the memorable week, but wrong about the cause. They thought the big news in Montana would concern grocery shopping.

All over the country that week, Americans were waiting in line to register for the newest ration book. The Office of Price Administration, the agency charged with preventing food hoarding and making sure everyone got his or her "fair share" of the country's limited supplies, had announced that it was time to trade in the first book for a more comprehensive version. Throughout the war, people would have to adhere to the rules of four different ration books. Besides ensuring that there was enough food, gas, and other goods for the military, the books helped keep citizens honest.

"Although most Americans don't try to chisel on their neighbors, there are some persons who will take advantage of their ability to get more than others," the paper said.

Though the ration books were intended to make everyone equal, the miners' families in Montana would get a little extra food than other folks. Just the day before, the state legislature had passed a bill increasing allotments of canned goods for ranchers and miners, whose jobs were considered essential for the war effort.

Getting used to a new book was yet another sacrifice Americans were being asked to make. In December, owners of the local dairy had placed an ad in the paper announcing that they had to stop delivering because their application for extra gas points had been rejected. There'd be no more waking to fresh milk on the stoop; folks without their own cow would have to go to the market or the dairy owners' house to get their milk.

In January the Office of Price Administration put a ban on sliced bread, ordering bakeries to sell only whole loaves as a way to streamline production and distribution. At the beginning of February the government decreed that women's heels could only be made a touch over two inches high. Other shoe-related manufacturing regulations: no men's patent-leather shoes, no women's formal evening slippers, no metal-spiked golf shoes, and no footwear in colors other than black, white, army russet, and town brown.

And now, people in their dowdy footwear would have to give up another convenience, since canned goods would be so hard to get.

"No more punching open a can of tomato or grapefruit juice for breakfast every morning," read an Associated Press article about rationing. "Less rushing home from a bridge game, ladies, to ready a meal by can opener."

The second ration book was more complicated than the first, which had only counted sugar purchases. It included pages of red and blue stamps: red for meat, dairy product, and oils, which would be rationed later, and blue for processed foods like chili sauce and cans of soup. Every citizen got a book, and the head of the household had to balance the books and stamps when planning meals and shopping for ingredients. The grocers would tear out the stamps in front of customers whenever they bought rationed items.

Besides explaining the new books, the ladies running the ration book registration tables asked people to declare how much coffee and canned fruit and vegetable products they already had at home. If someone admitted to having a stash, the registrar ripped out stamps equaling that amount before the holder could take the book home. They took the coffee stamps out of all the children's books because they were officially under coffee consumption age. The writer E. B. White, standing in the same kind of line all the way across the country in Maine, copped to a bottle of catsup and seven pounds of coffee and lost the corresponding stamps.

"Persons who should know are saying that the civilian population is just beginning to realize we are actually in a war and that the situation is really serious," the *Billings Gazette* noted.

Registration was a major happening in Carbon County that week. Classes let out early on weekday afternoons so people could register at the school buildings. On Saturday, even more people showed up with their old books and declaration forms. A Red Lodge teacher confiscated used books and issued new ones from a second grade classroom that morning. The room was crammed with people waiting their turn when the emergency whistle interrupted their chitchat. Suddenly, everyone wanted to get out and see who was safe and who wasn't.

The teacher sped up her work and was quickly processing people when two little girls ran into the room.

Something terrible has happened at the mine, they told her in scared little voices.

Their father, a tracklayer, was inside.

The teacher, accustomed to soothing riled children, tried to reassure and calm the girls. She told them not to worry, though who knows whether or not she was following that advice herself. All the adults were beginning to panic a bit, though they tried to keep their emotions tamped down.

When all the ration books had been distributed and so many of the people had flocked to the mine, the teacher walked the girls home to wait for their father. It would be a very long wait.

Once she arrived at the mine, Mary Wakenshaw headed immediately to the outside machine shop and began brewing coffee. The rescuers would need it to keep their energy up, and the trapped miners would need it to revive themselves when they got out. Coffee was good. Coffee was healing. Coffee kept Mary from thinking too much.

Bobby and Fannie met up with one of Fannie's best friends, Betty Hunter, who'd heard the news at the post office and had caught a ride to the mine. It was a crazy scene already, so no one noticed when the three of them slid down the snowy hillside to get a closer look at the inside of the mine. Maybe they'd see Bud walk out. But the closer they got to him, the closer they got to the deadly fumes emanating from the mine.

Thelma's uncle Lubes, who'd told his son that explosions happened all the time, couldn't stay in denial—or bed—for long. He grasped the gravity of the situation when his wife came home and told him about the smoke. She'd been one of several people at the mine picking up bimonthly paychecks when she saw the chaos firsthand. Lubes jumped out of bed while his wife bundled the whole family into the car. Together they joined the traffic heading to the mine.

Thelma's grandmother had already buried far too many children. Now she looked out the car window at the smoke and the people, the Red Cross truck that had just arrived and the doctors. She had three surviving children. One had driven her to the mine. Two were inside it. She prepared herself for the worst.

"They're all gone," she said.

9 The Rescuers

But they weren't all gone.

At that moment, with the winter sun still grinning down on Bear-creek, there remained life in the mine. Men battled: against nature, which assaulted them in the form of ancient methane; against themselves and the potent urge to lie down and sleep off their ferocious exhaustion; against dark, fear, odds, and time. Hearts pounding, eyes dilating, adrenaline surging, their fight-or-flight mechanisms cranked higher than ever, they struggled to see their children and wives and the sky one more time.

While the men on the surface had tried again to reach the miners by phone, a young tipple worker had noticed smoke curling out of the mine's mouth, as if it were alive and taking a cigarette break. Two boys ran to find Tom Freeman, the outside foreman, who'd been left in charge while his older and younger brothers, the superintendent and general manager, vacationed in California. He sent four surface workers into the mine to find out what was going on. One of them was the superintendent's son.

The men grabbed the only gas mask they could find. It was old, with a broken seal and a partly used oxygen canister. The company had barely any rescue equipment. Arnold had noted during the inspection that four blankets, two stretchers, and some dressing materials were the only first-aid supplies in the mine. The company kept five self-contained oxygen packs in a supply house, but they hadn't been used or maintained in years. They kept two gas masks at the mine, but the canisters that made them useful were damaged.

James Freeman knew how outdated his rescue gear was. In 1942 he sent a letter to the purchasing department of another Montana mine. In it, he discussed selling some oxygen breathing apparatus.

"These have been in our possession for ten years or more and have not been kept in condition and all rubber attachments have deteriorated to a point where they will have to be completely renewed," he dictated to his secretary.

He offered the damaged goods for the same price he paid for them, plus shipping costs.

As soon as the would-be rescuers entered the mine their heads began to seize up. A miner once said it felt as if the top of his skull were going to blow off when he worked in an extremely gassy mine. In fact, miners reported, the head pain was their best clue that they were immersed in methane. The ache was compounded by the awful smell, probably the rotten-egg scent of hydrogen sulfide, another gas common to coal mines, stinging their nostrils.

Tom Freeman had instructed the men to increase ventilation as they looked for the source of the smoke. They'd walked more than half a mile when they came to a door that they thought might lead them to answers. They pulled it open, looked down, and saw the crumpled body of Ignac Marinchek, the man who had collapsed while sweeping garbage out of his way. The men lifted Marinchek and carried him to a clear room, where one of them began trying to breathe life into him with mouth-to-mouth resuscitation. The rescuer would have to remember these steps: tilt head, pinch nose, place lips over patient's mouth, blow. Pray. Pounding and yelling wouldn't hurt, either.

Two of the men stayed with Marinchek, while the other two continued walking deeper into the mine. They soon spotted Houtonen where he'd collapsed on his way to safety. They also saw a light beaming from further down the passageway. They couldn't tell what it was, but they didn't have time to investigate yet. First, they had to lift and carry Houtonen to their makeshift rescue center and begin mouth-to-mouth on him, too. Marinchek still hadn't responded, despite the men repeating the procedure over and over. Tilt, pinch, blow. Tilt, pinch, blow. But Houtonen must have inhaled less gas. After ten minutes of resuscitation, he took a breath on his own.

This was excellent news. Maybe whatever had happened wasn't so bad after all. Maybe they'd all bounce back and be laughing about it over beers by nightfall.

The second set of rescuers headed back to the light they'd seen in the distance. It led them to Reid, whose last sensation had been of falling down something deep and dark. His headlamp was still glowing. Now, regaining consciousness for a second, he saw the rescuers. They were holding a lantern, except it didn't look like a lantern to Reid's gassed-up mind. It looked like a giant washtub was coming toward him. He passed out again, becoming dead weight for his friends to carry to the clearing. There they started trying to force life back into him, too.

News of the emergency started to spread. At some point, one of the first four rescuers had grabbed a phone in the mine and shouted for Tom Freeman to send more help. Freeman ran down the rocky hill to the main office, where he told the office clerk to start dialing. Emergency calls disturbed the Saturday-morning peace of Montana Coal and Iron officials and of union boss Tony Boyle. A phone tree began to sprout, with everyone contacted ringing up someone even more equipped to help. The clerk made calls to other mines around the state, asking them to send their specially trained rescue crews.

At the Foster-Creek mine, a smaller Bearcreek coal mine also owned by Montana Coal and Iron, work stopped. The miners were told to report to the Smith to help dig some guys out of a mess. It was just a cave-in, their superiors told them, but they'd better hurry. The mines were half a mile apart.

Someone called the funeral home and asked them to send their ambulance, a big Chrysler limousine that had been adapted to hold stretchers. The ambulance driver called the fire chief, who came with tanks of oxygen and his old Packard, which also served as an ambulance. They stood outside the mine with Dr. Oleinik and another local physician, waiting for patients.

Wives of night shifters continued to shake their husbands out of bed, breaking into their dreams to tell them they had to go back to the mine and help with a rescue. Former Smith Miners, who knew the layout of the mine and most of the trapped men, drove to the mine and offered to help. Anyone who worked on the surface, like Gil Sommerville, tried to pitch in.

Wait, they were told, it's dangerous in there. Everyone can't just rush in.

Someone alerted the press. City reporters from Billings packed up their pads and pencils and headed for the mountains. Photographers stuffed their pockets with film and joined them. The announcers at radio station KGHL in Billings interrupted their programs with news flashes. Not much was known at this point, but the announcers urged wives to stay away from the mine.

Fat chance.

Families continued to crowd around the mine, the women bringing blankets and fresh clothes for the rescued miners to wear, the men waiting helplessly. Bobby Wakenshaw leaned into the mine, breathing the same toxins that filled his father, and waited, as children always do, for his dad to come back. And Melvin Anderson, for probably the first time in his life, felt the terrible, out-of-the-natural-order burden of needing to save his father. But nobody would let him try. Not without the right equipment.

Emil Anderson could have used his son's help. He and his crew had piled everything they could find over the doorway of the room where they were sheltered. Only two feet of space remained open to the air, creating a little window for death to sneak through. There were five of them; they'd watched as a sixth crew member had tried to run to safety. He must have either panicked or believed there was no way they could shield themselves against carbon monoxide. When there was nothing left to do except wait for help, they began writing. The men who'd been rescued after barricading themselves in the Butte mine had written final notes too, just in case. Putting their thoughts down didn't mean they were going to die; it just meant they were doing all they could. Maybe after they got out, their families would preserve the notes so the miners could look at them every once in a while during their long lives, remember this ordeal, and feel grateful that they had escaped.

Emil and his friends ripped the sides off a wooden box that held explosive powder. Using the chalk they carried for making notations or signing their initials on coal walls, they composed messages. *Good-bye wifes and daughters*, one weak man wrote. John Sudar, the young man with the toddler at home, was so determined to get his feelings to his family that he wrote them on his helmet and on a board. His daughter, a little girl with blue eyes so pale they almost looked translucent, would read them one day. Emil, knowing these could be the last words his family ever got from him, included a clue about the crew's actions, an apology, and his love. He checked the pocket watch he always carried with him and wrote down the time.

Help was still hours away from Emil and his crew, who were about two miles from the mine entrance. The rescuers hadn't even reached all the men on the second level of the mine. While the first crew continued their revival efforts, more groups of rescuers had entered the mine, with only two gas masks to go around. They'd walked through the smoke until they spotted a forty-two-year-old rope rider who'd also been working in the second seam. He was lying on his back next to the thirteenth car of a train full of coal. His lunch pail sat between his legs. One of the rescuers reached down to take his pulse and noticed that his chin was quivering. The rescuers put his limp body onto one of the locomotives and let it coast down to the men performing mouth-to-mouth. They went to work on him, too, but the man's chin stopped moving. He never breathed again.

The rescue crews moved forward, trying, as they went, to repair stoppings that had been blown out. If they could get these barriers, which kept fresh air flowing through the mine, back into place they might be able to keep the toxic fumes from dominating. And they might have succeeded if they'd had gas masks and oxygen canisters instead of only wits and will. The unprotected men began to trip, fall to their hands and knees, and lose their minds, but not completely, so they knew to stumble out of the mine before it was too late. There, they called for reinforcements. For hours, strong men entered the mine and spent men staggered out.

They found Alec Hawthorne lying near the phone he'd used to make the first call for help.

"I'm getting the hell out of here," he'd said.

But he hadn't. He must have blacked out as soon as he dropped the phone, and now an hour and a half had passed. His rescuers breathed their air into his lungs. It worked. Hawthorne came back to the world. He was a miracle. He was hope embodied. But he wasn't the only one. Eli Houtonen had finally responded, too. The exhausted but adrenaline-fueled rescuers loaded him onto a stretcher and carried him out. And Willard Reid woke, then sat up, then allowed his friends to take him out of the mine. His older brother and cousin, men he'd spent his whole life with, stayed stuck somewhere in the mine's third seam.

It was about noon when some families' prayers began to be answered. After nearly three hours of waiting, they watched five men emerge from the mine, dirty but whole.

Initially, they didn't know who'd made it out. The previous night, a high school junior named Jane Laird had seen her father immediately before he washed the coal dust from his face. His skin was completely black except for two white circles around his eyes, that skin only clean because he wore glasses.

Now, seeing only a blackened face on one of the stretchers, Jane thought it was her father. She started running down the hill, screaming "Daddy! Daddy!" until her older sister, realizing the lucky man belonged to someone else, pulled her back.

Alec Hawthorne's wife spotted him and started to scream. She tried to scoot down the hill to be at his side, but she was so big and round that she slid and tripped down instead. Fannie and her friend pulled her up and steadied her as she made her way down the rest of the slope. But Mrs. Hawthorne, whose eldest son was still in the mine, still couldn't get close to Alec. She wouldn't have been able to talk to him anyway. He was alive and breathing, but wouldn't regain consciousness and realize what had happened to him until the next morning, when he woke up under the fresh sheets of a hospital bed.

The doctors on-site did all they could to treat the victims. They checked their vital signs and pumped pure oxygen into them. When they'd done all they had the knowledge or equipment for, they packed three of them into ambulances and sent them to local hospitals, not knowing whether they'd live to describe what had happened in the mine. Just because they'd been resuscitated didn't mean they'd survive. No one knew how damaged their bodies were.

Two of the men who were carried out of the mine that morning didn't go to the hospital. The doctors sent them on another journey. They hadn't really been rescued at all.

10 The Travelers

Once upon a time, Americans journeyed to California in search of gold. The Freemans were just looking for a tan.

The royal mining family of Carbon County, Montana, had been fleeing the wind and snow to spend a month or two by the shore for years. Before the war, they went away because there wasn't enough work to keep them at the mine. Then, when work and profits multiplied because of the war, they went away because they could afford leisurely vacations. Long Beach, a resort town a little more than twenty miles from Los Angeles, sits on the edge of the Pacific Ocean. Chilly folk came for the heat, for the amusement park with its giant wooden roller coaster, and for the chance to wake on winter mornings to birdsong. For the Freemans, such a sound surely beat the pierce of the mine whistle and the crunch of the coal-processing machines.

The Freemans' trip west was a big deal. Two newspapers, including the daily *Billings Gazette*, announced one family's departure in their society pages. Just a little notice, but enough to show the trip's significance.

"Mr. and Mrs. W. R. Freeman are vacationing in California," the *Gazette* printed.

Rich and poor folks notified the papers of their travel plans, but whether because the publications lacked space or the destinations lacked prestige, not all the itineraries made it into print. Fannie Wakenshaw, who'd gone to California that winter to get married, had hoped to see news of her trip in the paper, too. She'd asked Bud to save the society pages while she and Mary were away. But it wasn't mentioned.

W. R. Freeman, the mine superintendent, left Montana with his wife, Jeannie, on January 27, exactly a month before the disaster. His brother James, the mine's vice-president, had taken his family to Long Beach for the winter a few days earlier. The families rented apartments in a three-story complex that overlooked the beach. Though they wintered together, the brothers' clans weren't as close as would be expected. According to W.R.'s granddaughter, it was more a cordial relationship than a warm, deep one. Years later, the cousins descended from the Freeman brothers would completely lose track of each other.

Long Beach, unlike Montana, had been fairly diverse before the war. Hundreds of Japanese Americans, many of them farmers and fishermen, had called the city home until 1942, when President Roosevelt ordered them to internment camps. The government claimed that allowing Japanese people to live so close to important ports posed a danger to the nation. Since Long Beach was home to the U.S. naval fleet, it must have been relatively easy to convince citizens that this was the right thing to do.

On that last weekend in February, the jangling phone interrupted the Freemans' Saturday activities. It was Tom, the Freeman brother who served as outside foreman at the Smith Mine. He told them about the gas and the rescues and all those trapped men. No one knows what James did upon hearing the news. W.R. had a heart attack.

At least that's what his wife believed. She watched as he grew nauseated, went pale, and fell over with chest pains. There was no time to see a doctor, because W.R. insisted on taking the next train back to Montana. Evidence of an actual heart ailment would surface soon enough, though.

It was ironic that W.R. would be stricken while on holiday. His wife had worried that the pressure of running the mine would kill him on the job. Somehow, she'd persuaded him to quit completely to preserve his health. In the middle of December, the couple had sat down with a man named Bill Romek. Romek, Montana Coal and Iron's assistant manager, was one of the only men in management who wasn't related to the Freemans through blood or marriage. He'd been working for James, who was less than a year older than he was, for twenty-two years. He always called him *Mr. Freeman*.

Romek was an affable guy who seemed to befriend everyone, often over a glass of spirits. He peppered his written memoirs with tales of this bar or that, this drunken escapade or that beery outburst. He was so friendly, in fact, that another of his claims to fame was that he was the only member of mine management to socialize with union boss Tony Boyle, who had invited Romek to one of the union's Labor Day dinners.

W.R. had told Romek that he wanted to resign because he hadn't been feeling well. He was almost sixty-seven and starting to grow frail. Arnold's safety suggestions may have also played a part in W.R.'s plan to retire. According to one of his grandsons, Wayne, there was some tension between W.R. and James after the inspection. Wayne, who was only six in 1943, remembers hearing about fights concerning what should and shouldn't be repaired in the mine. It's conceivable, given their reactions to the disaster, that James insisted on protecting the bottom line while W.R. felt more responsible for protecting his men. That frustration might have pushed him to try to get out.

Romek convinced W.R. to stay a little longer. With so many men at war, the company couldn't afford to lose a superintendent. Whomever they promoted to the job would have to be replaced, adding to the existing manpower shortage. As it was, old men had been called out of retirement, and no one could quit without finding his own replacement. Freeman agreed to stay on, though he asked Romek to let him go as soon as possible.

While still on the job, W.R. had gotten his staff to make some improvements. Some of the leaky doors and stoppings were repaired so that more fresh air could reach areas where the men worked. Mine officials contacted DuPont about obtaining legally permissible explosives, and a team had begun testing new, safer ones inside the mine in mid-February. The main airway had been cleared and enlarged.

The biggest project W.R. oversaw was the building of a new air shaft from the third bed to the outside of the mine, a project that Arnold might have suggested verbally, though it wasn't in his written report. Workers had dug the shaft to within a few feet of the second bed, but they still had about four hundred feet to go before breaking through to fresh air. Then, inexplicably, the work stopped at the end of January, right before W.R.'s vacation.

No one really knows why the work was halted. The mine foreman he left in charge would later say that W.R. had told him to stop work on the new shaft until he came back from Long Beach. W.R. would later dispute this, claiming he had quit his job before going to California and that before he left he'd told the men to cut the new shaft through to the Number 2 level, then ask other managers how to proceed. Another miner would say he heard the work had stopped because management didn't want to buy another expensive fan to blow out the gas.

While W.R. breathed through his chest pains, James may have had an attack of a different kind. He, too, knew that dangerous conditions had gone uncorrected while he took in the California sun.

James essentially ran the business via post during his vacation, corresponding with Romek on a regular basis. Romek sent his boss a detailed letter every week. Some of the letters relayed excitement about profits, some solicited opinions and decisions, and some asked for forgiveness. On February 12, Romek admitted to misplacing a request from the purchasing clerk to get a priority rating from the War Production Board to buy a new coal crusher. He'd eventually found it buried among some other papers, but he assured James that he could make up for the delay his disorganization had caused and get the crusher delivered sooner than the quoted date.

In the same letter, Romek mentioned that an equipment salesman had told him to order a rock-dusting machine as quickly as possible, since the new federal inspections had created a demand for them. Someone at Montana Coal and Iron had contacted the American Mine Door Company of Ohio in December and asked for information about rock-dusting machines. The general manager of the door company had written three letters in response to the inquiry before he finally stated that he didn't want to become an annoyance and would stop corresponding if Montana Coal and Iron was no longer interested in rock-dusting. That clearly seemed to be the case.

"Just before you left for California, you stated that there was no hurry, so I would also appreciate your wishes on this matter," Romek wrote to James regarding the rock-dusting.

James confirmed that he was in no rush to get the expensive piece of rock-dusting equipment, despite Arnold's suggestion that it was essential for safety.

"The rock-dusting of coal mines is the most dependable method of combating the coal-dust explosion hazard," Arnold had written in his preliminary inspection report. He'd also told mine officials that as they increased ventilation, the mine would get even drier and dustier, making rock-dusting even more important.

Even so, James dictated a letter back to Romek: "I think you can let the rock-dusting equipment ride until I return to the mine, unless something should turn up that you think it is advisable to hurry this equipment."

In the next week's letter, Romek wrote James about a successful lobbying trip to Helena. He'd gone to speak against some bills being considered by the state legislature's worker's compensation committee. Everything went the company's way, he wrote, except that a bill to increase the burial allowance from $150 to $250 if an employee were killed in the mine would probably pass.

TOP: Mount Maurice, the mountain under which the Smith Mine ran. The winding road in the photo leads to and from Red Lodge, where many of the miners lived and where the rescuers were taken to a makeshift hospital. Photo by the author.

BOTTOM: Abandoned Smith Mine coal-processing buildings. Photo by the author.

TOP: The monument to the Smith Mine disaster in Bearcreek Cemetery. Photo by the author.

BOTTOM: Old and new gravestones for the Wakenshaw babies. The white stone is the original, and the gray was added by Bob Wakenshaw, their younger brother. Photo by the author.

TOP: Mary Wakenshaw standing beside the gravestone of her husband, Bud, and his father, Adam, shortly after the disaster. Photo courtesy of the Wakenshaw family.

BOTTOM: Bob and Fannie Wakenshaw around the time their father and two grandfathers died in the mine disaster. Photo courtesy of the Wakenshaw family.

Bob Wakenshaw (*left*), whose father and grandfathers died in the mine disaster, and Wayne Freeman, whose grandfather and great-uncle ran the mine. The men met at the Centennial Celebration for the town of Bearcreek in 2006. Photo by the author.

Virginia and Gil Sommerville, 1942. Photo courtesy of Virginia Sommerville Casey.

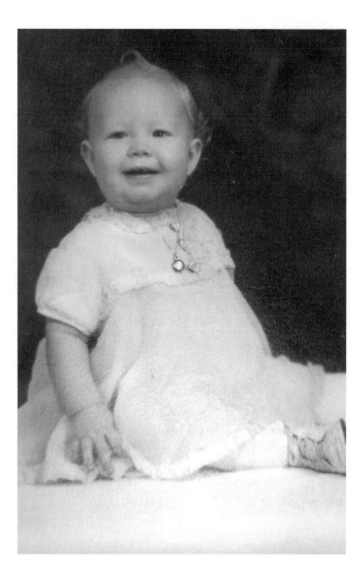

Connie Marie Sommerville, age 1, photo taken shortly before the disaster.
Photo courtesy of Virginia Sommerville Casey.

Connie Marie Sommerville's grave. Photo by the author.

Lula and Frank Mourich. Photo courtesy of Thelma Mourich Bischoff.

Thelma Mourich, around the time of the disaster. Photo courtesy of Thelma Mourich Bischoff.

The Bearcreek High School basketball team, 1942–43. Frank Mourich holds the basketball, and Melvin Anderson sits to his immediate right. Photo courtesy of Thelma Mourich Bischoff.

SMITH-MINE-EXPLOSION
A RESCUE WORKER R. COMING OUT.
2-28-43.

FLASHS-STUDIO
RED-LODGE
MONT

LEFT: A weakened rescue worker being helped across the trestle after his shift underground. Photo courtesy of Flash's Photography, Red Lodge, Montana.

BELOW: Nurses caring for gassed and exhausted rescue workers in the makeshift gym hospital. Note the basketball hoop. Photo courtesy of Flash's Photography, Red Lodge, Montana.

Bud, Fannie, and Mary Wakenshaw, mid-1920s. Photo courtesy of the Wakenshaw family.

"But it really doesn't mean a great deal," Romek assured his boss.

Romek also noted this cheerful news: he'd managed to hide some profits from the federal government.

"The net profit for the month was $24,473.16; however, I am charging Federal Tax Expense with $8,000, and making additional adjustments of $4,000 so the reports will show a net of $12,473.16 for the month, or approximately 19 cents per ton," he wrote. He went on to explain that the newly created net profit was now in line with the previous months' figures.

And on February 26, one day before the disaster, he wrote that the current workweek would be the last of the six-day weeks. The Saturday of the disaster was to be the final weekend day that men mined full-time.

"I am certain this will meet with your approval as we badly need the sixth day for maintenance and repair," Romek wrote, adding that "there is absolutely no profit in producing the sixth day."

Though the miners had been convinced that working around the clock was a way to support Uncle Sam, company officials apparently weren't requiring those hours out of a sense of altruism. They just wanted to earn more money. One Bearcreek rescuer and former miner, who would see such awful sights in the mine that week that he wouldn't ever speak of them, was certain of that.

"Big business isn't patriotic," he said when he was in his eighties. Talking about the disaster still brought tears to his eyes.

Indeed, records show that coal sales to railroads, the sugar company, the cement company, and smaller businesses increased nearly every month in 1942. The tons sold had more than doubled from the beginning to the end of that calendar year.

Also in the February 26 letter, Romek told James that two men had been killed in the nearby Roundup coal mine that week, for a total of three fatalities in less than two months.

"They certainly have had tough luck, and I sincerely hope that such luck avoids our properties," Romek wrote.

While Romek waited for the Freemans to come east, their nemesis headed north. G. O. Arnold was back in Salt Lake City when he got the news. It was just about lunchtime when the call came from someone at the Montana office of the Bureau of Mines. He'd heard about the explosion from a safety officer at a copper mine that would send rescuers to Bearcreek. Though Arnold wouldn't have been surprised to hear of a disaster befalling the Smith Mine before he inspected it, he thought the place was on its way to becoming safer. The Freemans and their employees had seemed to take his suggestions seriously, and had assured him that they would act on them. The last correspondence he'd received from James in December had identified several ventilation improvements that had already been made. And in mid-January, Freeman had written to the man who inspected the mine with Arnold and told him that the new air shaft was already a third of the way through. He never wrote, however, about workers leaving the project unfinished.

Arnold also thought the state mine inspector was on top of things. He'd sent this man, Ed Davies, his preliminary inspection report in December 1942 and told him what the company planned to do to make the mine safer. He had suggested that Davies help him by checking into whether the Freemans were really following his recommendations.

One month before the disaster, Davies inspected the mine and declared it safe. He didn't bother to address Arnold's concerns, though even if he had, he might have missed how truly dangerous the mine was. Everyone knew when the inspector was coming, so they spent the days prior to his visit working extra hard to clear gas and make the mine appear safer than normal.

Davies spent most of the inspection determining gas levels with a device called an anemometer, which takes readings of how much fresh air flows in a particular area. In some places the gadget showed tens of thousands of cubic feet of air, while other places contained just a thousand or so. When the device didn't pick up a reading at all, Davies would explain after the disaster, "it shows that something was wrong. Otherwise a reading would have been obtained there. That indicates clearly to those in charge of ventilation where the weakness is."

According to the report Davies wrote, posted at the mine, and sent to the State Industrial Accident Board after his inspection, he got no anemometer reading in eleven places in the Smith Mine. Still, he saw no reason to urge the accident board to shut the mine down and only suggested, at the end of his report, that "required quantity of air to be conducted to all working faces." The board issued the mine a safety inspection certificate on February 23.

Now Davies was on his way to Bearcreek, too, from his home in Billings. Before leaving, he'd called Tony Boyle and asked him to find a hundred men to help with the rescue. Boyle, making calls from his Billings office, mobilized miners from all over the state. Once he'd arranged for crews of helmet men to get to the scene, Boyle headed to Bearcreek, too.

Helmet men were trained to use bulky, *Star Wars*–like, self-contained oxygen units. These giant pieces of headgear allowed the men to stay alive for long periods in toxic conditions. At the Smith Mine they would repair the ventilation system and create new air routes so that gas could be blown out and fresh air brought it. The local Bearcreek rescuers, not a helmet man among them, had been entering the mine without any protection at all. The most experienced helmet crew came from the Butte copper mines.

The rescuers knew how urgent their task was. Many had been hearing about a mining tragedy for most of their lives. Back in 1917, 163 miners had died from fire and carbon monoxide poisoning in two giant Butte copper mines. Sparked by an open carbide headlamp, the fire and its aftermath had trapped hundreds more men for days. The rescuers heading to Bearcreek knew about the copper miners' grisly deaths, and about those who had survived by barricading themselves in pockets of clean air. If the Bearcreek miners were using the same self-preservation tactic, they'd need helmet men as soon as possible.

Besides, it was Butte's turn to try to help. At the time of the copper mine disaster, Red Lodge mine officials had sent special mine rescue cars to Butte, but the 250-mile drive took too long. The copper miners were dead before the cars arrived. Now, thanks to the miracle of aviation, their sons and nephews would try to reciprocate more successfully.

Twelve copper miners grabbed their rescue equipment and boarded Army transport planes that had arrived specifically to help them aid Bearcreek. The planes took the rescuers nearly two hundred miles from Butte to Billings, where they transferred to cars. Highway patrolmen escorted them the remaining sixty or so miles to the mine. People along the normally quiet route stopped what they were doing to watch the caravan of flashing lights and blaring sirens. This was more traffic than they'd seen in a long time, both on the ground and in the air.

Other crews around the state, who were also better prepared for an emergency than the Smith men, also streamed to the disaster site. The superintendent from the Roundup coal mine, who'd done rescue work during the 1909 Cherry coal mine disaster in Illinois, drove down with some of his workers. Almost half of the miners who'd been underground when the Cherry had caught fire had survived, no doubt due to rescuers' efforts. Miners from at least six other large Montana mines, plus the owners of private "truck mines," forgot their own lives and businesses and headed to Bearcreek to offer help. The Billings fire chief brought seven firemen and all the oxygen and respirators he could spare. The Yellowstone County ration board issued special gas points to anyone who'd been called to assist.

The whole world, it seemed, was journeying to Carbon County. People came from surrounding towns with blankets, flashlights, batteries, first-aid kits, woolen stockings, overshoes, and clothing for the trapped miners to change into when they got out. Friends, relatives, and men who'd worked in the mine before moving on to college or better jobs came to offer their skills. People who'd been in and out of the sleepy area all their lives couldn't believe the crowds. A young man who'd grown up in Bearcreek drove into Red Lodge at three in the morning to help with the rescue. He saw people roaming the streets and sitting around tables at the still-open restaurants. The activity reminded him of Las Vegas in the middle of the night.

"It was lit up like a Christmas tree," he said later.

The townspeople were nearly as wound up and buzzing as they had been on Christmas Eve, but the adrenaline wasn't from happy excitement this time. Fear and dread made their hearts pound. They tried to keep busy, but that wasn't easy either.

Mary Wakenshaw lost her coffee responsibilities when the Red Cross stepped in. Early in the day they took charge of food and drink in the mine's carpenter, or machine, shop. They organized a motor corps to drive families and rescuers around the county. They also turned a basketball court into a hospital ward.

The woman in charge of the Red Cross called on every high school boy she could find. She told them to go to local tourist camps and borrow cots, then set them up in Washington Hall, a Red Lodge gymnasium. Calls went out for pajamas for the patients to wear and blankets to warm then. Volunteers collected bandages, intravenous bags, and any other medical supplies that might be needed. By noon, the makeshift hospital was ready for patients. The boys had lined up fifty beds right under the basketball hoops. Four nurses stood ready to treat up to seventy-five men at once. The women had set up a second emergency kitchen, to feed medical workers and patients.

Food certainly wouldn't be a problem. Besides getting donations from a local grocery store and from individual cooks looking to do anything constructive, the Elks Club donated all the chicken and roasts and pies they'd planned to serve at a dinner that night. It was to have been a father-son banquet.

Virginia Sommerville waited for news with her mother-in-law. Though her husband, Gil, hadn't been in the mine at the time of the explosion, he was still in danger because he was back at the mine with the rescuers. With all that gas in the mine, a second explosion could happen anytime. Or the mine could cave in from the damage it had already sustained and smother the rescuers. Or falling rocks could crush their heads. There was plenty for a young wife to agonize over. But her mother-in-law had more concrete worries. No one had heard from her son or her husband, both of whom were still in the mine.

Maybe having Connie around would distract Mrs. Sommerville. The baby, who was starting to become her own little person, was developing all kinds of cute habits. She'd grown attached to a picture of a dog hanging in the house. Whenever she looked at it, she pressed her pudgy cheek against the back of her hand and smiled angelically, baby shorthand for adoration.

Margaret Meiklejohn was in a house full of people, too. She was measuring coffee and cutting sandwiches at the Cameron house, which had become something of a sanctuary from the chaos, albeit a crowded one. Friends and strangers were dropping in to collapse into chairs, use the bathroom, or park their kids.

Mary decided to take advantage of the last option. Bobby had been standing at the mouth of the mine all day, breathing in toxic vapors. He leaned against a wooden post that framed the entrance. That was as close as he could get to the shaft that held his father and grandfathers without actually stepping into it. With his hands in his pockets and his face a screen of worry, about the only thing that set him apart from the men who waited with him were his height and his blue jeans, which he'd rolled up to a few inches above his ankles. But his mother knew he wasn't a man yet and that he needed some rest. So, though she'd be staying at the mine until Bud came out, he was shipped to the Camerons'. Once he was finally in the warm house, everything—his breakfast, his fear, that gas—came up. He vomited for most of the night, without his mother or father to rub his back and tell him he would be okay.

Throughout the afternoon, Bureau of Mines officials and rescuers continued to arrive. Unprotected men continued to go into the mine to try to save their brothers, only to be tossed out by their superiors or their survival instincts before they could accomplish anything. Even Davies, the state mine inspector, who'd declared the mine perfectly safe, became extremely ill after spending time inside. He was sent to the hospital, where he would stay for two days before he could rejoin the search. Before the men entered the mine, the priest from the nearest Catholic church blessed each one of them, regardless of his religion. Maybe his prayers helped them, because on that day, none of the rescuers died.

Every half hour or so, a batch of men would emerge from the mine. The families' hopes would spike when they saw activity, then plummet as they realized they were only escaping the fumes, not bringing survivors out. They saw two men holding up a third, weak and wobbly from the gas, his arms balanced across their shoulders. They saw trucks normally used to transport laundry, meat, candy, milk, or groceries take the ailing men to the Red Cross hospital. But they didn't see the faces they yearned for.

Still, no one had given up. When a *Billings Gazette* reporter asked Bill Romek for a statement, he gave an optimistic one. He said that the trapped men were behind a rockfall, "but that isn't the major problem. We're hoping that they were able to get away from the danger area after the explosion and go to a safer place in the mine."

Everybody hoped that, but some knew better than others how unlikely it was. Even Romek couldn't have completely believed his statement to the press. He called the Western Union office in the middle of the night and wired a telegram to James Freeman. In it he explained where bodies had been found already, where rescuers would look next, and that the carbon monoxide was hampering their progress. He closed with four disheartening words.

"Situation appears very bad."

Arnold drove through the night with two other bureau men and a car full of rescue apparatus. During their eight-plus hours on the road, they probably took turns driving and sleeping and wondering what they were about to face. They must have known it wouldn't be pleasant.

The Freemans consulted train schedules. Their beach houses were twelve hundred miles from Montana. Mary Wakenshaw's trip to a more northern part of California right before the disaster had taken two days and nights. When James and W.R. finally arrived in their hometown, the springlike weather that had awakened Bearcreek on the morning of the disaster would be very old news. As men lay dying in the mine that first day, the immediate world went cold. The temperature sank, signaling the start of a record cold snap. Snow began to swirl and multiply, as if enraged. By nightfall, a full-blown blizzard made the rescue work even more impossible.

11 The Wait

Mary Wakenshaw waited.

She sat in the machine shop with her daughter by her side, both of them looking better than they should have after twenty-four hours of limbo. Mary wore cowboy boots, a skirt, and big button earrings. Fannie had tied a kerchief under her chin and swiped on fresh lipstick. Both of them leaned over their laps, resting their arms on their thighs for support. If they had drooped a few more feet, they would have been using their legs as pillows.

Everyone in the shop knew each other. They'd spent most of their lives together, usually during good times. On New Year's Eve they went First Footing, a Scottish tradition that involved popping into neighbors' houses and exchanging moonshine or whiskey, depending on which side of Prohibition the year fell. On the Fourth of July they hollered for the cowboys at the Red Lodge rodeo. And just four months earlier, many of them had put on their fancy clothes to celebrate Emil Anderson's elder son's marriage.

Emil's wife, Agnes, stood with her daughter and her daughter-in-law, whose father was also stuck underground. With their friends and neighbors surrounding them—some sitting, some standing, some holding drinks and talking quietly—it was a little like the wedding party, if everything had been turned upside down and blackened.

It was Sunday morning. A whole day and a whole night had passed since the explosion. None of the women were ready to give up yet.

"Emil knows every inch of that mine," Agnes said. "He'd know what to do. He'd protect himself."

Mary was equally certain that Bud would be fine. "I know they're coming out," she declared, holding her head and shoulders tall as if daring someone to contradict her.

It was cold in the shop. People hugged themselves and stomped their feet. They drank coffee and poured it for the rescuers, the hot cups warming their fingers for a few moments. They must have lost feeling in their toes and shivered as their bodies fought to create warmth. Few of them were dressed for a blizzard, but who dared to go home for a warmer coat or an extra sweater? What if her miner came out while she was gone?

The women and children had been told that the rescuers were doing all they could to free the miners, but they hadn't heard any real news in hours. At two that morning, word had spread that the crews had found four men. All were dead, three of them killed violently. No one knew who they were yet or exactly what had happened to them, but the news was enough to drain the women's optimism a bit. Wives who had been so calm and restrained throughout the first day finally began to weep.

To pass the hours until more reports came, it's likely that the women shared stories about unusual events that had happened the day before. Premonitions and ironic twists. Odd glances that they'd never forget.

Pete Giovetti had started for the door three times the morning of the explosion, his wife remembered. Before he finally left, he turned and told her he loved her.

It wasn't his usual parting phrase, but maybe he'd just been happy about what lay ahead. It was to be his last day in the mine. Giovetti, who was already wheezing and choking from black lung disease, was retiring. Sometimes when he drove his locomotive down the rail tracks he noticed that the coal dust coating them was two inches thick. His lungs couldn't take much of that anymore. He needed pure air. That's why he was about to move his wife and kids out of Bearcreek and take over a relative's cattle ranch. He had the luxury of leaving the mine because he'd managed to get a replacement for himself, a rare prize in those days. The new man was supposed to have started on the day of the explosion, but he'd called Giovetti the night before. He couldn't make the Saturday shift, he explained, so could Pete do it one more time?

As Giovetti walked down the front steps of the house, he turned and waved.

"Last time for this," he said with a grin. "It's down on the farm for us."

John Sudar's young wife remembered his face more than his words. He'd given her a long and penetrating look at breakfast the morning of the explosion. He was in a particularly good mood, more jovial than usual, she remembered, even though he'd overslept because they'd been out at the movies the night before. He was excited about a road trip they'd be taking to visit their folks in Roundup after work. A friend had asked him to switch shifts that day, but John had said no. He didn't want to rearrange the Roundup plans.

"I'll see you tonight," he said. Then he got into his car and drove away.

And now he was underground with Emil Anderson, the good-bye note he'd composed just in case he didn't make it out lying beside him. His bride had been planted in the machine shop since she'd learned about the explosion; she would stay for most of four days and nights, only leaving to take care of their toddler and make coffee for some of the rescue workers staying at their house.

One of the motorman's wives may have thought of the argument they'd had that morning. Her husband was sick and she wanted him to stay home. He insisted on going in.

"I can't miss a time-and-a-half day," he said.

"Can't you let the work go for this one day and rest until you're feeling better?" she asked.

"Tomorrow is Sunday," he said. "I'll rest then."

During the afternoon, a group of men entered the shop. The governor of Montana, Sam Ford, had arrived. If anyone needed confirmation that the disaster was indeed a big deal, here it was. The governor certainly had better things to do on a stormy Sunday than come all the way from Helena just for some publicity. He wasn't even running for anything.

He was impressed by how calm everyone seemed. Maybe he'd expected wailing and chest beating. But, as many of the news stories patronizingly reported, the women weren't hysterical at all. Later, the governor would call the women "some of the bravest I have ever seen. As they stand at the head of the shaft, dry-eyed, their courage is remarkable."

He walked over to two of those remarkable females, sisters who attended Bearcreek High. One was seventeen and the other fourteen. Their mother had died twelve years earlier while the rest of the family was burying the baby she'd lost in childbirth. Their father was their world. They kept house for him. He worked in the mine to buy their food and school clothes.

The governor spoke privately to the girls, then shook the younger one's hand.

"Be brave," he told her.

Then he headed to the mine office to talk to the men in charge of the rescue operation. He, like everyone else, wanted to know what was taking so long.

Most of the stoppings that controlled the flow of air in and out of the mine had been destroyed in the blast. Without them, fresh air entering the mine had no clear path. It flowed into rooms at random instead of staying in the main shaft. The rescuers needed breathable air in that shaft if they were going to reach the survivors, so they had to plug up hundreds of gaps with temporary stoppings before they could advance. It was torturously slow and dangerous work. As they hung the stoppings—actually, curtains of brattice cloth—they knew that another explosion or a rockfall could kill them. A cave-in had already spooked them and stalled progress on Saturday night.

The helmet men were in much less danger than the locals. Their forty-five-pound helmets came with canisters that provided between one and two hours of clean air. The Bearcreek men, who had to hang back because they didn't have a source of supplemental oxygen, shouted instructions about where to look for survivors or what direction to take at forks in the road. This was their mine and they knew where their brothers had been working. If they'd had their own rescue supplies, they might have saved them already.

At one point, a local miner who'd used a rescue helmet years before asked one of the men giving orders if he could use one now. He couldn't take the helpless waiting anymore.

"You're too old," the supervisor told him.

"I don't know," he argued. "I think I can take a chance to go in and try to rescue those men to see if we can bring them out alive."

Like his co-workers, he knew they could be barricaded someplace safe, and he knew how to reach those sanctuaries better than any of the outsiders.

"No," the official said again. Case closed.

As the helmet men cleared sections and moved further into the mine, they lifted their safety lamps to check the quality of the air in front of them. It was incredibly unstable.

"There was places there where you could stand in one place and be alive and five or ten feet farther along it would knock you out immediately, it was so bad," one rescuer would tell people later.

Even with their special equipment, the helmet men couldn't move as swiftly as they wanted. They had to wait while workers removed a fan from another Montana Coal and Iron mine and installed it in the Smith to replace the one destroyed in the explosion. For some reason, this project hadn't even been started until Sunday morning, which, coincidentally, is when Inspector Arnold arrived. It would be twenty-four hours before the fan was working properly.

Whenever local rescuers popped out of the mine, families rushed at them, pelting them with questions. *Did you see him? Any word from my Dad? When will we know something?* The men, who still had little information to share, just shook their heads and walked away. Most of them desperately needed a hit of oxygen or a fast ride to the hospital.

Nurses in starchy white caps bustled around the Red Cross hospital holding wrists as they counted pulse beats and soothing men who couldn't catch their breath. They'd already treated forty-one patients by Sunday morning, and before the day ended they would see twenty-four more. They'd finished off a large tank of oxygen. Many of their patients were local men who'd run into the mine immediately after the disaster, though even more were from other mines around the state. The nurses examined them and wrote down one of two diagnoses in a logbook: gas shock or exhaustion. Some were treated and sent right back to the rescue lines. Others lay on cots, their filthy coveralls replaced by fresh pajamas that the national Red Cross office had sent over. High school boys scurried around the beds and followed orders. They delivered trays of food and medicine, changed sheets, and filled hot water bottles. As busy as they were, they kept watching the door for a sign that someone had survived. But none of the many vehicles arriving from the mine had brought one of those victims since the first five men had been retrieved.

A fleet of Montana highway patrolmen drove patients and rescue workers between the mine, the hospital, and their homes. Because of the storm, even people who had their own cars could no longer navigate the hilly roads safely. Everything that the sun had started to melt before explosion had turned to ice.

Fannie Wakenshaw's friend Betty Hunter, an energetic high school senior, hopped into a patrol car. She settled into her seat and began to tell the officer at the wheel when to turn left or right and when to stay on a this loopy road or to stop at that front gate. Betty, like all the Bearcreek kids, knew where everyone lived, so she could easily direct the cops in and out of the different neighborhoods. They certainly weren't going to know Chickentown from Stringtown from Scotch Coulee—only a townie could make those distinctions. She was a good choice to navigate because she had a clearer head than many of her friends. Her father wasn't trapped in the mine. He'd already died there. Eight years earlier, a rockfall in the Smith had killed him. Now her mother was engaged to one of the rescuers.

The patrolmen weren't just transporting people. They delivered groceries, too. They brought beans and tomatoes to two women who kept busy cooking pot after pot of chili for the rescue crews. Those ladies made so many steaming pots of chili that most of the plaster peeled from their kitchen ceiling. Later, the police picked up the cooked chili and delivered it to the canteen, where volunteers added it to the array of sandwiches, juices, homemade donuts, and pies—the offerings from people who were powerless to help in any other way.

This is how communication with the boys in the service was supposed to work: the good news came from home, and the bad news came from the front. Parents dreaded hearing from military officials, but their sons didn't usually have to worry when the post arrived. So their guards were down when superiors handed out telegrams that week. MINE ACCIDENT, the stark messages may have said, FATHER TRAPPED.

The local Red Cross sent and received sixty-two such bulletins, contacting soldiers, sailors, and marines in fourteen states. They sent two telegrams under military code to men at sea. They sent one with happy news to a soldier in New Guinea, telling him he didn't need to come home because his father and brother hadn't been working the doomed shift. At least twenty-six servicemen who hadn't gone overseas yet managed to get emergency furloughs. They arrived at the Red Lodge train station from Texas and New Jersey and Kentucky. Some even made it in time to shed their uniforms and help with the rescue.

The station was full of old faces. Friends and relatives from all over the country had paused their lives and come back to Bearcreek. One man, who'd worked at the Smith Mine and helped organize its union before moving away, packed a bag in Rhode Island and crossed the country to volunteer on a rescue crew. His nephew was trapped, along with many old friends. As the out-of-towners hopped off the trains, they ran into residents waiting in line at the Western Union office. The man in charge typed madly, and the delivery boy rushed in and out with stacks of queries and replies.

Reporters used the office to call or wire their stories to copyboys in distant city rooms. The tragic tale was starting to radiate across news wires. All the major Montana dailies ran it on the front page. United Press sent it around the country. The *New York Times* ran the most misleading United Press account. Besides containing many misspelled names and factual errors, it reported that rescuers had already made contact with the trapped men.

"They are apparently in pretty good shape," the article said.

Other newspapers around the nation ran photos of rescuers waiting to go into the mine, of families waiting in the cold, of Mary Wakenshaw looking like the quintessential western girl with her leather boots and lovely face. Photo services and news outlets from Chicago, Colorado, and Seattle called the owner of Flash's photo studio in downtown Red Lodge and begged for pictures. The Seattle people even offered to pay for a car to fetch the shots.

Folks with ties to Bearcreek read the news and panicked. They sent urgent telegrams asking whether their former neighbor or cousin or playmate was safe.

Olga Marinchek didn't have to wonder anymore. The telegram she received held the grimmest news: her father was dead. Ignac Marinchek, the man who'd fallen backward instead of forward as he tried to run out of the mine, hadn't responded to all those hours of artificial respiration. Now his daughter would have to find a way to get home from Cheyenne, Wyoming, where she lived with her husband and new baby. They never would have made it on their normal gas rations, but a friend who owned a gas station broke the rules and filled their tank. Olga made it home in time for the funeral.

The man found with his chin still quivering had died, too. But the three other men who'd been pulled out of the mine were coming around.

Alex Hawthorne and Eli Houtonen shared a room at Adams Hospital in Red Lodge. They'd been too sick when they came out of the mine to go to the temporary clinic in the gym.

"I don't know where I've been," Hawthorne said to the strangers hovering around him.

He'd been unconscious all night, but finally cracked his eyelids on Sunday morning. Reporters stood by his bed asking what he remembered. He told them about the sound, the wind, the phone call to the surface. His voice was sluggish.

"He's still a little woozy," Houtonen whispered to a reporter. "He's been trying to keep up his spirit. He's got a son, Jimmy, still inside."

Houtonen was more alert than his roommate, but still weak and achy. Black and blue marks had bloomed where Willard Reid had kicked him as he tried to get Houtonen to stand up in the mine.

Reid was the strongest of the survivors. He was well enough to recuperate with the Red Cross nurses, though he, too, was banged up from rolling around in the mine. He kept complaining about a bitter taste in his mouth.

"Have you got any gum?" he asked a nurse.

She managed to find some licorice-flavored Black Jack, but that didn't help much. Later, the local pharmacist came for a visit. Reid told him about the horrible taste, most likely a remnant of the gas he'd inhaled. The man left Reid's bedside, headed to his drugstore, and returned with a case of spearmint gum.

Reid's wife knew how lucky she was to be able to touch and see her man. She did what she could to give back to the others, bringing cans of pheasant and elk and beans from her pantry to the canteen. But she couldn't give them answers or their own bruised men to fuss over.

On Monday, the first day of March, Mary still hadn't left the machine shop. People kept trying to get her to go home to rest, but she refused.

"Want to meet Bud when he comes out," she said.

Two days had passed since the women in the shop had spoken to their husbands. How many times had they made mental notes to tell their men about some detail of this ordeal when they saw them again? How many times did they replay the last conversations in their heads?

The night before the accident, Ned Laird had been scrubbing the black coal dust off his face, blowing it from his nose, and spitting gray gobs into the sink.

"All we need is for someone to light a match," he'd said.

A tracklayer had complained to his family because his mining partner had been late to pick him up the morning of the explosion due to a flat tire. The tracklayer, a normally calm man, drank two cups of coffee and fidgeted as he waited.

"If Bill doesn't get here pretty soon, we'll miss our trip down," he'd said, aggravated and impatient.

When his partner, Bill Pelo, finally drove up, the man ran down the steps to his car. They made it in on time.

The rescuers were finally getting closer to bringing those men out. They would make a long loop through the mine, starting down the western side until they reached the farthest mined point, then coming back on the eastern side. With the fan working, they could traverse the route a little faster, but because there was still so much gas in the mine, they couldn't use electricity to power the mantrips. They would walk more than a mile as they searched for life, stepping over debris and maneuvering around cave-ins, balancing rolls of brattice cloth, and waving flashlights in the dark. On Monday afternoon, helmet men reached the shop inside the mine. Two rigid bodies sat at the bench where they'd been working when the power went off. Four people who loved those men ferociously waited outside for them, but they'd keep hoping for happy reunions for a while longer. Since the helmet men didn't recognize the corpses, they weren't officially identified until later in the week. Their remains wouldn't even be brought out of the mine until Friday when the mantrips were running again. It was too arduous to carry a dead man through all those obstacles and over all that distance. Besides, they were in too much of a hurry to try to find live men.

Though a few men had been discovered, the outcome for the rest didn't look good. On Monday, assistant mine manager Bill Romek, whose statements to the press had been so positive over the weekend, told reporters it was "almost beyond hope" that anyone was still alive in the mine. A rescue worker admitted to reporters, "Even if the men had reached an area where clean air remained, it must by now have been all but used up."

But the wives and daughters wouldn't accept that.

"I know they all must be alright," said the older of the teenage sisters who'd talked to the governor. "We're all praying for them. God will hear us, I know."

She was answering questions from a redheaded *Billings Gazette* reporter. The reporter, who usually published on the women's pages, had been sent to get the female point of view. She, too, couldn't believe how quiet the women were, how stoic and strong. Outside the machine shop, she had seen a rescuer come out of the mine, sit down by himself, and cry. But these women weren't breaking.

"We can't stop hoping," Emil Anderson's wife told her. "We won't."

Bud had once told Mary that he didn't worry about dying in the mine. *When your time's up, it's up*, he'd said. But she couldn't believe this was his time. Not yet.

"Everyone's doing all that can be done," Mary said. "I have all the confidence in the world."

It was dark again, close to midnight on Monday. Mary had been in the machine shop for more than two and a half days. Her faith may have been superhuman, but her body wasn't. She finally agreed to go home and lie down. Four hours later, before the sun rose again, she was back.

12　The Games

Melvin Anderson should have been kicking Red Lodge's butt on Monday night. His high school basketball team was scheduled to play its biggest rival, and the boys had been waiting a month to get revenge on their neighbors. In January, Red Lodge had given the Bearcats their first loss of the season, with a final score of 29–26. Melvin and the boys had sunk twelve baskets during the final quarter, but they couldn't catch up.

That must have hurt. Bearcreek was known all over Montana as a basketball powerhouse. The *Billings Gazette* had recently run a long feature story about Bearcreek basketball in the Sunday paper. The article had begun by describing the mining town and lauding its all-American spirit. "Recently, as a patriotic effort, the employees of the mine contributed one day's work to the government," the reporter had noted.

The story went on to review Bearcreek's basketball history. It referred to Bearcreek High as "the cradle of champions" because of all the talented players it had groomed and sent on to college teams. Two of those big shots, brothers who'd worn the orange and black in the thirties, were in the mine now looking for their father. Most of the 1925 team, which had brought Bearcreek its first trophy, was also struggling because of the disaster. That squad had included Willard Reid, who'd been rescued already; one of the mine superintendent's sons, who was on the rescue crew; Mary Wakenshaw's older brother, whose father was still in the mine; and two other men waiting for their fathers underground. A player from the 1928 team was also among the missing. Only the state champions from the 1938–39 season seemed to have been charmed: oddly, none of the starters on that squad was stuck in the mine or waiting for fathers who were.

The article mentioned the current team, too. Melvin's coach proclaimed that the 1943 squad was better than average, and the reporter used the word *stellar* to describe Melvin and his buddy, Frank Mourich. Stellar: pertaining to the stars. He and Frankie, already the vice-president and president of the senior class, were officially stars. It said so right in the paper.

But neither of them got the chance to sparkle on Monday night. The game was canceled because the players and fans for both teams were busy with the rescue. Melvin and Frank were busy shifting their feet outside the mine, waiting for a chance to go in and help their fathers.

None of the Bearcreek kids was doing what he or she was supposed to be doing that week. Melvin's sister, Doris, wasn't delivering daily papers to the nine customers on her route. How could she, particularly over the weekend, without her father around to pick up the bundle of papers at the mine and bring them home for her to distribute?

Frank's sister, Thelma, wasn't juggling boyfriends or making crank calls. She was sitting around with relatives like all the other women and children. Their mother, aunt, and cousins waited for news at their grandparents' house. None of them knew it yet, but Thelma and Frank's father had already been found. Their father's brother, whose thirty-sixth birthday was the day after the explosion, was still in deep in the west side of the mine.

Bobby Wakenshaw wasn't sledding down the hill near his house with his border collie, Rags, trying to yank him off the sled by the pants leg. He was at the Camerons' too. His stomach had settled and he felt well enough now to tease Jessie Cameron, his best friend's kid sister, as he often did. Driving her crazy must have been a distraction from wondering about his dad and his grandfathers and from wishing he were home. He liked the Camerons and they were being really kind to him, but it was crazy in that house.

By Bearcreek standards, the Cameron place was quite nice. Shaped like an L, it had a big front porch, a basement root cellar with shelves full of jarred preserves, cheery wallpaper depicting chickens in baskets and red and yellow flowers in sky blue vases, and a full bathroom. But with so many neighbors clomping in and out to deliver food or to use the bathroom, the house must have felt small and chaotic. Plus, it was getting messy from people tracking snow and mud onto the floor. Not that the Camerons minded. Opening their house made them feel useful, just as giving food did for others.

Guido Marchello, the grocer who used to forgive tabs when people ran out of money and hand out fresh fruit when they paid their bills, came to the Camerons' back door carrying packages from his market. It was one of several trips he'd make to the kitchen that week, no doubt completely disregarding the nonsense with the ration books.

Having all those people together could have been fun under different circumstances. Take these folks, change the season to summer, throw them into the town pool, and things would have been fine. Like so many Bearcreek institutions, the pool was less than traditional. No town-wide vote or official recreation committee for this project. Just some miners with a clever idea. A house had been jacked up and moved, leaving a perfectly good cellar. Why not clean it out and fill it with water? So they did just that, working as a team and sweating through their shirts just as they did in the mine. They strung a rope across the middle for kids to hang on. The pool became a central spot for escaping the summer boredom and heat.

Different kids kept charging in and out of the Cameron house. A cross-eyed girl who went to school with Bobby had some news for him.

"Your dad is alive," she said.

Another child was getting good news, too. Her name was Cheri, and she wasn't from Bearcreek. She'd come down from Roundup with her mother to see her father in the Red Cross hospital. Her father was an important man. He was the superintendent of his mine. Besides running the Roundup mine, he sometimes went to Mine Operators Association meetings. That December, he'd been among the group that had listened as Tony Boyle pleaded for the union men and the mine operators to jointly support a bill that could have turned some of Arnold's safety recommendations into law. Her father had voted against it.

Now he lay on a cot recovering from gas inhalation. He'd hurried down to offer aid, but ended up needing it instead. Six-year-old Cheri, wearing a dressy coat and a hat with an upturned brim, flung herself onto his chest and wrapped her arms around his neck. His slender young wife kissed him.

"I'm alright, Cheri," her dad said.

It was a scene that many families hoped to repeat. A photographer snapped a picture of their reunion that ended up in papers all over the country, including the front page of *Chicago Daily Tribune*. Anyone who saw it would have thought things were going well over in Montana. They would have been wrong.

If there had been a church in Bearcreek, people might have drifted over to it. They might have sought comfort in its familiar pews or in the faith a minister could inspire. But no one had ever built a church in town, despite the rumor that someone had run off with a collection that the townspeople had saved for one. Not that people were completely without religion. Occasionally, a priest from out of town performed a mass in an abandoned boxcar, and some of the pious ladies led Protestant services and held Sunday school classes in houses, clubs, and vacant classrooms around the valley. Still, there was no official place to hold a meeting with God.

The Sommervilles didn't mind. Virginia's mother-in-law prayed for her miracles at home that week. She had eleven relatives trapped in the mine, and they needed as many holy favors as possible. She and her husband had found the Lord through an evangelical sect and often worshipped at tent revival meetings. Religion had saved Virginia's father-in-law, who was now trapped in the mine with his son, by inspiring him to give up alcohol. As with so many families, drinking had long been a problem for the Sommervilles. Booze was so prevalent that they even gave it to the children, and not just to treat bad coughs. When Gil was little, he had a beautiful singing voice. At family functions, folks would coax him to get up and give them a song, then they'd reward him with some whiskey. Fortunately for Virginia, Gil's drinking didn't appear to be a problem.

As Mrs. Sommerville beseeched God to save her son and husband, Virginia comforted the baby. Connie looked just like a little Sommerville. In her birthday portrait she wears a pink party dress with a locket around her neck, white leather shoes, and a big smile. Her two front teeth have a healthy gap between them that would close as more teeth came in. Virginia had brushed a lock of her blond hair into one curl on the top of her head.

"Mama," Connie said. It was one of her two words: Mama and Dada.

Virginia wasn't crazy about exposing the baby to the frigid air that swept in whenever a visitor arrived. People just kept coming and going, asking how they were holding up or whether they'd heard any news. Virginia worried that Connie might catch a cold. When her sisters arrived from Billings to see how they could help, they offered to take Connie back home with them, away from the confusion and the drafts. Let Virginia focus on her mother-in-law, and Gil, who was part of the rescue crew. Virginia agreed. As much as she'd miss the baby, she kissed her plump cheek and sent her off to the city. That made one less person for her to fret about.

Melvin and Frank missed another chance to play hoops that week when the annual district tournament was postponed because of the disaster. But basketball *was* being played in Montana, and one game was for their benefit.

The Billings Junior Chamber of Commerce organized a tournament of independent teams from around the state to raise money for a disaster fund. John Barovich, a legend from Bearcreek's 1932 team, asked if he could play on one of the teams. Though he'd been working with the rescuers, the basketball court was where he could best contribute. Barovich, who'd gotten scholarship offers from four colleges, had graduated and was now coaching a high school team. The military had rejected him due to a broken eardrum, but that injury didn't affect his aim or balance on the court. He scored his team's first five baskets during the fund-raising game, making eleven in all before the ref blew the final whistle. His team won, and the tournament raised $650 for Bearcreek.

That didn't help Barovich, though. Before the proceeds had been counted, he learned what had happened to his father. He'd been waiting to go in with a fresh rescue crew when an outgoing shift emerged from the mine.

"Find my dad?" he asked one of the men.

"Yeah," the man answered, simply and conclusively.

At least Barovich knew that the curt acknowledgment meant his father hadn't made it. At least, despite all the pain that would follow, he hadn't been misled like Bobby Wakenshaw. When the girl had told him his dad was alive, he thought his nightmare was over. He thought he'd get to see his dad and hug him and get back to watching the Bearcats together again. But the girl had been wrong. They hadn't found Bud yet. He'd been missing for three days.

13 The Beloved

All through the Smith Mine, men who were once vibrant and rau-
cous lay as still as stones. It was Tuesday morning, and the rescue
crews had finally routed fresh air to the sections where the men had
been working. Because some electric power had been restored, the
rescuers could now ride mantrips into the mine, but they still had to
walk from tunnel to tunnel and from room to room as they searched.
They climbed around the bulky, heavy fans and locomotives that
had been blown to new resting spots, and hiked over floors that the
blast had completely cleared in some places and piled with junk in
others. In each working area, they waved their lights around to il-
luminate the wreckage. Sometimes they just saw dust and debris.
Other times they saw men frozen, as if a spell had been cast. There
was a switchman sitting upright between two mantrip cars, wedged
into the exact place where he had fallen. A row of men sitting along
the track, where they'd been instructed to wait until the power resumed. An engineer with his clothes completely blown off and coal
dust embedded into his body.

Lives changed as the men absorbed those sights; carefree souls
grew heavy, images too gruesome for language becoming forever chiseled in their minds. Some of the rescuers would try to flush out the

memories by speaking about them whenever asked. But some would lock them in, along with other parts of themselves they'd once shared openly. Those who could explain some of what they'd seen in the mine frequently mentioned the smell.

After people die, the bacteria in their bodies begin to digest organs and tissues from within. This creates gases, which causes incredible swelling, which distorts faces and turns limbs into discolored clubs. Skin can split open from the internal pressure. Less than forty-eight hours after a death, some bodies are so swollen they can't be identified on sight. The odor that results from these biological processes has been described as indescribable, but it is unmistakable after one exposure.

Since the helmet men hadn't known the victims in life, they couldn't identify even the least decomposed of them in death. But the local crews usually could. They found their union president in the first large group they came upon. He'd lost much of his vision after being slammed by a rock in the mine in 1928. Maybe that's why he'd spent extra time and energy pushing to keep the other men safe. Just a week earlier, he'd made a trip to Tony Boyle's office in Billings to discuss the gas problem. *It's getting really bad*, he told Boyle. *How about another inspection?* Now he was on the west side of the mine with five of his brothers from the local. Before the noxious gases had snuffed them out, they'd walked more than a thousand feet. The group also included the fifty-seven-year-old grandfather of Thelma and Frank Mourich, a man known for playing the accordion and singing Scottish songs. He rested near a thirty-one-year-old who should have reported for military duty that very day.

When they couldn't recognize the bodies, the rescuers dug into pockets and pulled on belt loops until they found the numbered brass discs every man carried. They would later compare these to the identical discs left above ground. They felt for other pieces of evidence they really didn't want to discover, too. Sometimes, they spotted a familiar coat or watch and knew they'd located their friend or father. Despite the trauma of finding clusters of dead men, the rescuers didn't have time for more than silent prayers. If they were going to find survivors, they had to take care of these bodies quickly and move ahead as soon as possible. Because it was humane and because it kept the odors and fluids contained, they wrapped the bodies in the canvas brattice cloth they'd been using to fix the stoppings. The helmet men then proceeded on, while six-man recovery crews carried each body—sometimes as far as a mile—to the mantrip cars at the parting. There, just like the coal, they awaited transport out of the mine.

It was brutal work. Without ventilation, the air stagnated. Without pumps, water seeped in from the mountain streams. Soon the rescuers were soaked. That Tuesday was the coldest day of that cold month, with one reading of twenty-five degrees below zero. The men were sweating from exertion and freezing from moisture at the same time. Paths from sweat—or maybe tears—lined their blackened cheeks.

At the end of each six-hour shift, they dragged themselves back onto a mantrip for the ride up to the surface.

"Boys, take a drink of whiskey," one of the rescue foremen instructed. "It's going to be cold on the trip."

Before the afternoon crews could complete their shifts, Arnold ordered them out of the mine. He was suspending the operation until he and his team of federal officials could inspect the ventilation systems. They would walk through the mine taking air readings until they were satisfied that it was safe enough for the rescuers to go back in. Arnold, who'd been in and out of the mine constantly since Sunday, then needed to find some time to work on his inspection report. That day he'd received a wire from the Washington office of the Bureau of Mines. Though he'd filed and distributed the preliminary Smith Mine inspection report back in December, he hadn't quite finished the final report. The higher-ups wanted it now. Though most of the report was already typed, he spent the hours between 2:30 and 4:30 Wednesday morning writing the remaining recommendations by hand. At dawn he air-mailed the document to the Salt Lake City office. The complete report contained even more distressing facts than the preliminary one had. Arnold had described safety hazards such as liquid chemicals stored in glass jars and kept on shelves, required safety meetings that had never been held, and improper and ineffective warnings about gas accumulations. Montana Coal and Iron officials would later accuse him of composing the entire seventy-four-page final report during the rescue week, even though he'd been working twelve-to-sixteen-hour days overseeing the job. They would claim he exaggerated the report to deflect blame for the explosion from himself.

At six on Wednesday morning, Tony Boyle called in a telegram for John Lewis, the legendarily bushy-browed president of the United Mine Workers of America. Lewis had done so much for America's coal miners that many of them hung framed photos of him around their house. Bobby Wakenshaw wanted to grow his eyebrows just like Lewis's.

"We have no further hope of finding men alive," Boyle told Lewis over the telegraph lines.

The *New York Times* had already run a snippet of gloom that declared hope was flickering out for the miners. And the politicians seemed resigned to the worst as well. The governor asked the state legislature to appropriate five thousand dollars for "a thorough examination" of what had happened in the mine. The House and Senate passed the request quickly, then formed a committee to draw up "a proper resolution of sympathy with the people of Carbon County." One of the men on the new committee, a Carbon County state representative, had voted against Boyle's "no blasting" bill after the mine operators' lobbying campaign.

But the Bearcreek families weren't the type to accept defeat so easily. Melvin Anderson and Thelma Mourich and Margaret Meiklejohn still had reason to believe they had complete families. As far as Mary was concerned, she was still a wife. She wasn't reading newspapers or speculating with politicians. She was focusing on the facts: nobody had found Bud yet, or either of their fathers. No bodies meant there was still hope. They could be tucked away in a pocket of fresh air, just waiting to be rescued. They'd be a sight when they came out—exhausted and filthy and starving for dinner—but they could still come out.

The rescuers continued to work their way deeper into the mine, checking for life or corpses, wrapping and moving them, pushing forward. They entered the 6 West panel. Room 1 was clear. Room 2 was not. Five bodies slumped very close to the coal face. All of them had been burned to some extent, and judging from the chaos in the room, they'd died from a violent blast. A rescuer flashed a beam of light on a dead miner's watch. One of its hands had been knocked off, but the other one pointed a tiny bit past the halfway mark. The rescuer showed it to the men around him. Given that first word of the emergency had come sometime before 10:00 on the morning of the explosion, and that the watches had probably been destroyed almost immediately, they figured the timepiece had stopped at a little after 9:30 a.m. Nobody knew *what* had happened to kill all these men, but at least now they knew *when* it had.

One of the men in the group was Jimmy McNeish, a sixty-five-year-old grandfather with a great big grin who could dance so beautifully it looked like he was gliding on ice skates. His son Jake was on the crew that spotted him. In some traditions it's an honor to tend to a parent's body. But not like this; no son should have had to see this. Jake would never be the same again.

They found a tracklayer, two machinemen, and an old man who had started every day with a soft-boiled egg: Adam Wakenshaw.

The rescuers secured the bodies and headed to the next section. They found a cap and an open light six hundred feet away from the man who'd worn them into the mine. His clothes were charred. He must have tried to run for safety while the fabric burned off of his body.

Before they could locate anyone else, a man looked up and saw smoke. It was pouring out of an old opening that had led to another Montana Coal and Iron mine. He warned the rest of his crew, all of whom knew that if the smoke came from a fresh explosion, poison gas could instantly start surging into the shaft. They could all die if they didn't get out immediately. When Arnold got word of the discovery, he and the other supervisors called all the rescuers to the surface. It was five in the afternoon. Outside, they stood around waiting, wasting time, while helmet men searched for smoke. They never found it. The man who'd started the panic must have seen a puff of dust and thought it was smoke, an easy mistake given how edgy they all were.

Still, everyone wanted to help, whether they were desperate to find a relative or thought they could do a better job than the other rescuers. Many of them were turned away. When W. R. Freeman arrived from California, his chest pains had settled down, so he dressed to go into the mine. The men running the operation in *his* mine told him he wasn't strong enough for it. As soon as Willard Reid left the makeshift hospital, he tried to get into the mine to search for his cousins and his brother. *Nope*, was the answer, *not after what you've been through*. Instead, they sent him to help with supplies. A reporter caught up with him and asked if he'd ever enter a coal mine again. Sure, he told him, he'd be back on the job soon. "One mine is just like another," he said, "and I'll always be a miner."

Melvin Anderson worked nearby. High school kids and men who were either unskilled or physically unstable kept busy with chores like loading brattice cloth onto coal cars and running to other mines to charge batteries. Melvin wanted to do more. He asked to go into the mine to find his dad. The older men shook their heads. "We'll find him, but you are not going down," they said.

For some reason, Melvin's good friends Frankie Mourich and Leo Hodnik were allowed underground. Frankie, whose father was still in the mine, and Leo, whose brother was, picked up bodies, heaved them onto stretchers, and carried them to the mantrips. The air was cool, but that didn't make inhaling any easier or the sights any more tolerable. The bodies were heavier than they could have imagined. After two days of the work, the young men bowed out.

"Up for another trip?" a man asked them.

"No," Frankie said. "I can't do her anymore."

Leo agreed. There was only so much teenage boys could handle.

By Thursday morning, the methane content in the air had finally drifted below the explosive level. The rescuers could use full electric power again, meaning they could ride all through the mine instead of walking. Finally, they could get to the men faster.

They found five bodies in 8 West, all of them burned and killed instantly, probably from an explosion. One was still sitting on his Goodman loader, having expired in the act of running the coal-scooping machine. Frankie and Thelma's uncle was crushed against a coal car.

Nine men who'd spent their last few moments trying to scramble out of the shaft rested in various states of decay nearby. Some had been burned, but those who had died from the gas were still whole. Leo's big brother was tall, husky, and quiet. He was also one of the best bowlers in town. Every day after his shift, he had practiced in an alley under a Red Lodge hardware store. His pinsetter would always remember how well he tipped. He rested near the single father whose two teenage daughters were waiting in the machine shop and whose basketball phenom sons were trying to find him. He had pushed his seven children to make it out of the coal-mining life. He insisted they get educations. And though he'd never get to see them all grow up, they achieved his dream: one son became a career naval officer and all the others graduated from college, most going on to work as white-collar professionals.

Mercifully, the group around 8 West would be the largest the rescuers would have to face, but throughout the day they found individual men and small groups scattered throughout the tunnels. They found Frankie and Thelma's father in the underground machine shop where he'd started his shift at least ninety-six hours earlier. He and his workmate had actually been discovered early in the week by the helmet men, but they hadn't been identified until now. Their bodies would stay in the shop for still another day.

The rescuers reached the furthest point in the mine, more than two miles into the mountain, late in the day. Three men had been preparing to carve the mine even deeper. Two of them had been drilling a hole in the coal, and one had been preparing the charge that would blast it down. Before he could put the explosive in its crevice, it had blown up in his hand. He flew fifty feet, fire ravishing him. The flames had also wounded the others, but not as severely. Their caps and closed lamps had blown toward the coal face.

All of their faces were pretty distorted, but the rescuers who'd worked in the mine knew who had been on this job. One of the men had been a grandfather to nine. Another hadn't parented any children yet. The third had been unconditionally beloved. He'd started life as an orphan and met the love of his life at a baseball game. He wasn't finished raising his only surviving son yet. His name was Bud Wakenshaw.

The rescuers unfurled the canvas and wrapped it around Bud's big frame. They'd leave him and the others where they'd fallen for now. The parting where they had been depositing the bodies was getting too crowded.

A very busy lady named Mrs. Cassidy was running Red Cross operations in the makeshift hospital when someone pulled her aside. *Tonight*, he told her, *we'll be moving the bodies out of the mine. We need you to send a few folks to help. Have them come to the mine entrance at midnight*. It was a secret, he added. They wanted to wait until most of the families had gone home for the night before bringing the men out. No need for a scene, the authorities figured.

Mrs. Cassidy quietly enlisted some nurses and drivers for the mission. There weren't nearly enough ambulances in town to bring all those bodies to the morticians, so they'd have to borrow other vehicles. She contacted all the companies that used vans and pickups to carry out their businesses and asked for their cooperation. Then she continued to work for the rest of the day, trying not to let the secret distract her too much. At a little before midnight, her posse of helpers drove through the swirling snow to the mine.

The nurses posted themselves outside the mine entrance. The drivers stayed on the side of the road. Most of them were teenagers. A boy who delivered groceries and a girl who picked up laundry sat tensely behind the steering wheels of their work trucks.

The nurses stood in silence until they heard the rumble of wheels. The mantrips, loaded with thirty-two bodies, were emerging. Steam rose from the canvas-swathed bodies and the stench spread, permeating even the nostrils that had been stuffed with formaldehyde-soaked cotton. The rescuers, who'd spent hours loading the bodies onto the mantrips, hopped off. They were grim-faced and shaken, pale under the grime on their skin. Their hands trembled. The nurses helped steady them so they could grasp straight shots of liquor, the best medicine the ladies had for this kind of wound. Luckily, the Montana Liquor Control Board had lifted rationing restrictions on a Red Lodge liquor store, so there was enough for everyone. The men gulped it quietly, then went back to their task of transferring bodies to hearses and milk trucks.

It was bleak work. Bodily fluids leaked from the canvas. The rescuers wore white cotton gloves to protect themselves. As soon as they loaded a body onto a vehicle, they pulled off their gloves, threw them to the ground and grabbed another pair. Eventually, it looked as if they were walking back and forth over a white carpet.

When the trucks had all been filled, they began their eerie caravan to the Red Lodge mausoleum. Brownie the dog, who had waited every day for five years for his owner to emerge from the mine with half a sandwich, finally trotted off. He had been hanging around since Saturday morning, mainly in the mine office. He sniffed all the men who came in, then flopped back down onto the floor with a sigh when he didn't pick up the scent he wanted. Now, without anyone telling him, he knew his master had finally come out. The man's remains were in one of those trucks.

Despite the plan to hide the transport from the families, everyone knew what was going on. They heard the trucks chugging up the hill. They saw them out their windows. It was an awful sight because of the truth it held: more than likely, all the men who'd gone to work on Saturday morning had died. Mary now knew that Bud was among them. He wouldn't be walking out of that mine, and she wouldn't be running to greet him ever again. She could finally go home.

Her brother and sister-in-law had picked up Bobby and brought him home so he could sleep in his own bed. Mary went into Bobby's room, past the Popeye lamp, past the stash of Walnettos. She lay down next to him. The boy woke up and Mary took him into her arms. *Dad's gone*, she said gently. Then she held him tight and they both cried until they fell asleep.

14 The Good-byes

The Red Lodge funeral directors had never seen so many bodies at once. Even during 1918, the year of the flu epidemic, only about 160 people in the entire county had needed their services, and those poor souls certainly hadn't arrived at the mausoleum all at once.

The two funeral homes stored around ten caskets between them, so the morticians put out rush orders for scores more. The boxes came in on trains, and the railroad agents unloaded them and stacked them on top of each other. Soon the coffins began to take up too much space at the station, so the agents stood them up on their ends instead. Every so often, men would arrive from the funeral homes and thin the grisly forest of boxes, but soon a new shipment would fill it out again.

When faced with all that hard evidence of death, everyone's hope began to wither. The families who had continued to wait at the mine started to accept the worst.

"Come," said a woman to her three little children. "We'll go home now. Thank God we know they are no longer hungry or thirsty."

Another woman told her son, "I'm going. When you see Dad's tag, let me know."

But the rescuers meandering through the mine couldn't stop believing they'd find someone waiting for them.

"Do you think they might be alive?" a young rescuer asked one of the more experienced men on Friday as they approached a room that hadn't been searched yet.

"Well, they could be if they knew what to do," the older man said.

He wasn't just trying to give the kid false hope. Based on the way the ventilation had been set up and where he thought the explosion had originated, the man believed that the men in this part of the mine could still be alive, as long as they'd stayed inside the room.

"Well, my dad and brother are in there and my dad is an old time miner and maybe he would know [what to do]," the younger rescuer said.

There was only one rescuer whose brother and elderly father were still in the mine: Gil Sommerville, Virginia's husband.

Gil and the other men on his team quickly built themselves a pathway into the room with some brattice, then headed in. They heard none of the sounds living men would make—moans or wheezes or even weak pounding—but that could have meant they had fallen asleep or passed out. Some of the rescuers might have held onto that fiction when they walked into the room and saw the miners lying down, but within moments they would have realized that all twelve miners remained where they'd died as they started to leave the mine. They hadn't stayed put at all, so none had survived. Ten of the men had walked distances of between sixteen hundred and two thousand feet from where they'd been working. The other two, a motorman and a nipper, had been thrown about fifty feet from their locomotive. Their twenty-ton motor had been blown off its track.

Gil glanced from body to body until he found his father, David, and his brother, John. The old man was lying on the ground with his son's head in his lap. They had walked quite far before lying down together. Maybe they decided together to lie in that position while waiting for death. Or maybe David had collapsed and John knew he'd be next, so he rested his head on the older man for a touch of fatherly comfort during those last moments. Gil would get no such solace.

Tall, thin Ned Laird had landed near the Sommervilles. Laird, who'd complained the night before the explosion about all the coal dust he was scrubbing off his face and spitting into the sink, lay sideways on his lunch pail. One of the rescuers removed Laird's glasses, cleaned the dust off them, and put them back on his face. They weren't even bent.

Gil and his crew swaddled and lifted these men, plus nine others found in the section. The dead included the vice-president of the union local and a particularly conscientious pumpman. He'd taken the time to shut off his pump before grabbing his jacket and lunch pail and leaving his workplace, and had lasted the amount of time it took to run a thousand feet. One of his hands was already decomposing.

The rescuers moved to the next tunnel, 9 Southeast. They found two bodies in one room and a third by himself in another. This was among the most gruesome scenes they'd encounter. One of the men was lying thirty feet from his electric lamp and belt. He'd obviously been hit hard and his clothes were burned. But that was nothing compared to his companion's appearance. The fifty-one-year-old track-layer, a native of Italy, had landed atop of pile of coal, surrounded by a spike bucket and some pieces of wood and canvas. He was naked, burned, and mutilated. When the rescuers turned him over, they found a hammer underneath his body. He must have been pounding nails into track with it when the explosion occurred. He had managed to hold onto his tool as the force of the explosion propelled him through the air. His charred clothing had remained where he'd been working, and his battered open carbide lamp had rolled about ten feet away. The man was alone on the heap of coal, and alone in the world. He'd grown up an orphan and died without a wife or child to grieve for him.

In the next room the men spotted a helmet and a safety lamp very close to the coal face. Their owner had flown forty feet away from them. He was Dave Murray, one of the foremen on the shift. He had probably been testing for gas at the face. He'd certainly found it.

A rescuer named Matt Woodrow stood over Murray's short, stocky body. Woodrow, a sixty-one-year-old Scotsman, had worked in the Smith Mine for decades as a mechanic and foreman before retiring to build vacation cottages in Red Lodge. He had come out of retirement to fill in for younger miners who'd gone off to war. Over the past six days he'd sucked in gas, come out for fresh air, then gone back in over and over again in an attempt to save his buddies.

"Dave!" Woodrow cried. "He came from the old country in the same boat with me. My pal! Now I'm living and he's dead."

It wouldn't be long before Woodrow, who was engaged to a woman who'd lost her first husband to a Smith Mine accident, would join him.

The rescuers found eleven men in the next tunnel. Some had died alone and some had clustered together in their last moments. Almost all of them had tried to leave the worksite before the gas flattened them. One was pitched forward with his lunch pail in his right hand and his jacket still hooked over his left thumb and slung over his shoulder. Another was discovered and carried out of the mine by a crew that included his uncle from Rhode Island.

Margaret Meiklejohn's father was in this group, his brilliant white hair setting him apart from the others. The bustle of the Cameron home had kept Margaret occupied all week. She and her fiancé had gone back to her house on the third day so she could change her clothes for the first time. She made meals for rescuers and waiting families, and most likely entertained the little kids who were also waiting for word about their dads. Now she would receive the same awful news they had. Every daughter gets only one father in this life, and the pain of losing him isn't age-specific. So Margaret, at twenty-four, and Mary Wakenshaw, at thirty-nine, who was about to find out that her father had also been discovered that day, would have felt just as kicked in the gut as those kids.

The junior men on the shift, the ones who were hardier and conceivably more likely to survive the blast, were also found on Friday. Twenty-one-year-old Andrew Jordan had been working at the Smith while he waited to be drafted. He'd helped raise his younger siblings after their mother had died. He was handsome and charming on the dance floor, but a bit of a hothead off it. He sometimes got into fights because of his temper. It was a tendency he probably would have outgrown.

Herman Mejean, twenty, was the youngest man on the shift. The tall redhead hadn't had an easy childhood. He lived with his aunt and uncle because, allegedly, his parents hadn't treated him well. Like so many damaged children, he was a bit of a loner, but he'd managed to catch the heart of Thelma Mourich, one of the most popular girls in town.

"He didn't have many friends," she said. "But I was his good friend."

She would remember Herman fondly for her whole life. His relatives had the word SON carved into his headstone.

As the rescuers headed up the tunnel, they found two men halted in the act of taking an empty mantrip toward freshly blasted coal. The motorman had been knocked off, but his assistant had kept right on riding as the car drifted down the rail. They were found very close to the unfinished rock slope that could have provided an airway or escape route if the Freemans hadn't stopped production on it while they vacationed in California.

Later, the Freeman family would have to answer for that decision. But James Freeman was already trying to cover himself. As his remaining employees ground themselves down trying to find those he had put in danger, he wrote to one of the officers of Montana Coal and Iron. "We have had a little trouble with gas occasionally during the past ten years, but our mine was not considered gaseous," he claimed. "Since Federal inspectors were here in November, we have been unusually cautious, as they found sufficient gas to recommend the use of electric lamps."

He didn't mention that workers still weren't using those lamps because they'd just been ordered a few weeks earlier. Nor did he mention that the mine was indeed considered gaseous, which is why it had been the first in the state the Feds had inspected.

A couple of days later, Freeman wrote a letter to the president of Montana Coal and Iron in which he expressed his opinion that a "small gas pocket" had caused the explosion and that coal dust had fueled it. He also said that the mine was drier and dustier than usual because of the cold winter air, though he neglected to admit that he had put off ordering the dusting machine that would have ameliorated the hazard. Finally, in case the president was worried about him, he ended the letter with a medical update. "Outside of a slight headache, I feel quite well," he wrote.

Emil Anderson and his crew were decidedly not feeling well. In fact, they hadn't felt well since ninety minutes after the explosion. That was when they'd begun writing farewell notes to their families from the shelter of their blocked-off cave. The experienced rescuers heading toward them had been right: it was possible to find a pocket of clean air and build a barricade against the gas. This group was the only one that had even tried. As the rescuers approached their hideaway, they found the one man who hadn't thought the barricade was a good idea. He'd fallen about a hundred feet from where the other men had piled the boxes and rocks and canvas designed to save their lives. Heading away from his body and toward the barricade, the rescuers spotted footprints in the coal dust. It looked as if Emil and his crew had, at first, left their work area and tried to make it to safety. They had also been working close to the unfinished rock slope. If it had been completed, maybe they would have continued running and made it out. But when they realized they'd never outrun the gas, they doubled back to where they'd been able to breathe and began building their shelter. The gas hadn't arrived yet, but it soon followed them in.

The rescuers traced the same path and ran toward the barricade. They must have frantically torn it down, hoping the whole time they'd find someone with at least some warmth left in his flesh. But they didn't. Later, one report would say that a loosely hung brattice indicated that they hadn't tried very hard to protect themselves. If their work really was substandard, here was evidence that the lack of adequate emergency training had done them in.

Emil and the four other men had died lying with their heads on their crossed arms, a position that gave them the best chance to inhale air at ground level. Lying beside them were the notes.

The rescuers held them up and tried to decipher the scrawl. The miners had written in chalk on small boards ripped from the sides of explosive boxes.

"Goodbye wifes and daughters," they wrote. "We died an easy death. Love from us both. Be good."

It was signed by Walter J. and Johnny S. and had been dropped next to their bodies. Johnny had taken the extra time to locate a pencil and inscribe the same message on his helmet.

The rescuers picked up another board.

"We try to do our best but we couldn't get out," it said, and four men had signed their names: Frank Pajnich, Fred Rasborschek, Walter Joki, and John Sudar.

Rasborschek, sixty-one, had already lost his wife and daughter, burying the girl when she was still a child. Joki, thirty, had left mining to ranch, then returned because of the war shortages. Sudar, besides doting on his blue-eyed little girl, was a musician in a two-man band and a fantastic yodeler. He was tall and lanky with dramatic waves in his blond hair and a mouth that turned up at the corners even when he wasn't smiling. His sister-in-law had dreamed about him the night before the disaster. In her sleep, she'd seen John sitting on a white horse. Then he waved good-bye to her and rode off.

All the men except Emil had worked together on the notes, possibly to conserve their energy. But Emil turned one of the boards over and wrote his thoughts privately. He was dying, but he still managed to use proper cursive as he pressed the chalk into the wood. Two rescuers carried the boards out of the mine and delivered them to one of the Freeman brothers in the mine office. The assistant, Romek, and Tony Boyle were there, too. This is exactly what they read from Emil's final message.

"It's 5 min, Pass 11 o'clock. dear Agnes and children. I'm sorry we had to go this God Bless you all. Emil with lots Kiss."

Later in the week, someone drove over to Emil's house with his belongings. They knocked on the door and handed Agnes the pocket watch he always carried, the lunch box he'd never opened on his last workday, and the board bearing his final words. She would keep this proof of how much Emil had loved her and their three children, and how sorry he'd been to leave them, for many years. Eventually, Elmer would donate the board to a museum so everyone could see how much love his family had shared and lost.

In the early hours of Saturday morning, the bodies of Emil and fourteen of his co-workers were taken out of the mine, eased onto the delivery trucks, and driven to the morgue. For the second night in a row, people woke to the sound of trucks rumbling back and forth over the gravel roads.

Red Lodge's two morticians, Edward Olcott and R. G. Martin, now had more bodies to officially identify. They'd begun the job the day before. In many cases, family members had to come to view the bodies so there would be no doubt about who was being buried. It had been a week since the men had died, so their faces weren't recognizable. One man identified his son's body by his left boot, which he'd repaired himself after the young man's ax had fallen on it and sliced through the toe while he was working at a Civilian Conservation Corps camp. A friend of Margaret Meiklejohn's had to go to the morgue twice to try to identify her father's body. His right index finger was gone, but the friend recognized his distinctive white hair and a ring on one of his remaining fingers.

Other bodies were too mangled to offer any clues, but the items in their pockets served as calling cards. One man had stuffed a house key and a silver dollar in his coveralls pocket. Thelma's family identified her father by the knife he'd always carried. Her mom took the knife home and put it on the porch because it smelled too foul to keep inside. The cold air didn't dilute the stink much either, so she buried one of the last things her husband had touched in the backyard.

Another family had only a pair of boots and the top of a lunch pail as proof of their loss. The morning of the explosion, the man's daughter, who happened to be the sister of James and W. R. Freeman, had watched him walk into the mine behind the mantrip. He was on foot so he could inspect the rails. He'd tucked that same lunch pail in the crook of his elbow.

It must have been awful for the morticians to prepare all those remains. They had to rip the lovely satin linings out of the coffins to wedge the bloated bodies inside. Those linings, sewn in to gild the spectacle of death, weren't necessary anyway. There would be no open-casket funerals. Some of the corpses had split open and the canvas they'd been wrapped in had oozed fluids. Morticians are accustomed to unpleasant juices. They're used to the smell of death. They know how to cope with these parts of their job. But this odor was so intense that Martin eventually had to repaint the walls of his building to get rid of it.

And those professional men, trained to keep their emotions hidden and to offer solace to others, had to deal with their own memories, too.

In September 1941, an old man had died after a long illness, and a normal funeral had ensued. Six strong, vital men served as pallbearers. They lifted the coffin, working to keep their faces from showing the strain of the weight and the responsibility, and carried it down the aisle. They walked past their neighbors and relatives and saw the body into the ground. Now, five of those six pallbearers—plus the son and son-in-law of the man who had been buried that day—were dead, too. The morticians had known all of them. They had shaken their hands and given them instructions on how to manage the coffin. Now they were enclosing them into their own boxes.

While the undertakers worked and the families began making funeral plans, the rescuers continued to hunt for trapped miners. Not that anyone thought they'd find survivors now. A full week had passed since those men had started their ordinary workday. Even if they'd found those elusive pockets of untainted air, how could they have lived that long without enough water?

The rescuers were being hailed as heroes. The lead editorial in the *Billings Gazette* that morning lauded their bravery and persistence in looking for the "missing in action" miners. "Their spontaneity, their eagerness, their industry and their willingness to give what they had to save a life wrote a wonderful commentary upon mankind in the dramatic story unfolded with tragic climax," the editor wrote.

But the rescuers couldn't have cared about accolades. They just wanted to find every last man. Two were still missing.

One of them, a fifty-three-year-old bachelor, had been overlooked the first time they combed the mine. But on a second pass, they found him. It seems that he'd known about a breakthrough between the seventh and eighth entries on the southeastern side of the mine and had tried to use it as an escape route. He never made it through the passage.

But that still left one man to find. At first, the rescuers didn't even know whom they were seeking. They initially thought they'd lost track of a pumpman, so they looked in all the places he would have worked. Then word came that the pumpman had already been identified. The only man who hadn't been accounted for was Elmer Price, the foreman.

Price knew the mine well. If anyone had a chance of escaping, it was this seasoned man. He'd managed and inspected every bit of that mine for years, though now he spent most of his time surveying and mapping the mine. He only went underground every few days, when he needed to check on safety issues. He'd earned enough money as he rose through the ranks to feed and clothe five children, though he wasn't completely finished with that job. One daughter still had a college degree to secure.

Later, when the officials would argue about whose actions had caused the disaster, Price's name would be thrown around quite a bit. Not as a culprit, but as a tragically ignored hero.

Now that the searchers knew whom they were looking for, they had to figure out where he'd been at the time of the blast. They narrowed the possibilities down to 5 Southeast, where Emil and his crew had tried to hide. But that area had been thoroughly explored already, so they began looking elsewhere. They spent most of the day hunting for Price with no luck. As the sun went down, one of the rescuers insisted on going back to 5 Southeast to look again. Inspector Arnold wouldn't hear of it.

"No," he told the man. "We are not going to kill you. You've had it for the day. You better go home."

That rescuer, a Smith foreman and fire boss named Loren Newman, was tired. He couldn't fight anymore.

"Well," he said, "Elmer Price is just as dead now as he will be tomorrow anyway, so it don't make any difference."

As Newman exited the mine, W. R. Freeman asked when he'd be back for another shift. Arnold was still looking out for him.

"This man isn't coming back for three days," Arnold said. "He's had it."

"Well, I can tell you where Elmer is," Newman said before leaving.

They pulled out a map and he pointed to a breakthrough between two rooms in 5 Southeast. Sure enough, that's where they found Price the next day.

The final search party entered the mine at around 1:00 p.m. and spotted Price at about 3:15. He had been knocked against the rib of the room and probably died instantly. But like the captain of a ship, he'd somehow managed to remain in the mine until all of his men had been brought out. They carried him to the surface at six that night and declared the recovery operation complete.

15 The Grief

The day after they found Price, the rescuers peeled off their coveralls, scoured the filth from their skin, and slept. Those who'd come from other states and towns headed home to their families, whom they would appreciate a little more, and to their own mines, where they would be a little more grateful each time they inhaled outside air at the end of a shift. They would go on with their lives and try to forget all the preview of hell they'd seen in Bearcreek. The local men had no such luxury. After a tiny respite, they would be digging graves and carrying coffins all week.

Already, seven of the miners had been buried, starting with the two men found just hours after the explosion. By the end of the week people would be going to two or three funerals a day. Even when they had a break, they couldn't escape the sounds of death all around them. They heard the plaintive notes of "Taps" wafting from grave-sites during ceremonies for miners who had fought in World War I. They heard the chop-crunch, chop-crunch of shovels cracking through the snow and frozen dirt as men hollowed out graves. Their figures dotted the sloped Bearcreek cemetery as they bent and stood, sinking lower and lower into the ground as the holes deepened. The laborers were friends and relatives of the dead, people who should have been sitting quietly with their sorrow instead of fighting with the earth. But the regular gravediggers couldn't handle all the work. The many servicemen who had rushed home to bury their fathers didn't expect it to be a literal job. Later, they would stand tall in their dress uniforms as preachers read prayers, but first some of them would sweat through this undignified task.

The local newspapers had replaced the urgent updates on the rescue with simple death announcements. Obituaries dominated the pages. If just one of these men had died, his story probably would have been long and detailed. But with so many deaths to chronicle, the notices were relatively basic. They included the man's name, age, birthplace, burial location, pallbearers, and survivors. The editors must have decided that there wasn't enough room to print the sadder details, such as specific cause of death, though the *Carbon County News* managed to find the space to run its weekly installment of a serialized story called "They Were Expendable."

When a man in a small town dies, the community usually rallies around his wife and children. The women bring cakes and hot casseroles, wipe the kitchen counters, and make sure the mourners try to get some sleep. The men do their best to fill in for the departed, offering to fix loose screen doors or mow the overgrown lawns come spring. But when everyone in the community is grief-stricken, there is no one to hold up the weak, no one to distract them from their emptiness and take care of the details. Nearly everyone in Bearcreek and Red Lodge must have been numb with shock. Across the ocean, people in countless European communities walked around in similar trances after their cities were bombed or their neighbors were murdered. But Bearcreek may have been the only American town in such a wounded condition.

That Monday morning, Mary Wakenshaw took a ride into town. "Keep pushing" was her motto, and things needed to be done before Bud's funeral. Bobby sat beside her in the car. It was his twelfth birthday.

"What do you want for your birthday?" Mary asked.

"I want my dad," Bobby answered.

She kept driving through a fresh batch of tears.

There was a requiem high mass for the miners that morning at the Catholic church in Red Lodge. Everyone was welcome, of course, but it was a tiny building that couldn't fit all those who needed comfort. Most people would wait until Tuesday and go to the community-wide memorial service.

They had to hold that in the Roman Theatre, the biggest auditorium in town. Just before two in the afternoon, people started to arrive. The room was a long rectangle, and each row of seats featured an art deco pattern. The narrow red leather seats were set very close together: a good thing for sweethearts sharing a wooden armrest, but a bit claustrophobic for people trying to contain their sobs.

Thelma Mourich sat with her mother. It was strange to be in the theater, where she had spent so many good times with her dad, for something like this. The Mouriches sat a few rows from the Freeman family. Thelma's mother was furious.

"It was more important to take a vacation than take care of the men!" she said loudly enough for the Freemans—and everyone else—to hear.

Thelma was mortified. She wanted her mother to stop, to sit sedately like the other widows. But she knew her mother had many reasons to be angry. She'd lost her husband and her father in the disaster. And maybe that *was* the Freemans' fault. Or maybe one of the miners had made a terrible mistake. It was even possible that her mother was angry with herself. Two years earlier, around the time he'd gotten gassed after the mine fire, her father decided he'd had enough of mining. After nearly three decades underground, he quit. The family packed up and moved west to Washington, where Thelma's father found work in a shipyard. He could labor in the open air and see the daylight, but somehow it wasn't enough. He never really took to the job. He and Thelma's mother both missed the people and memories they'd left in Montana. Frank quit the shipyard and they moved back to their old life, where he rejoined his friends in the mine. If only they hadn't left Washington, her mother must have thought at least once. If only.

The preachers stood at the front of the room as everyone settled into their seats. The Red Cross nurses scanned the crowd. They'd been called to this service—and to the Catholic mass—to stand by in case anyone fainted.

Bill Romek's wife sat before a keyboard and played as a soloist sang "The Old Rugged Cross" and "Good Night and Good Morning."

The second hymn had been composed by a grief-stricken mother after she'd buried her young daughter.

"Good morning up there where cometh no night," she'd written to her baby.

Thankfully, all the Bearcreek children were still alive. At least they had that.

The Methodist minister read from scripture. Then the pastor from the Congregational church rose to give a sermon.

First, he recited the usual funereal boilerplate. He spoke of how none of them could put their grief into words, and reminded them that Jesus himself had overcome death. Then his message became more specific. He praised the Bearcreek miners for taking on such dangerous work and for keeping "the wheels of war industry" turning.

"They had erected a sign urging men not to miss a single shift in order that coal might be supplied in abundance for the war machine," Rev. Seebart said. "You see, they were like real soldiers fighting on the battle lines. The only difference was that they were fighting on a home battlefront instead of a foreign strand."

He couldn't blame any one person for the tragedy, but he could blame the war.

"It may be possible that the haste to get production, in order that the battle be quickly over, led to some oversight which reduced below normal their margin of personal safety," the pastor continued. "In such case, they were all the more like military heroes and are therefore entitled to stars on our service flags."

Then it was time to wrap up. He needed to give these people some guidance, some tips for carrying on after mass calamity.

"And now what shall we say to those who are left behind, those who must face the long and arduous task of reconstructing their lives?"

He must have struggled to find an answer. He must have hovered over his writing paper for hours the night before, trying to compose just the right message. But some of what he came up with couldn't have helped much.

"Do not think of them as dead—just away for a while," he said.

He tried to convince the bereft that their losses would spare others and that their men may have been martyrs.

"We need to remember that costly and terrible as this accident was to us, our sacrifices will lead to the introduction of safety devices and the taking of precautions which will eventually save the lives of literally thousands and even millions of workers," he said. "When one looks at the situation this way, we can say that these men died that others might live. There is great comfort in that thought."

He might have been correct. Maybe this event would lead to rules that would save other lives. But there remained the troubling fact that safety devices and precautionary laws already existed. The mine operators had just failed to make use of them.

Could the people in the theater even absorb these messages? Mourners often can't, lost as they are in silent trauma or messy hysteria. The reality of all they'd lost must have hit some of them as they looked at the crowd, which was so much thinner than it should have been. They might have realized in those moments that holidays would never be the same. Because so many of the families were related by blood or marriage, at every gathering from now on there would be empty chairs and forgotten punch lines. Everyday life would be changed forever. When a man walked into a saloon expecting to see the usual faces, he'd be reminded of this horrible week. Sitting on his stool, he might notice far too many clean glasses behind the bar, or wonder when it would be okay to tell a racy story again. Simple things like card games would be forever tainted with memories of better days. One foursome had been reduced to a single player, after his three companions were killed in the mine. And the town itself would never operate with the same precision. Among the dead were a school board member, two councilmen, the chairman of the Carbon County Selective Service board, a justice of the peace and, of course, the constable.

Mary sent Bud to heaven with a graveside service at the Bearcreek cemetery on the same day as the group memorial service. He was buried alongside his father, Adam, as Rev. Daniel McCorkle said prayers for both of them. McCorkle, who would preside over seventeen burial services for twenty-one of the miners, had been in town since early in the rescue mission. Though he lived hundreds of miles away, near the top of the state, he had called Bearcreek home from 1920 to 1930. He worked in the mines for two years, taught grade school for one year and high school for seven, and served as pastor of the nearby Presbyterian church for four of those years. He'd since moved on to politics, and now sat on the State Welfare Board.

He happened to be working on a case in the Senate chamber in Helena when he heard about the disaster. He immediately phoned other members of his board and convinced them to grant ten thousand dollars in relief funds for his former neighbors. Then he headed back to Bearcreek to do whatever he could.

Mary stood by the open graves as McCorkle blessed the bodies. Her brother was there with his wife. Some friends, her mother-in-law, Mag, and her children huddled around the gravesite that until now had been marked only with the babies' white stone. There were thirteen inches of snow on the ground to muffle their voices. Bobby noticed that the dirt that would cover the coffins wasn't in piles, but in great big frozen chunks. Fannie watched the ritual with her new husband, who'd gotten leave to come home and lend his support. Bud hadn't even seen them together as man and wife.

The Wakenshaws' was one of many joint funerals. Who knew what was harder: facing it all in one day, as Mag was, or spreading the ordeal out, like Mary would. Her father, Frank, would be buried on a different day in a different cemetery, near her mother. She'd go through this all over again, and she wouldn't be able to spare her children, either. Bobby had been close to Frank, who'd been his roommate for years. He'd built the boy a basketball court in the yard, spending hours out there clearing the space with his shovel and wheelbarrow. And he'd delighted Bobby just this past December with a Christmas surprise. As usual, an excited crowd waited for Santa Claus around the big Christmas tree in the center of town. He always drove up with a truck full of candy and dried fruits, courtesy of the union, and passed them out to the children.

Bobby had already discovered that his father usually dressed as Santa, but this year Bud was standing in the crowd. Who could replace him, Bobby wondered. Then Santa finally arrived, yelling, "Merry Christmas" in an accent that hadn't been cultivated at the North Pole or in Montana. It was the voice of Bohemia, and Bobby knew immediately that Grandpa Frank was under the white beard.

The Wakenshaws listened to the school superintendent sing "The Old Rugged Cross" at Bud and Adam's funeral. They wiped their eyes through the final blessings, then headed home. McCorkle checked the next name on his list. That day he would also bury Margaret Meiklejohn's father in the Bearcreek cemetery. One of W. R. Freeman's sons was scheduled to be a pallbearer.

McCorkle's attempts to comfort Margaret earlier that week hadn't been very effective. When he saw her, he'd been holding the sheet music for the song "Someday We'll Understand." He asked Margaret if she was familiar with the tune. She said she knew it.

"Someday we *will* understand," McCorkle explained.

"Well, right now I sure don't understand," she shot back at him.

The Pelo kids and their cousins buried their fathers on Tuesday, too. The joint service was awful, for them and for their mothers. How many sisters become widows on the same day? The families had just eaten dinner together the Sunday before the disaster. One husband had complained about all the gas in the mine. His brother-in-law, Bill Pelo, had agreed with him. There was so much gas building up, he'd said, that one day the whole top of the hill would blow off. Pelo had almost missed the shift because he had a flat tire; he might still be alive if he hadn't been so fast at changing it. Pelo's eldest son forced himself to smile as he emerged from the Congregational church after the service. He wanted to show that he was still strong. It was the hardest thing the twenty-two-year-old had ever done, including telling his six-year-old brother that their dad had died. Pelo had always saved a piece of cake or some cookies in his lunch pail for the little boy. As soon as his dad got home, the boy would dash up to him, pull the pail from his grip, and run off to gobble his treat.

There were at least fourteen funerals that day, and at least ten the next. One thirteen-year-old girl didn't think she could cry anymore after her father's service; how could she have any more tears, she wondered. Her father was gone, and she'd had to watch her grandparents bury their second son in less than two years. Both had died in mining accidents. But she still had more funerals to attend, and she managed to cry just as much for the other kids' fathers as for her own.

As much as they hated it, at least most of the children had the chance to say graveside good-byes. One young Coast Guard man wasn't even there. Clem Lodge's family had decided to notify him of the death by regular mail, but he'd been on a convoy ship for a destroyer and wouldn't receive their letter until the ship docked months after the disaster. He was waiting in line for mail call when a shipmate who'd already collected his correspondence walked past him. This fellow, who hailed from a town near Bearcreek, was reading about the disaster in the local newspaper his family had sent. He asked Lodge if he knew one of the men mentioned in the article. Lodge recognized the name as someone who had worked on the same shift as his father.

He immediately felt that something terrible had happened to him. When the line moved and Lodge got his mail, the letter from home confirmed his hunch. He wouldn't get back home until August, six months after the disaster.

His uncle had also died in the disaster, but his son—Lodge's first cousin, Jimmy Laird—had made it to the funeral. The cousins, who were born a month apart and grew up side by side, had joined the Coast Guard together. They'd made it through basic training together, too, before being separated. Lodge was assigned to the convoy ship. When the commander called for one more volunteer for the mission, he nudged his cousin.

"Come on," Lodge said. "I'm already going!"

"Go to hell," Laird said.

Jimmy Laird ended up on an ammunition ship. Because of his decision, he was free to go home to bury his father, Ned. But deciding not to join his cousin's ship also doomed him. Lodge survived the war and went on to enjoy a long life. Laird went down with his torpedoed ship in 1945.

On Wednesday, Rev. McCorkle bowed his head with the large Mourich family. Its patriarch had helped to build the mine buildings, and now the old man held himself together while burying his sons. They buried Thelma's other grandfather in the Bearcreek cemetery that day, too. Her Mourich grandparents had one son left. All of their grandchildren surrounded them, some big enough to carry coffins and some still little enough to hold their mother's hands during the service.

Thelma and Frankie got through the day, but going home wouldn't be easy. As soon as they walked into the house, they'd see the hat rack in the kitchen. Their dad always tossed his cap onto it when he came home for the day. He'd watch it land, then tell the dog, "Get my cap! Get my cap!" and the dog would hop up and pluck it off the rack.

During the second half of the week, the Bearcreek families went to more than a dozen other funerals. Emil Anderson was buried in his only suit, the one he most likely bought from Peter the tailor in Red

Lodge. He'd been handsome when he wore it, with his blue eyes and brown hair and gold-rimmed glasses. His daughter, Doris, chose the same golden frames when she needed lenses that school year. One day, after a bath, she'd accidentally grabbed his glasses instead of her own and went out to play wearing them. She didn't even notice she was wearing the wrong pair until Emil pointed it out. It was a mistake she'd never get to make again.

Rev. Seebart officiated during Emil's graveside ceremony, doing his best to console the sweet man's many relatives. They gathered at the Red Lodge cemetery, a wide, level field framed by stately mountains. Doris had her mother and Elmer had his new wife for comfort, but Melvin was alone. The snow on the ground was so deep that it obscured people on the cemetery paths almost completely. Melvin's mother could only see their heads passing.

On the same day that Melvin said good-bye to his father, his basketball team went back to work. They'd already forfeited one tournament game, but the coaches in the league had fiddled with the schedule so they could make this one.

Five players started. Despite all that time away from the court, they played fiercely. No one could have been surprised, though, by all the fouls called on the boys. They were tired and angry and without their star players, Melvin and Frankie. But they didn't give up. They led for the first three quarters, not losing stamina until the fourth. The other team pulled ahead, but the Bearcats tied it up with a swish at the buzzer. The scoreboard read 30–30 when overtime began. Bearcreek still had a chance to win and advance to the semifinals. Then one player got a personal foul and headed for the bench. Then it happened to two more players, the ref's whistle blasting their decline, until there were only two Bearcreek men left. They lost 37–30 and were eliminated from the tournament.

The season was over, and soon the funerals were, too. Or so everyone thought. A week later, the Wakenshaws pulled on their best clothes once again and said good-bye to another loved one. Bud's grandmother had died.

16 The Clues

As his neighbors put their people back into the earth, a man named Harry Owens sat down at his desk to type a letter. Owens was Montana Coal and Iron's office manager. He'd worked for the company for more than twenty years, plenty of time to learn just about everything that went on in the suit-and-tie end of the business. Enough time, also, to know where his loyalties lay. But he had something to say about the tragedy. So, rather than blab his opinions around town and risk his job, it was safer to put the words on paper, fold them into an envelope, and send them to another part of the world. His son, Jim, was a corporal in the Marine Corps at the time. He was stationed on Tarawa, a Pacific base about halfway between Hawaii and Australia that would be the site of a major Marine battle later that year. Owens wrote the missive eleven days after the explosion.

Dear Jim:

I got your letter of February, 28th yesterday and was sure glad to hear from you. I will tell you what I can about the disaster here.

Conditions down in the No. 3 vein have been getting worse, lots of gas and things not being looked after like they should have been. Old W.R. had pulled out for California and had been away for about five weeks without leaving the bosses any instructions and the airways were in very poor condition. They never made any attempt to clean up the wasted coal and there was slack and dirt every place. They were having an awful time to keep the gas out and what I think happened was as follows:

Some one lit some gas in a room; it raised a lot of dust which exploded after the gas in various parts of the mine. All the stoppings were blown out and the men who were not killed by the explosion died from the gas after effects. Emil Anderson and four others left written messages on powder boxes for their folks. . . . The first I knew about it was when someone came in the office and said that there was smoke coming out of the mine. I looked and there was a little smoke, but nothing like the time of the fire.

In the last sentence he was most likely referring to the mine fire that had gassed Frank Mourich a few years earlier, the one that had lasted eight days. Owens wrote a little more in the letter about some of the men who'd been saved and some who had not, about a horse he might buy and the cows that were toughing out the cold weather, then ended with his love. His son would read it, cram it into his duffel bag, and bring it home at the end of the war. Its damning words would remain tucked away from the public for fifty years.

If only Tony Boyle had read that letter when it was written. If only Boyle, who would later turn out to be quite good at breaking the law, had thought to pressure the postmaster into handing over all personal letters mailed by company officials during those weeks after the explosion, things might have turned out differently. Boyle would have had proof from a company insider that the mine had indeed been unsound and its managers negligent. He could have read the letter aloud to a courtroom full of people and called Owens and Freeman to the stand to explain and defend it.

But Boyle didn't have access to the letter, and he would be long dead before it surfaced. So he had to try to prove in a more round-about way that the company didn't care about the miners. He had to convince people to say it for him.

As followed most violent or mysterious deaths at the time, officials scheduled a coroner's inquest to find out how the miners died. Assistant County Attorney George Smith, a coal miner's son, was assigned to the case. He came to Red Lodge before the inquest, expecting to find something he could dig into. Surely, someone would have gathered up a pile of folders, some background documents, and the names of witnesses he could depose. Instead, he arrived at the courthouse to find virtually nothing that would help him prepare for the hearing. He had, he'd say later, "serious misgivings" about accomplishing anything worthwhile. Fortunately, Boyle had been collecting evidence on the mine's owners and its conditions for years. He knew the union players and the knowledgeable townspeople. Boyle met with Smith and offered his connections and his wisdom. Smith gratefully accepted, and Boyle dove into the job.

Boyle had been craving this opportunity for years. Finally, he might have thought, he could stick it to the mine owners. And, as a bonus, he could show off his leadership skills. Though union god John Lewis was busy trying to secure a two-dollar-a-week raise for miners all over the country and monitoring sporadic strikes in several regions, he was also paying some attention to Boyle's efforts. So were many miners whose support Boyle would need as he tried to move up the United Mine Workers hierarchy. He must have known that he wouldn't rise on his charms alone. Even the most arrogant of men know somewhere deep inside whether they are liked or not. James Brophy, whose family owned the independent Brophy Mine in Bearcreek, said Boyle's father, a coal miner, was "one of the nicest men you ever met and he raised the three most rotten kids you'd ever know."

Brophy remembered a typically unpalatable move Boyle had made while he was district president. One Montana local still belonged to the United Mine Workers of America autonomously instead of falling under the local district's control. Boyle wanted to change that, so when the small local refused to join his district he arranged for its national dues to go up. And when the members gave in and let him control them, he raised their dues even more.

He never would have become district president if he hadn't had such chutzpah. In the early 1930s, he'd quit mining. When he decided to return a year later, he claimed seniority at the mine he'd left. The mine's manager wasn't about to give it to him, but Boyle persisted. He was a hothead with a short fuse, so the arguments must have been fierce. Eventually, the manager asked the union's and company's executive boards to mediate the case. But on the day of the hearing, the manager never showed up. Boyle regained his job and his seniority, which led to his district presidency. Montana Coal and Iron's Bill Romek, who was at the hearing, doubted Boyle would have prevailed if the manager had testified. If not for that curious absence, Boyle might never have rejoined the coal business that led to his ascent.

Romek was one of the few Bearcreek folks who had a good relationship with Boyle. Even after all that would happen later, he'd maintain that, "as president of the United Mine Workers in Montana [Boyle] was a straight-shooting, honest American."

And he might have been Bearcreek's only hope for justice.

The miners didn't go back to work until all the funerals were over. A large crew of them clocked in again on Sunday, March 14. They were essentially on cleanup duty that week. They'd been instructed to take out all the salvageable mining equipment for use in Montana Coal and Iron's other mine, the Foster, which would ramp up its output to compensate for losing the Smith's. They spent time scrubbing the helmets and lamps the rescue crews had worn, and they cleared the passages enough so investigators could traverse the whole mine. Several teams of officials—from the federal government, the state, the company, and the union—would spend more than a week trying to figure out the cause and trajectory of the explosion. As the working miners tidied up, they must have unwittingly disturbed evidence. They also would have had the chance to alter some of it if their bosses ordered them to, though nobody would ever discuss such malfeasance.

The people of Bearcreek embarked on the challenge of surviving without those who had anchored their lives.

The children went back to school after the funerals. As if their lives weren't horrible enough, the grade school students had to start on a Saturday to make up for time lost during the disaster. The high schoolers could stay home that day, March 13, but the free day didn't make up for a new blow, particularly to the seniors. Their senior ball had been scheduled for that night. A full-page notice in *The Bear Facts* with a sketch of a girl wearing an off-the-shoulder gown and a tiara had provided all the details: music by the Nite Owls; admission prices set at $1.10 per couple and 35 cents for "extra ladies"; anyone and everyone invited. The prom crew must have planned the gym decor already. Girls had surely chosen their dresses, and boys may have mentally rehearsed their extra suave moves, but neither gender got the chance to wow each other. The ball had been canceled for no discernible reason except for sorrow.

At least they could go to the movies again. The Park Theatre in Red Lodge, which had shut its doors early in the rescue mission "out of respect to the miners of Bearcreek–Red Lodge and their families," according to an ad the owners placed, reopened that weekend. Among the Park's offerings that month was a film that had been released in January. It was called *City without Men*.

The widows, besides trying to shut out the refrain that must have been blasting in their minds—*What will I do now? How will we live without him?*—needed to restore some sort of structure in their lives. They bid their guests good-bye, put away the extra blankets, and may have begun to sort through their husbands' belonging. Or maybe they couldn't face that yet. Was it easier or harder to see his razor by the sink, his socks in the wash pile, his summer hat on a high shelf?

They put the funerals behind them by submitting notes to the

Carbon County News, which ran "Card of Thanks" notices throughout its pages.

"Words cannot adequately express our deep appreciation for the
many kind and sympathetic acts that came to us at the time of our
recent bereavement. We also appreciated the beautiful floral offerings," read one.

"Our recent sad loss leaves us with grateful hearts toward neighbors and friends," another widow wrote on behalf of her large family.
"Their comforting expressions of sympathy and thoughtfulness will
always be remembered by us."

The messages might have been impersonal, but it wasn't as if the
widows had the time or energy to compose eloquent tidings. They
were the heads of households now, with all the paperwork that job
entailed. One woman didn't even know how to cash her late husband's final paycheck so she could buy groceries. Some needed to
meet with lawyers to go over wills and life insurance policies. Each
widow was busy collecting documents which proved that she had indeed been married to her late husband and that he was the father of
her children. It was another burden, but at least the hassle of digging
through dresser drawers and desk cubbies would keep them solvent.
If the accident had occurred seven years earlier they would have received nothing from the government, but the 1937 Social Security Act
had granted miners Federal Old Age and Survivors Insurance coverage, which provided widows and dependent children with monthly
checks. The Social Security officers were doing all they could to help
the women win their benefits as quickly as possible. They'd set up a
temporary office at the mine so the women wouldn't have to travel far
to prove they had lived full, secure lives just weeks before.

Boyle was busy preparing for the inquest, so it wasn't until the end of
March that he met officially with union members. They gathered at
the Bearcreek Union Hall, the familiar aura of sadness following each
man in and settling beside him. Federal Inspector Arnold was there,
too, though neither man could give the miners much information.

Arnold told them how important it was to form a safety committee to deal with the mine owners and the workers when dangerous conditions arose in the future. Boyle stood to read a condolence message that John Lewis had wired.

"International officers are shocked to learn of the great tragedy that has befallen so many members of our local #858 at Washoe," Boyle read in his shrill voice. "These brothers have died in the service of their country as truly as any soldier upon a remote battlefield. Our hundreds of thousands of members will grieve with the members of local union #858 and the members of the families of the deceased brothers."

Well, that was nice, the members must have thought, but are they going to help us?

Boyle continued: "The international officers are placing at the disposal of president W. A. Boyle of district #27 certain funds to be used for the relief purposes in this great disaster. Please convey our profound sympathy to each member of the bereaved families."

He looked up from the telegram and announced that the union had released $7,400. It sounded like a lot of money at first, but divided by seventy-four families, it came to only $100 each. Still, that was one hundred times more than the company was offering.

Montana Coal and Iron appeared to be honing its image. The company, which would later claim to be too strapped to help any of the widows, donated $500 to the local American Red Cross chapter as thanks for its help during the rescue effort. The check arrived with a letter from Romek. He gushed his appreciation for the ladies' aid, then flipped to false humility.

"We only wish that circumstances permitted it to be a more substantial amount," he wrote.

James Freeman also continued to work on damage control, this time by blaming the federal inspectors. In a letter to a company officer, written just after the last body was recovered, he had claimed that the explosion was caused by dust accumulation that had been exacerbated when the federal inspectors made the company increase ventilation. Just days earlier, during the rescue effort, he had told the company president in a letter that he believed gas had caused the explosion. Now he'd reversed himself again. In a second letter to the company president, Freeman blamed the dust and claimed that the dust hazard "heretofore has not been in the minds of Federal and State inspectors." Of course, he knew very well that this was untrue. Arnold had recommended methods for controlling the coal dust in his preliminary report, and he would also maintain that he specifically warned company officials in November that increasing ventilation would dry out the mine and intensify the coal dust explosion hazard. Besides being deceitful about the coal dust warning, Freeman knew that he had personally postponed the purchase of a rock-dusting machine, which would have curtailed the multiplying dust. Still, he attempted to make himself appear proactive. The inspectors may not have concerned themselves with coal dust, he asserted, but he would.

"We have decided that it would be best to rock-dust our Foster Creek mine before we start operations there," Freeman wrote.

No one knows whether James Freeman ever went into the mine after the explosion, but he definitely wasn't there for the investigation into what destroyed it. He sent Romek, two mine foremen (Loren Newman and Martin Rapp), and his brother Tom, the Smith's outside foreman. On Monday, March 22, they gathered outside the mine entrance with two other investigative teams. Arnold and Fred Bailey, a senior mining engineer, represented the Bureau of Mines. State inspector Davies, recovered from being gassed on the first day of the rescue mission, showed up with Ben Henry, a state metal mine inspector, and Archie Browning, the foreman from the Griffin mine in Montana. Tony Boyle brought along three union men: international board member Joe Masini, district board member Joe Yanchisin, and Joe Boone, secretary of the Foster mine local. Four Montana Coal and Iron employees also joined the officials, either to serve as tour guides through the dismantled mine or to provide background information along the way.

Each team would try to piece together exactly what had happened. They would examine charred areas of the mine to try to pinpoint where fire erupted. They would take clues from the way the dust had blown and look at items that had moved to try to determine what direction the explosive forces had taken. For example, a drill press, which weighed at least a thousand pounds, had moved about ten feet north of its usual spot, showing that the force in that area traveled north. Sixty-pound rails and a booster fan were also blown outward, as were the shelves and supplies in the machine shop. Three loaded mine cars were turned on their sides. But the investigators might have done better by just guessing. Much of the evidence was baffling, with equipment tossed in all directions. Even if it had landed in more helpful positions, this type of reconstruction was unreliable.

"Determining the point of origin of an explosion by noting the direction of its forces is far from being an exact science," Davies wrote in his report of the investigation.

Still, with no living witnesses, it was all they had to go on.

The men donned helmets and squeezed onto mantrip benches, as the miners had on their last day of their lives. They would check out the mine systematically, starting down one side of the main tunnel and coming up the other, just as the rescuers had when looking for survivors. But this search was even more tedious. The rescuers had faced the dramatic yet uncomplicated task of finding warm bodies. The investigators weren't even sure what they were seeking, so they had to examine everything they saw. There were hundreds of rooms, and each one had to be searched.

They started in 2 West, but moved on after realizing they couldn't read the explosion's force or find any indications of heat or lingering gas there. They found traces of gas in 3 West, but no other leads. If this kept up, they'd come out with nothing. There was more to chew on in 4 West, though none of it very enlightening. In one area Davies figured that the explosion had traveled both east to west and west to east, but when he looked at the stoppings the forces appeared to have gone north to south. The investigators found remnants of intense heat and spotted a pile of ash that had once been a sheet of canvas, which proved there'd been a fire. But despite spending quite a while pondering the contrary forces, they didn't reach any conclusions. And since they knew that no men had been working in the area at the time of the explosion, they decided to eliminate it as a possible ground zero.

With literally miles to go before they had combed all of the mine's working places, the teams agreed to stop for the day. They left the mine and went back to their respective homes and hotel rooms, some of them probably running into each other over dinner or whiskeys that evening. Most to them were professionals, men required to wear suit coats and felt hats to work. They would have behaved civilly around each other, especially in public. But there was no question that the investigation wasn't just about finding the truth. It was also a competition. Depending on what they found, one team could come out looking guilty and the others innocent of killing all those men.

On Tuesday they trudged into 5 West. They found a loading machine and six loaded cars. Someone had turned the machine off, meaning one of three things: no one was using it at the time of the explosion, the worker had had time to shut it down before leaving the area, or one of the rescuers or cleanup crew members had shut it off. But none of these scenarios pointed to explosion's origin. The investigators knew that the men who'd been working in 5 West— including Thelma's grandfather—had walked about a thousand feet before the gas had asphyxiated them. That and the fact that there weren't signs of heat proved that there hadn't been an explosion or fire in that entry. They moved on.

Adam Wakenshaw and four other men had been found in 6 West, all of them killed instantly. The investigators traced the force there from east to west and assumed that since it entered from another location, it must have originated elsewhere. In 7 West they wagged a safety lamp in the air to test for gas. Despite all the time that had passed since the disaster, there was still an explosive amount of gas floating around. Again, the men calculated that the force had come from the outside, eliminating that entry, too.

At the end of the day, they went home without making progress and met again the next morning to resume where they'd left off. According to reports filed by the night-shift fire boss, the first two rooms in 8 West had been deadlined in the early morning hours of February 27, meaning that there had been too much gas present for men to work there safely. But men *had* worked there, possibly because the deadlines had been removed sometime before the explosion. A tracklayer's tools and lunch pail were found in Room 1, but his body had been recovered from Room 5. There was still explosive gas in Room 5, though the fire boss hadn't reported any on the previous shift. Davies took this to mean that the gas had accumulated the morning of the explosion, possibly after miners sliced into a new side of coal. A wall had caved in nearby, compromising air quality, which could have exacerbated the gas accumulation. Many pieces of equipment had blown out of the room, and the men killed in 8 West had died instantly from an explosion. Davies thought he'd found the answer. The tracklayer, who had worn an open light, must have put his supplies in Room 1, then walked out for some reason. As he moved through the area, his light collided with the newly released gas and sparked an explosion.

At first, Arnold thought Davies's explanation sounded reasonable, but as the investigators moved to other rooms he began have doubts. They found another blown powder box, more blasted-out doors, and fresh pockets of gas. They reached the farthest point in the mine, eleven thousand feet into the mountain, where Bud Wakenshaw and his crew had been preparing to drill a new hole. There they found a car full of at least 150 pounds of illegal pellet powder, all of it burned, along with some exploded detonators and sizzled fuses. But they ruled out that section of the mine as the starting point of the explosion too, because all three men had worn closed lights and the shot-firer, who'd been holding the charge, hadn't been a smoker.

Finally, they arrived at 9 Southeast and headed into Room 5. This was where the naked miner had been found atop a coal pile with his track hammer still in his hand. The two other men in the corridor had died violently as well. There was still a combustible level of gas in the room, and judging from the condition of the walls and equipment, it had been the site of something very hot and very violent. Gas had been found in the room on all but one of the seven days before the explosion, and coal had been freshly drilled and shot from the room the night before the explosion, probably releasing even more fumes.

The tracklayer had been laying a switch at the time of the blast. Arnold looked at the ceiling above the switch and saw something unusual. Unlike the ceilings in the other rooms, fungus was growing on this one. The rescuers had noticed rings of the same fungus forming around the decomposing bodies as they wrapped them up, but this was the first time anyone had seen the stuff sprouting on the coal. Arnold looked from the ceiling to the coal pile and came up with his solution to the puzzle. The trackman, who was wearing an open light, had met up with the gas, he surmised. Maybe the gas had been there for a while, but he had been the first person with an open flame to enter it. When his flame kissed the gas, he was thrown right out of his clothes, up to the roof, then down and across the room for sixty feet, where he landed on the coal pile. The fungus on the roof had grown on fragments of his flesh.

Arnold was sure that the forces had blown outward. But Davies disagreed. The way he saw it, the explosion couldn't have started in 9 Southeast because the force did *not* blow outward.

The teams of investigators continued to search for six more days, only taking Sunday off. They saw a massive motor that had been blown off its track, a booster fan that had flown 235 feet, and a partly burned coat that may have belonged to Meiklejohn. In one section, the clues were so confusing that Davies seemed to have difficulty describing them.

"The evidence and indications in these entries in regard to the directions of explosive forces traveled are so conflicting and contradictory that no other statement in regard to them can as adequately and satisfactorily explain them," Davies wrote of the chaos they discovered.

Eventually, they'd eliminated every place in the mine as a starting point except 8 West, Davies's choice, and 9 Southeast, Arnold's. They agreed to check them out again on Tuesday and Wednesday. But after tracing and retracing all the leads until they were sure they'd seen everything, Davies stuck with 8 West, and Boyle's group agreed with him. Arnold stood by his 9 Southeast position. The company team, oddly, expressed no opinion to the other groups as to where or how the disaster had begun.

When they were done, the men shook hands, took off their hard hats, and drove back to their offices. They would distill the notes they'd scrawled in the dark into separate explanations about what had happened. The reports wouldn't come out for months, but most of these men would be back in Red Lodge in two weeks for the inquest.

17 The Exodus

Virginia Sommerville seemed to be one of the luckier ones. Though her father-in-law and brother-in-law had died in the mine, her husband, Gil, was alive. They had their baby, Connie, their new apartment, and years and years ahead of them to spend together. Thank goodness Gil had been working in the processing plant that morning instead of underground. He was grieving terribly and needed her support, but she could handle that. It was nothing compared to what the widows must have been going through.

During the weeks of rescue and funerals, five out-of-town relatives had stayed at the Sommerville house, but now they'd finally gone home. It was time for Virginia and Gil to resume as normal a life as possible. And the first step was bringing Connie home.

They drove down to Billings to pick up the baby from Virginia's sisters' house. After two days in the city, they planned to head back to Bearcreek. Gil needed to start working again, and Virginia needed to serve as woman of the house until her mother-in-law could function again. On the drive back, Connie started to fuss. It wasn't normal tired or hungry fussing, either. Clearly, the little girl didn't feel well, which figured. Virginia had sent her away so she wouldn't catch a cold from the icy drafts whooshing into the house, but she'd come down with one anyway.

As they rolled into Bearcreek, Virginia and Gil decided to make a stop at a Red Lodge doctor's office. The doctor looked into Connie's ears and mouth and pressed his stethoscope to her chest so he could hear her heartbeat and breath sounds. There was some congestion.

"Rub her up," he advised, and sent them home.

Virginia smeared a gob of Vicks on Connie's chest and covered the icy salve with a flannel. The normally mild-tempered baby didn't make caretaking easy. She kept fighting her mother's ministrations, pushing away anything that got close to her face. She didn't cough or scream, but she sure was irritable. Gil's mother decided to add a home remedy to the treatment. She prepared a poultice and laid it on the baby's chest. The common folk poultices of the day—cooked onions wrapped in a cloth or mustard seed mixtures—were designed to dissolve the gunk that was clogging up Connie's lungs.

Connie had youth and vigor on her side, qualities the town of Bearcreek had possessed just a few weeks earlier. Now the thirty-seven-year-old village seemed as ill as the child. If a place can lose weight and go pale, if it can sag from exhaustion and struggle to breathe, Bearcreek was unquestionably sick.

Losing seventy-four men had depleted the town enough, but now entire families were leaving. Some simply couldn't bear to stay. There were too many memories and too many sad faces. Anytime Bearcreek High School junior Jane Laird's mother met someone in the street or at the store, a crying fest would break out. Mary Laird understood everyone's pain—she felt it herself every day—but she couldn't stand living that way much longer. She decided to leave town soon after the April inquest. With her husband dead, her oldest daughter married, and her son overseas somewhere, she just had herself and Jane to worry about. They would borrow money from Jane's sister and ride the train out of Montana. First they'd spend time in Indiana, then head to Michigan, where Jane would sacrifice her senior year of high school to become a riveter on B-24 bombers at the Ford Motor Company.

Thelma's mother was thinking about moving, too. The house was so quiet now. After his father's funeral, Frankie Jr. had taken tests to determine whether his body, mind, and intelligence were fit for the Navy. Only four of the twenty-five draftees passed all the exams, and Frankie was the only high school student to manage it. He'd already left for Seattle, where he was now a Naval Aviation Cadet. Thelma was back in school, working on the paper and going through the motions of finishing her junior year. Her mother's sister lived in California. Maybe when school got out for the summer, they'd go there to escape all the ghosts.

Margaret Meiklejohn, who was supposed to get married that March, postponed her wedding and made plans to visit with relatives in Washington state after the inquest. It wasn't that she didn't want to marry her fiancé. She just needed some time to heal from her father's death.

Blast survivor Willard Reid needed to get far away, too. Even before the inquest, he packed up his family and drove to live near relatives in California. He would get a job in a sugar refinery. Even though he was the sturdiest of the three survivors, he wouldn't testify at the inquest. He might not even come back to close up his house. He just filled a couple suitcases and shut the door behind him.

Such an abrupt exit wasn't uncommon. Some people took their entire houses with them, jacking them up on giant wooden beams and towing them up to Red Lodge or to other small towns in the area. But others just abandoned the buildings. Years later there would be rumors that, knowing they'd never be able to sell them, people had burned the houses for insurance money.

Mary Wakenshaw wasn't that rash, but she couldn't wait to get out of Bearcreek either. Her father had been wise enough to buy a life insurance policy, so she had a fat $500 check with which to start over. She knew exactly how to spend it. After all those decades as a country girl, she would return to her city roots. She might not run into organ grinders on the streets of Billings, but there would be traffic and office buildings—things that wouldn't remind her of Bearcreek at all. She drove to Billings and walked through houses for sale until she found the right one. It was located in a safe neighborhood on a long street and was within walking distance of a baseball stadium, a park, a hospital, and a city swimming pool. The little white house was long and narrow, like her Bearcreek home, and had only two bedrooms, but for the first time in her adult life, Mary would have an indoor bathroom. She could squeeze a twin bed onto the enclosed sun porch for Bobby, and give her mother-in-law the tiny guesthouse at the back of the lot. Mary signed over her insurance money as a down payment. Her monthly mortgage bill came to $40. Somehow, the Social Security number crunchers had decided that the average monthly payout to the Bearcreek survivors would be $20.73 per widow and $13.88 per dependent child. That wouldn't even cover her mortgage, never mind groceries, clothing, and heat, so Mary, just like all heads of households, went to work.

"I wasn't trained for anything but housework," she said.

But she managed. She took in roomers, which added to her housework, and landed her first paying job. It was a natural transition from housewife to hotel maid. The hours and uniform were more formal, but she was still making beds and polishing faucets as she had for her family for all those years. She would eventually waitress, stuff wieners at a packing company, work in a laundry, and get a job as a saleswoman at the Gambles department store. The higher-ups must have noticed her intelligence and efficiency because they promoted her to a desk job in the company's billing department. She would stay there, in relative contentment, for many years.

Mary was so anxious to get away from Bearcreek that she left before the end of the school year, pulling Bobby out of sixth grade and transferring him to a Billings school. He had no say in the matter, but at least he could do one thing to make his new life easier. His parents' views on discipline had differed slightly. Bud had rarely resorted to corporal punishment, and the few times he had, he'd just used his hand to spank Bobby. Mary applied the razor strop when necessary. Bobby wasn't planning to give her cause to use it, so, he reasoned, why not start fresh without it? Before they packed the last box into the car and pulled out of Bearcreek, he grabbed the strop and hid it under the house.

Connie wasn't any better the morning after the Vicks and poultice remedies, so Virginia called Dr. Oleinik. He came right over, looked at and listened to the baby just as the other doctor had the day before, and grew concerned. Oleinik, convinced that she was sick enough to warrant prescription medicine, opened his black bag and pulled out a new sulfa drug. Sulfadiazine, which had just come out in 1940, was one of the drugs of choice for respiratory illnesses in those days. He would have filled a syringe with the medicine, pierced Connie's satiny skin, and pushed the solution into her muscle. The pain would have made her cry, but he had every reason to believe it would cure her.

Doctors had been performing miracles with sulfa drugs since they had been introduced in the 1930s after German scientists discovered that a certain red dye could kill bacteria. In December 1936, one of President Roosevelt's sons, twenty-two-year-old Franklin D. Roosevelt Jr., had such a severe strep infection that doctors predicted he'd die. But they revived him with a sulfa drug. During the war, all U.S. soldiers carried a packet of sulfa powder with them. They'd been instructed to immediately sprinkle it on open wounds to slow infection. And later in 1943, a sulfa drug would cure Winston Churchill of pneumonia.

After Dr. Oleinik left, Virginia continued to do everything in her power to soothe the baby. She held her and walked her and brought her over to the picture of the dog she loved so much. But even that didn't help.

While it seemed that everyone in Bearcreek was suffering, there may have been a few people whose lives had actually improved since the disaster. They wouldn't confess it to anyone, of course, and must have suffered terrible guilt because of it, but one or two of the widows may have been relieved that their husbands weren't coming home. At least one of the dead miners had been a mean drunk. There may have been other forms of abuse going on behind the floral curtains and rickety wooden doors—slaps and bellows that would stop now that the perpetrator was gone. Sometimes even a tragic death can be a blessing. But those so blessed were still forced to start new lives.

Their desperation for work came at a good time. The federal War Manpower Commission was encouraging women with children older than fourteen to get a job. The *Billings Gazette* ran an article predicting that eighteen million American women would be working outside their homes by the end of 1943, and they wouldn't all be Rosie the Riveters. Women were needed to run restaurants, stores, laundries, hotels, and transportation businesses. Once employed, they could consider themselves "total war soldiers," the commission spokesman told the paper.

The Bearcreek women hardly needed such a patriotic lure. They just wanted a paycheck. So, like Mary, they took whatever they could at first. One widow got a job as a telephone operator. Another rang up orders at a market. They found work hawking blouses at Penney's, pulling sodas at drugstores, taking orders at diners, and cooking for strangers. Some women supplemented their Social Security payments by babysitting the children of other working widows. Even Mary's mother-in-law, at age sixty-one, got a job in a hospital kitchen washing dishes.

On the third day of her illness, Connie still hadn't improved. A cold would have begun to dry up by now, but this was something different. Dr. Oleinik came over again, though now he had nothing miraculous to pull out of his bag. If only she'd gotten sick a couple of years later, he might have had a magic potion. Penicillin was so new in the winter of 1943 that it was still only used by the military, and there wasn't even enough to meet half the Army's needs. Scientists had just begun figuring out how to manufacture and use the drug when the war broke out, though it was still confined to lab use and experiments. After Pearl Harbor, production was rushed and the limited dosages were used in military hospitals for wounds and infections that didn't respond to sulfa drugs. In March 1942, a year before Connie got sick, a thirty-three-year-old Connecticut woman was dying of a streptococcal infection. She had a fever of 107 and was delirious. Sulfa drugs, blood transfusions, and surgery hadn't touched the bacteria. Her doctors decided to try penicillin, making her the first civilian to receive it. Overnight, her fever dropped and the delirium faded. She lived to be ninety years old.

But the War Production Board's Office of Penicillin Distribution still controlled the country's stash, and any civilian usage had to be approved by a Boston doctor who first required a dossier explaining its need. It wasn't until March 15, 1945, almost two years to the day after Connie fell ill, that surplus military penicillin was released for public use. But even if Dr. Oleinik had tried to appeal to that doctor, the response wouldn't have come in time.

He put on his hat and walked out the door. It was dark, and his headlights lit up the mountains as he headed back to Red Lodge. Virginia laid Connie on the couch. Less than three weeks earlier, the mine had exploded and Virginia's little family had been spared. Now it turned out that they hadn't been lucky at all. Just late. Connie's blue eyes were closed, her little words locked inside her forever. She was thirteen months old the night she died.

Three days later, Virginia and Gil sat in the front pew of the Olcott Funeral Home chapel. There were flowers everywhere, but they couldn't distract from the little white coffin at the center of everything. Five women stood to sing songs and hymns, including one cruelly called "Life at Best Is Very Brief." At the end of the service, four pallbearers lifted the coffin. They were all women, and three of them, including Margaret Meiklejohn, had just buried their fathers. Jane Laird, one of Virginia's best friends, knew she would never forget that beautiful baby. She proved it later by naming her own daughter Connie Marie.

The group of mourners moved to the Red Lodge cemetery for burial. Some of the ladies from the Sommerville's church had made a beautiful dogwood wreath to drape on the grave. Virginia had ordered a gravestone with two white baby shoes carved into the top. They looked as if they were waiting for their owner to wake up and step into them. The entire funeral had cost sixty-four dollars, almost exactly the amount Virginia had saved to buy Connie toys and clothes as she grew up.

18 The Inquest

Margaret Meiklejohn climbed the front steps of the simple brick courthouse and stepped under a promise.

Justitiæ Dedicata, the words over the doorway read. Dedicated to justice.

Margaret and so many others whose lives had been shaken by the mine disaster had come to the Carbon County courthouse in Red Lodge on that warm April morning for the coroner's inquest. The purpose of the inquest was to determine how the men died and whether anyone was responsible for their deaths. It would be run like a typical trial with lawyers, witnesses, evidence, and a jury, but instead of a judge, the county coroner would control the theatrics. Though no one had been charged with a crime, the jury could make recommendations for criminal charges and name guilty parties, if they chose to.

The courtroom was unpretentious, like everything else in the county. Margaret took a seat in the spectators' section behind a wooden rail. Witnesses, including the Freeman brothers, the state and federal inspectors, local miners, and out-of-town rescuers, filled the seats around her. Closer to the front of the room, important-looking men pulled files and legal pads out of their briefcases and settled behind long tables. The county attorney, E. P. Conwell, and his assistant, George Smith, sat together, as did Montana Coal and Iron's three lawyers. Tony Boyle sat with the United Mine Workers lawyer. In still another part of the room, the jurors waited for the show to begin. There were nine of them, all men, including an insurance agent, a grocer, and several coal miners who worked at a privately owned Bearcreek mine. A court reporter sat with a pad, ready to record everyone's words in shorthand. Coroner Edward Olcott presided over what would be known as "The Matter of the Inquest Over the 74 Bodies of Certain Persons There Lying Dead."

Assistant County Attorney George Smith, who would be directing much of the trial, asked the assistant coroner, Walpas Koski, to read the names of those certain persons.

"Yes, sir," he said. "The names are as follows."

The room was quiet. It would take three long minutes to list all the men.

"Frank Mourich," he began. "Jack Philip Mourich. Emil Anderson."

When he finally finished, Smith asked for a number of the dead.

"There were 74," the witness said.

But that wasn't technically true. Seventy-five men had died as a direct result of the mine disaster, the last one lingering until just three days before the inquest began. Matt Woodrow, the former Smith Mine foreman who had rushed to the scene to try to save the miners, had been gassed three times during the rescue week. He lived for nineteen days in a hospital bed before joining his men. He would forever be known as the disaster's seventy-fifth victim.

A recent development in a similar situation may have encouraged the miners' families to believe the words above the courthouse door. The previous day, a Boston jury had convicted the owner of the Cocoanut Grove nightclub on nineteen counts of manslaughter resulting from the fire that had killed 492 people in his club the previous November. The fire, started after a busboy lit a match while trying to replace a lightbulb, spread to highly flammable decorations and lashed through the club. One thousand people, more than 25 percent over the legal limit, had been in the establishment that night. They tried to escape, but throngs of them were trapped, trampled, and burned. They found exit doors locked, a large window boarded up, and staff who demanded they pay their checks before letting them leave. The club's politically connected owner had cut corners on safety measures. But he didn't get away with it. The Boston jurors found him responsible for the deaths because he'd packed the club with ticket-buying bodies while neglecting to consider their safety. They believed that he'd put profits over lives and should be punished for that greed. More than a few people in the Montana courtroom thought that the Smith Mine's owners had done the same thing and should face the same consequences.

There were no opening statements to wind up the jury because, officially, there were no "sides" campaigning for a victory. So once the names of the victims had been read, Smith called his first witness: G. O. Arnold.

It had been five months since the inspector had spent a week making the state's first federal inspection, and four months since he'd sent back a preliminary inspection report. Smith asked Arnold to state the purpose of that report.

It "embodies matters that should receive attention prior to the completion and distribution of the final report," he said.

Smith introduced the report as Coroner's Exhibit 2 and stood by while his boss read it aloud. It was the first time many of the families heard exactly how dangerous the mine had been, the first time they learned that the mine operators were supposed to apply rock dust, "substantially" increase the air shaft so that more than half the necessary fresh air would begin reaching the men, stop allowing explosive gas to accumulate, and give every man a closed light, among other things.

"Now, there are a few things here that maybe we laymen do not understand," Smith said after the report was read. "I should like you to explain some of them."

Arnold gave a basic primer on ventilation, explaining that while enough fresh air had been entering the mine, it was escaping through leaks and open doors before it could reach most of the men. Gassy mines need more ventilation, not less, to keep the percentage of gas to no more than .5 to 1 percent, Arnold said. But, air samples he had collected during his initial inspection showed the Smith air contained an average of 1.5 percent gas. By itself that wasn't terribly explosive—5 percent is the explosive concentration—but it certainly indicated a potential problem.

"The hazard is the possibility of gas accumulating quickly in any place—where you know so much is being generated—because of a disruption in the ventilation," Arnold said.

Which is exactly what was happening in the mine, according to Arnold and subsequent witnesses. One miner said that brattice cloth curtains, intended to direct fresh air to working places, were regularly left up for at least an hour while men loaded coal, allowing gas to seep in. The gas could build up at any time, though the Smith staff didn't seem aware of this possibility. In testimony later that day, a fire boss said that if the night shift had just left an area, he "naturally" assumed it would be clear of gas for the next shift. Not so, Arnold confirmed. He testified that even if the fire bosses *hadn't* found high gas levels the night before the explosion, the noxious fumes could have built up after their inspections.

The Montana Coal and Iron attorney interviewed Arnold next. His goal was to show that the Smith's higher-ups were dedicated to safety, but his line of questioning backfired.

"Did the officials of the company also indicate to you they would cooperate in carrying out the recommendations?" the attorney asked.

"Very wholeheartedly," Arnold replied, proving either that Freeman and his minions been deceiving him with their enthusiasm, or that their best efforts had proved inept.

After lunch, Smith called state inspector Edward Davies to the stand. His testimony was a bit more helpful to the company.

"From your experience is the present state coal code adequate to cover all conditions that exist in a mechanized mine such as the Smith Mine?" he asked Davies.

"No, sir," replied Davies, a slight man who had okayed the mine's safety a month before the disaster. The code had been written when mining was still done by hand, he admitted.

"And, of course, until such time as the lawmakers of the State make a change, there will be conditions that cannot be controlled by anybody at the present time, is not that true?" Smith asked.

"That is true," Davies said.

Smith also led Davies to illustrate that even appropriate laws couldn't be followed. He asked how Davies had determined the amount of gas in the Bearcreek mine.

"Under the law the state coal mine inspector is required to make those tests, but the equipment has never been provided for," Davies said.

"That is another case of there being a law there, but of there being no way to carry it out, is that right?" Smith asked.

"Yes."

The jury could have inferred from Davies's answers that mine operators couldn't hope to protect their workers without proper laws or the means to follow them.

This would have been a great argument for the operators' lawyers to build on if only the Smith's bosses *had* been obeying all the laws on the books, no matter how flimsy. But testimony given during the inquest would show that Montana Coal and Iron was already breaking several laws. The 1911 laws stated that shots could only be fired at end of a shift except in certain areas; that leaving doors open was forbidden; that coal dust should be removed "as often as necessary" and not be used to tamp drilled holes; and that in gassy mines or in mines where gas was likely to accumulate, "no light or fire other than a locked safety lamp shall be allowed or used." But repeatedly during the inquest miners would testify that the company had been guilty of all of these infractions, both before and after Arnold's inspection. Fines of twenty-five dollars per day should have been imposed on the company for years.

Davies certainly wasn't imposing those fines. He didn't seem to be doing much of anything. Smith entered Davies's January 27 inspection report into evidence. It showed that he'd found ventilation problems in the area where Arnold believed the explosion had originated, and that a room in the area Davies himself chose as the point of origin had been deadlined because of excess gas during his inspection. Still, Davies hadn't been alarmed.

"The condition of the mine appeared to me to be normal," he said.

When assistant manager Bill Romek testified, he claimed that he'd gotten the go-ahead from James Freeman to order a rock-dusting machine right before the disaster. He neglected to mention, however, that Freeman had told him in a February letter to hold off on the rock-dusting equipment, because he didn't deem it necessary.

The company's defense team planned to call James Freeman later. First, though, his brother W.R. would answer the state's questions. The thin, gray-haired grandfather, no longer the vigorous man Arnold had met in November, maintained that he and his men had improved ventilation after the inspection, but that he didn't think the mine needed to be rock-dusted, despite Arnold's strong recommendation to do so.

"When I left I did not know of any place that I would call dusty enough to be serious or anything," Freeman said.

"Is it not a fact that to increase the air through there made for a dustier mine?" Smith asked.

"The flow of air in the severe cold weather would make more dust," Freeman admitted. "After I was away I do not know just what occurred. There was snow every morning. In my experience, those things will occur."

Freeman's departure from Bearcreek and whether it was permanent would be disputed in testimony to come. Freeman claimed he had essentially quit in December and had only stayed on a month longer at Romek's request. He said that before he left for California, he told the crew to keep working on the new ventilation shaft and gave Elmer Price, who would take over his responsibilities, permission to hire and fire employees.

Untrue, said two Smith coal miners who fully expected Freeman to come back to work. One of them testified that about a week before the explosion, he heard Price talking about wanting to hire eight more men. He said that there were men "rustling work" at the mine but that he couldn't make any hires until Freeman returned. A man whose brother had died in the mine testified on the second day of the inquest. He said that work continued on the ventilation shaft after Freeman left, but when the miners reached a certain point, they stopped. Price told him they wouldn't finish until Freeman got back, implying the man's certain return.

Tony Boyle, who was questioning the man at the time, must have gone crazy. Finally, he had something to grab hold of.

"Mr. Freeman resigned on the 26th day of January," Boyle said, citing the day Freeman left for California, "and [your claim is] in direct reverse to the testimony that he gave yesterday—that he was not expecting to return and that he had resigned on the 26th of January and the escapement shaft development work was not stopped. Now you testify that Mr. Price told you that work was discontinued until the return of Mr. Freeman?"

"Yes, sir."

"Is that what you want to testify?"

"That is what he told me, that the shaft would not be continued until Mr. Freeman returned," the man said.

Boyle asked whether he knew why they didn't finish the shaft.

"Only from what I learned this morning from the fellow who was constructing the shaft, that they did not want to blow it through, that probably there was a large quantity of gas up there and the fan would have to be changed," he said. Replacing the fan was a potentially expensive undertaking.

Later in the inquest, another miner would also challenge Freeman's honesty. Freeman had insisted that the men didn't shoot down coal until the end of a shift, when most of the workers had left. But Alex McDonald, a driller who worked the February 26 night shift, said that they regularly blasted during shifts.

"We fired on shift for years that I know of," he said in voice tinged with Irish and Scottish inflections.

In fact, he said, he fired off about eleven shots in three different places the night before the explosion. Boyle seized on this, repeating that Freeman had "testified to his knowledge that shooting on shift was not going on down there."

"He was wrong in his statement," McDonald said.

Several other miners testified to shooting on shift as well. One said it was done two or three times a week on management's orders. The shooting couldn't always wait until the end of a shift because they were in a hurry to collect as much coal as possible, McDonald explained.

"All we had to do when we went on shift was to hit the ball and keep going until quitting time," he said.

"What effect did that have on the safety of the miners—the men?" the union attorney asked.

"We never thought much about the safety of the men," McDonald replied.

Now he was angry about that. He said he hadn't realized how dangerous the mine was until he heard Arnold say from the witness stand that the air contained 1.5 percent gas. There was no indication of when Arnold got those air analysis results back from Pittsburgh or whether he could have gotten the information to the miners before the explosion.

"I want to say this," McDonald said, "that if those 74 brothers killed in the Smith Mine—if they had known there was one and one-half percent of gas in the air, they would not have been in the mine. I know I would not. I know the rest of the brothers would not either."

The crowd erupted in applause so enthusiastic that the court reporter characterized it as "vigorous."

Without hard numbers to guide them away from the gas, the miners had to listen to their bodies. One man said that in some parts of the mine "we had awful bad air. If we did not feel like going in, we did not go in."

"How does a miner determine that the air is good and that the air is bad?" Smith asked.

"The way I determine—if it knocks me down, I would not go on. I would get out of there."

Not all the miners used common sense on the job.

"How did you light your shots?" Smith asked one miner. "Did you work with the closed light or the open light?"

"With a closed light."

"You worked with a closed light?"

"Yes."

"How did you ignite your shots?"

"With an open light."

"With a carbide lamp?"

"Yes, sir."

"You worked with a closed light for safety measures because there might be gas in there?"

"Yes."

"Then you turned around and used an open light to light the shots?"

"That is right."

A well-spoken union secretary who ran a Goodman loading machine for a living said the air in the mine had been more plentiful immediately after the federal inspection than at any other time in his fourteen years of working in the Smith. But he could tell the quantity decreased as time went on.

"I believe around three or four days before the explosion we did not have the volume of air that we had before," he said, explaining that the smoke from day-shift shooting hadn't dissipated by nighttime because there hadn't been a healthy air current to blow it away. The miner also admitted, under Boyle's questioning, that the air was better right before the state inspector's quarterly visits because they worked harder on ventilation prior to his inspections.

Not all the miners' testimony made the company look bad. A couple of men maintained that ventilation had gotten and stayed better since Arnold's inspection and that men were much more diligent about keeping doors closed to maintain good ventilation. Some supervisors, who were considered company men rather than union brothers, swore that they insisted on doors and brattices remaining tight.

Dr. Oleinik couldn't have been surprised by all the conflicting accounts. He was the last man to give testimony on the second day of the trial, and his was possibly the most credible testimony of the entire week. Besides having the gravitas granted to most physicians in those days, he had numbers. And he wasn't worried about the ramifications of his honesty.

"You have a mine contract," the Montana Coal and Iron attorney asked Oleinik. "As an employee are you not afraid that they might fire you?"

"No, they would not," he said, and the people in the courtroom laughed. "But the miners pay me. They make the deductions."

It was clear that Oleinik was on the miners' side. Under oath, the forty-two-year-old said he treated between 175 and 200 miners a year, mostly for symptoms of gas poisoning. He told the jury about analyzing his patients' blood just a month before the explosion and confirming his hunch that it was loaded with carbon monoxide. And he said he'd been seeing more men with similar maladies right before the explosion, leading him to believe that "the ventilation was getting more insufficient."

He'd examined one of the dead miners the night before the accident.

"He showed clinical manifestations—weakness, headache, backache, aching knees, palsy, heart palpitations—all symptomatic of gas poisoning," the doctor said. "I did a gas analysis—monoxide, carbon monoxide—and I found his content was around 20 or 22 percent."

Had the concentration been double that figure, the patient would have collapsed before ever making it to the clinic.

Oleinik told the court about the Smith Mine gassing case he'd helped bring to the Industrial Accident Board and about testing his own blood to give further proof that everyone in the mine was absorbing excess carbon monoxide. But the accident board had ruled as if Oleinik had never said a word.

"They refused to give him compensation on the basis that it was impossible for a man to be gassed with the carbon monoxide in the Montana Coal and Iron company mine because there was no gas," Oleinik said.

There wasn't much more the doctor could offer. There'd been gas in the mine and gas in the men and now they were dead. All parties could sleep on those facts until the next morning. Court was adjourned.

The final day of testimony dawned mildly, like the day of the explosion. The temperature would reach the seventies by the end of the afternoon, almost ten degrees warmer than the previous day. The courtroom was more packed than ever with families, witnesses, and reporters. The newsmen came from the *Carbon County News*, the *Billings Gazette*, and the *Picket Journal*, but they clearly weren't interested in bringing their editors a scoop. All the coverage was extremely superficial. The journalists didn't bother to question the many inconsistencies the witnesses uttered or to report family reactions. Faced with a room full of emotion, they chose to file the driest of stories.

So far, the inquest had revealed that the mine had indeed been gassy, that many involved had known about it, and that mining practices at the Smith were unsafe. But there had been little discussion about what had occurred in the mine the day of the explosion. One of the three men who had lived through it had moved to California, and one was apparently still too weak to take the stand.

Only Alex Hawthorne was able to describe that morning, and just barely.

"I will make my examination very short since I understand you are not feeling very well," Smith said.

"No, I am not," Hawthorne said,

He recalled the mine going dark and the air rushing in.

"Now you spoke about the wind blowing," Smith said. "Was that a strong wind?"

"I'll tell the world it was," Hawthorne answered.

"You might say it reached the proportions of what you might call a gale, or something like that?"

"It was worse than that, I think."

"Then was there debris in the air along with the wind?"

"What?"

"Debris or pieces of . . ."

"Oh, there was everything a-coming."

"That, of course, was different from any condition you had ever experienced in the mine before?"

"That was the first time I ever seen anything like that, and I hope it is the last."

Smith asked about his phone call to the surface.

"I called the outside on the telephone and said there was something radically wrong and I was getting the hell out of there," Hawthorne said.

"Were you able to get out?"

"It seemed like I was not."

"That was the last you knew? Did you lose consciousness?"

"I must have lost everything, because I do not know anything about it."

All Hawthorne wanted now, the assembled would learn later, were some new tires so he could drive to California to recuperate. One of the federal inspectors who'd helped with the rescue vowed to try to get him the tires.

Though no one was left to tell what else had happened in the mine, some people still wanted to know what *could* have happened had circumstances been different: the women.

The union attorney wanted to show that the mine owners could have run a safer operation but had chosen not to. But he knew that even his best attack on the suits couldn't trump having a widow lash out at them.

"If your Honor please," the union lawyer asked, "one or two women are here who would like to ask a few questions. If there are no objections, may they ask those questions?"

"Well, if there is no objection," the coroner said before pausing for a moment. "Very well. You may proceed."

Agnes Anderson, who had been married to for Emil twenty-one years and one month on the day of the disaster, stood up. She had beautiful eyes that flashed when she grew angry. The man on the witness stand had helped with the rescue efforts. She asked if proper rescue equipment could have saved Emil, whose 11:05 note proved he hadn't died instantly.

The witness, a short, dense man who filled out his suit like a weight lifter, said it might have.

"You think he had a possible chance to get out?" she asked.

"Yes."

"The company had no masks and no equipment for them to take in there with them, [but] they could put up brattices or barricades and try to help themselves, and naturally they could have waited for help from the outside to come," she continued.

"Yes," he said.

"I think the company should have had some equipment to go after those men with to help them. They had to wait for all that to come from Butte," Agnes said.

"Correct."

"They had a fighting chance, if there had been equipment for my husband."

"I think there would have been a chance to save some of the men," he said.

"Otherwise, they did not have a chance at all."

"No," he said. "There was no chance at all."

Agnes walked back to the spectators' benches and sat down. She'd effectively shown that the company had screwed up by being so unprepared. Later in the day, another widow emphasized that point. Mary Laird had a firm jaw and a warm smile, though she wouldn't be using it as she questioned a witness. She left her seat behind the rail and sat at Boyle's table. She was holding a pair of glasses.

"Would you think that at the time of this explosion the equipment that the Smith Mine had was good enough whatever to save any of these 74 lives?" she asked.

"No, I do not believe so," the miner on the stand said. "In fact, I made the statement yesterday that I did not see no equipment so far as the company had."

Laird's husband, Ned, had been a handsome man with a slightly receding hairline and gentle eyes. His shiny wire-rimmed glasses, which had protected his eyes from coal dust the day before the explosion, had given him a distinguished look. Put him in a three-piece suit and he could pass for a banker. Now, she held up those glasses.

"I have my husband's glasses, and they never were even broken on his face," she said. "So far as I am able to understand, he was found with 11 other men huddled together in a room, and I feel that if this company had had the equipment to go in there at the moment this happened, those 12 men could have been saved. I have his glasses here, if the jury wants to examine them. There is not a mark on them of any kind and Mr. Olcott will testify that these glasses were given to me at the morgue and were taken off my husband's face when he was over at the morgue. That is all."

She gave the glasses to a juror to pass around.

"Be careful not to bend them," she instructed.

Then, unable to stop, she added, "His body was not mangled in any way. Nothing came in contact with him at the explosion. I believe—that is, I have every conviction that if they had had the equipment to go after him, he may have been saved."

The women's questions certainly upped the emotion in the courtroom, but the idea that their husbands would have lived if only the company had supplied the proper rescue equipment turned out to be too simplistic. Arnold returned to the stand to explain why.

"If rescue apparatus had been available at the mine at the time of the explosion and men who were trained in the use of the equipment had been available, it would appear highly probable that all the men in the Number 2 bed might have been saved," he said.

In other words, the men who died after receiving mouth-to-mouth resuscitation from the early responders probably would have lived. Further, Arnold noted, if the local rescuers had had the right equipment and could have used it immediately after the explosion, they might have gotten to the interior of the mine a day earlier than they did. Some of the trapped miners might have been able to wait for them.

"There were a couple or three locations in the mine wherein it might have been possible for the men to barricade themselves in relatively unaffected areas and to live until we got there if they had done so," he said.

But, he countered, even with the right rescue helmets the extreme heat may have acted like a slamming gate.

"This extremely hot air is very noxious to a person and even though it may not contain poisonous gases, the heated nature of it would make it impossible almost for a man to pass through," Arnold said.

Arnold was also asked if self-rescuers, which contain chemicals that neutralize carbon monoxide for about thirty minutes, would have helped the trapped men. Again, he said that the men in the Number 2 seam would probably have been able to walk out if they'd had self-rescuers. But the others probably had too far to travel. The self-rescuers wouldn't have lasted as long as the journey, so it was unlikely for any of the men in the Number 3 seam to get out in time.

"It is something we would like to believe possible," he said. "But we know that it is impossible."

One more woman stood up in court that week. Unlike the others, she wasn't a wife and mother with years of life experience and a solid sense of her place in the world. She was just a twenty-five-year-old orphan with an inordinate amount of bravery.

Margaret Meiklejohn was determined to find out what had happened to the black book her father had used to record the gas levels. It seemed to have vanished, though the pencil he used had been returned to her with his belongings. She'd already caused a bit of a ruckus regarding the black book earlier in the inquest. When fire boss Loren Newman doubted whether such a book had ever existed, Margaret called out from the audience.

"Yes, he did carry a book!"

"It is possible he did," Newman said.

"I know he did," Margaret said. "For a fact he did."

"He could have had one without my knowing it."

"He carried a small memorandum book," Margaret persisted.

"If that book was on him, it was probably picked up by the men who found him," Newman countered.

"I know it was on him," Margaret continued, "and it was in the locker with half the pages torn out, like somebody had torn the pages out."

Newman finally acknowledged that Meiklejohn might have carried a notebook, since he had a lot of details to keep in his head.

"He did," Margaret said. "I know that because he told me that he could not positively remember everything that he had to remember, and so he started to carry this book."

Another miner backed her up. He said he'd seen Meiklejohn taking notes in the mine.

"He told me that he was not depending on memory, but the book," the miner said during his testimony. He also brought to light the disagreements Meiklejohn had been having with Newman about the gas that winter, and that Meiklejohn had told him the arguments stemmed from the fact that he was finding more gas than the other fire bosses.

Now Margaret rose to formally interrogate Newman. Maybe she could get the jury to see that the notebook contained incriminating evidence on the cause of the disaster. She led up to her point calmly and deliberately, like a real prosecutor. First, she asked her witness to name all the places her father covered on his shifts. Then she asked about the gas reports he'd made. Finally, she tried to corner Newman.

"If he was in that mine seven hours, would it be possible for him to remember all that by the time he come out of the mine?" she asked.

"I do not know," Newman said arrogantly. "Maybe. I always did."

"I do not think my father did," Margaret swiped back. "I think he kept that notebook."

"Well, Miss Meiklejohn," Newman scolded, "in connection with that, your father's report was in the same part of the mine every day."

"Yes, I know," she said to the nonsensical statement.

"And as to anything he might have put in a notebook in that mine, I would rather think if he used one it was not on this—not on his body. It was possibly in one of his jumpers where he always left it."

Margaret said she'd been told the notebook was in her father's coat, which he'd been wearing. Newman, who was starting to get angry, began to describe in detail what Margaret's father had been working on before the explosion, though she hadn't asked about it. Then his diatribe turned personal.

"I cannot imagine that there was anything in a book that would be involved here in any way, for this reason, that regardless of what

[was] said the other day on this stand, your father and I were good friends," Newman said. "He confided in me and . . ."

"I disagree with you," Margaret interrupted. "He told me that you and he . . ."

The coroner cut her off. "This is off the record," he said.

The stenographer's hand stopped. A conversation ensued. When Margaret and Newman could speak more civilly, the stenographer resumed his scribblings.

The seasoned miner and the young woman continued in calmer tones. Her anger spent for the moment, Margaret's tough surface cracked.

"I thought there might be something in that notebook—that he realized he was going to die, or that something was wrong, and he might have written in the notebook," she said. "That is what I was trying to find out."

The temperature outside rose even higher as the inquest wound down that afternoon. The state and the union finished with their witnesses, and at the last minute the company lawyers decided not to call James Freeman, surprising even the man himself. Boyle reminded the jury of his failed attempts to get stricter safety laws passed and asked them to remedy that with their verdict. He would bask in a round of applause after giving a soliloquy on protecting miners' lives.

The nine jurors began deliberating at 4:30 in the afternoon. They returned more than six hours later. Their conclusion: the men "met their deaths due to concussion and to gas poisoning caused by gas and dust explosion."

The jury also officially recommended new state mining laws to cover the gaps that the inquest had revealed. Among their requests: all coal mine inspectors gain the power to close dangerous mines; blasting be restricted while men were working in the mine; all underground employees get self-rescue equipment; the mine companies keep enough helmets and working gas masks on-site; rescue crews receive proper training and equipment; all coal mines be rock-dusted; and companies improve ventilation systems as soon as inspectors tell them to.

They were sound suggestions, and some of them would eventually make it to the law books. But they fell short of pinning the blame on anyone. Despite all the evidence about unsafe mining practices and excess amounts of gas, about laws the company wasn't following and shortcuts they were taking, the jury hadn't mentioned a thing about charging anyone with a crime.

There remained one more chance for justice. The governor had appointed a committee to investigate the disaster. This time, three different out-of-towners—men who hadn't helped with the rescue or inspected the mine or sobbed over one of the victims' graves—would look into what happened with unbiased eyes. They would begin their investigation the next day. Maybe if they found evidence that someone was to blame for the disaster, there would be a way to make the culprit pay.

19 The Blame

Two days after the inquest ended, James Freeman sat down to write a joyful letter to his boss. He had great news for the company president: the inquest jury hadn't blamed anyone for the explosion!

"They did not prove where the officials of the Montana Coal and Iron Company had in any way done anything contrary to the present mining laws of the State of Montana," Freeman bragged.

No one would ever say why the jury chose not to hold anyone responsible. Maybe some of the jurors didn't believe the witnesses who'd described the violations. Or maybe they'd all agreed in the privacy of the deliberation room that it wouldn't be in the community's best interest to skewer the company. But while the families would pay in countless ways for the rest of their lives, the men who ran the mine were officially debt-free. And they intended to prove it by pinning the blame on Gerry Arnold.

"It's a good place to go to blame somebody," Emil Anderson's nephew, Leonard Anderson, would say sixty-four years later. "Far away from home."

Arnold's final report on the explosion probably didn't help. Prepared for the governor's committee and his own department, it may have provoked the company to lash out at him. Besides explaining his theory that the explosion occurred when a miner with an open light walked into a cloud of gas, he repeated the many safety recommendations he'd made that the company had ignored. In fairness, he also listed the few items they'd addressed, and admitted that the company might not have finished the new ventilation shaft before the day of the explosion even if work on it hadn't been suspended while the Freemans were in California.

But his general conclusion negated any compliments he may have bestowed upon the company: "It is evident from the foregoing discussion that the most elementary safe mining practices were being disregarded in the operation of this mine," he wrote near the end of his report.

Thus began a lengthy battle fought through business letters and formal reports. Though James Freeman couldn't dispute Arnold's specific arguments about what actions he and his staff had or hadn't taken, he could raise a new topic that would make Arnold look equally negligent. In the company's final report on the explosion, Freeman pinned the disaster on Arnold and an order he had allegedly given them after the November inspection.

He claimed that Arnold told them to erect thick concrete stoppings in front of certain abandoned entries, or working places, to trap any gas that might accumulate there. The company didn't want to block the entries in case they decided to work them again later, Freeman's report said. But Arnold had insisted, so he had complied. Then, Freeman claimed, on the day of the explosion a rockfall pushed over a stopping and released all the built-up gas, which then slithered out until it reached an electric fuse that had just blown. Sparks met gas, and the tragedy unfolded. Freeman and his cronies were apparently certain of this chain of events, but they told their surviving staff members not to mention any of it during the post-disaster inspection or the inquest, despite all parties agreeing to disclose their theories and evidence.

"The Company withheld its views at the Inquest, expecting that the final report of the Federal Examiners would change the Management's theory as to where the explosion started," they explained in their report.

Later, Freeman would claim he omitted the theory to protect the federal inspectors. "The company, on account of feeling so greatly indebted to the Bureau of Mines for its splendid effort during the rescue work, refrained from introducing certain testimony at the Red Lodge inquest that might prove embarrassing to your inspectors," he wrote in a letter to the chief of the federal coal mine inspection division in Pittsburgh.

Arnold might have appreciated that protection—if he'd needed it. But he insisted in a rebuttal report that he'd never told the company to put up the stoppings. "The entries in question were well ventilated at the time of the inspection in November, the inspectors did not find any gas in them, there was no apparent reason for sealing them off, moreover, the inspectors did not recommend sealing them off," he wrote.

The company would maintain for years—and convince many Bearcreek citizens—that the abandoned areas had been harmless until Arnold forced them to put up the stoppings. They would claim that Elmer Price, the foreman who was the last man recovered from the mine, had argued with Arnold about installing the stoppings, predicting that they would lead to problems. But in an interview years after the disaster, fire boss Loren Newman said that the gas in the entries had been a concern *before* Arnold's arrival. He said that when Price found out Arnold was coming to inspect the mine, he asked Newman if he could clear the gas that had been building up in the entries for a couple of years. Newman suggested blasting a hole through the coal there to let more air circulate, but Price thought that would be too much trouble, according to Newman. The next thing Newman knew, the stoppings were being erected, though he was never sure exactly who authorized the job. Price's daughter, Tharen, would always remember hearing that her father had been opposed to the company installing the stoppings because he believed the gas behind them could lead to an explosion. But she never knew who ordered the stoppings or when they were erected.

Regardless of who decided to build the stoppings, nobody except the company believed they caused the disaster.

"The difficulty in accepting the Company's conclusions is that two miracles were necessary in order to bring about the sequence of events which they believe led to the explosion," Boyle wrote in the union's final report on the explosion. "The cave over the stopping in the back entry which they declare took place couldn't have happened."

Boyle explained that the roof couldn't have just fallen in unless the stopping collapsed first. Evidence would show that the foot-thick stopping didn't move until an explosive force coming from elsewhere in the mine had pushed it over.

"The other miracle was the blowing of the fuse at the shaft at practically the same time that the cave over the concrete stopping occurred," he wrote. "If this is not a miracle, it could be described as a most remarkable coincidence."

Arnold also found the blown fuse explanation incredible. "It is obvious that the fuse burned out as a result of a short circuit near one of the rotary-converter stations immediately after the explosion," he wrote.

Even if part of the company's secret theory could have been explained logically, it was compromised by their cover-up.

"We are of the opinion that if such an extraordinary cave had occurred, the company officials would have brought it immediately to the attention of other investigators, and the necessity of straining their imaginations would have been avoided," Boyle stated in writing.

The company's report contained other weak explanations. Regarding smoking in mine, they wrote, "it was not reasonable to expect the men not to smoke as long as they had to use open lights, due to the fact that electric cap lamps were not available."

They also claimed that the rock-dusting machine wouldn't have arrived in time, even if they'd ordered it in November, and that they got no credit for "trying so hard" to obtain it. But documents indicate they didn't try terribly hard. Montana Coal and Iron wrote one letter of inquiry to a rock-dusting machine company, the American Mine Door Company shortly after Arnold's inspection, but apparently didn't place an order then. In December and at the end of January 1943, American Mine's general manager wrote letters in response to Montana Coal and Iron's initial inquiry to prod them to order the machine. He was clearly trying hard to make the sale.

"We will be glad to receive your order, but if you decide otherwise, we do not wish to occupy your time nor annoy you with correspondence in which you are not interested," the general manager wrote.

The company officers hadn't even ordered the machine after the disaster. On May 3, Freeman told the Bureau of Mines he expected rock-dusting equipment to arrive any day, but American Mine wrote again on July 30 to remind Freeman that he still hadn't purchased a machine. The letter included a guilt-inducing sales pitch that may have stemmed from the Bearcreek disaster.

"Every time that we remind an inquirer who has a tendency to procrastinate, we are reminded of the terrible explosion at one mine, which could have been averted has the decision been made promptly," it said.

Still, Montana Coal and Iron didn't get the machine. In an August 10 letter, Freeman told American Mine that he'd misplaced their quotation for the rock duster and needed another one, plus pamphlets describing the machine and an estimate of how long it would take to arrive. American Mine officials wrote back at least two more times nagging Freeman to make the purchase.

State inspector Davies also tried to blame the disaster on Arnold. Davies noted in his final report that Arnold, "lacking police powers," would have had to tell him if the mine operators refused to take immediate action on safety issues. Since Arnold didn't ask him to take such action, he must not have considered the mine very dangerous,

Davies implied. But Arnold had no reason to ask Davies to use his police power, since the company never actually refused to do what he'd suggested.

Boyle attacked Arnold as well, though it's unclear why. In a series of letters he sent the following fall to the U.S. Chief of Health and Safety Services, he accused Arnold of fabricating his theory for the explosion. He also said that based on the air sample results, Arnold should have accepted the company's offer to close to mine until improvements could be made based. But Boyle's argument made no sense. The results weren't available in November, when the conversation about closing the mine allegedly took place, and the company later disputed the results anyway.

The safety chief wrote back and defended his inspector. If the company had followed Arnold's original recommendations, he wrote, the gas would have been diluted enough to prevent the explosion.

Arnold didn't address Davies's or Boyle's mudslinging in his rebuttal, but his response to the company was fierce. The company claimed in its report that "the preponderance of the testimony at the Inquest" indicated that doors and brattices were not being left open and that the mine's air had been "substantially improved." Arnold disputed this by quoting seven examples of testimony stating otherwise. He challenged the company's claim that the mine wasn't particularly gassy by reprinting details of the December 15 letter that informed Freeman about the gas that had showed up in the air samples. And he defended his decision not to order the company to close the mine "because [we] found no imminent hazards in the mine that could not be taken care of immediately."

Finally, he attempted to shame the company for not taking care of the mine's problems either before or after his inspection. "The means for preventing gas ignitions and widespread coal-mine explosions are known, and the safety standards of the Bureau of Mines relative to such matters are public information," he wrote at the end of his rebuttal. "It would seem that operators who desire to protect the lives of their employees and mine property as well would not wait for Federal inspectors and specific recommendations but would apply the safeguards that are known to be necessary if coal-mine explosions are to be prevented."

The governor's committee consisted of three men with extensive mining experience: Richard Dalrymple, chief coal mine inspector of the state of Utah; William Redshaw of Billings, who had been a miner and mine operator for forty-eight years; and Abe Douglas of Roundup, who'd been on the job for fifty-five years and still earned his living underground. The day after the inquest ended, they met with Montana governor Sam Ford at the stately Northern Hotel in Billings. Then they drove up the hills to Red Lodge, where they sat down to discuss the case with all the concerned parties. The next day, they traipsed into the ruined mine to have a look. The report they filed that summer ranged from stern to brutal and attacked the mine operators, the state inspector, and the state itself.

The report denounced Davies for neglecting to follow up on Arnold's safety recommendations during his January 27 inspection; if he had, the men wrote, he would have seen "how rapidly the mine was getting out of control."

They criticized the weak Montana legislation that led to such chaos, and suggested much tighter laws, like Utah's, which required rock-dusting, prohibited smoking and open lights, and defined permissible electrical equipment.

"The Smith Mine Disaster is a stigma, comparable to cancerous proportions, to your State's proud record," the men wrote.

They also chided the company for basing its safety practices on the state's vague and outdated laws.

"The Montana Coal Code may not have been so worded as to name every potential hazard which is known or otherwise related to coal mining, nor does any other State code," they wrote, implying that common sense and compassion were mining tools. too.

Not surprisingly, the Montana Coal Operators Association had little interest in seeing the laws amended. "We do believe that existing State Mining Laws are fairly complete and in need of little change," the association's secretary wrote in a memo to the governor's committee.

Though Montana Coal and Iron had gotten off with nothing but a finger-wagging from the governor's committee, most of the involved parties refused to move on. The Coal Operators Association asked the governor to reconvene his committee before releasing its report to the public. James Freeman also wrote to the governor to object to the report, particularly its criticism of Inspector Davies, which he blamed on Arnold's input.

"There is evidence that Mr. Arnold of the Bureau and Mr. Ed Davies, the State Coal Mine Inspector, were not on the best of terms during the rescue work at the Smith Mine," Freeman wrote.

When the governor refused to change the report, Freeman complained again about unfair treatment and threatened that his company's directors "may wish to talk to you in the near future" about the case.

"Personally, Mr. Freeman, after considering the matter from every angle, I feel both you and Mr. Davies are unduly excited about the content of the report," Ford replied.

It's perplexing that there was so much interest in protecting Davies. If the company was defending him in the hopes of getting more favorable inspections, it wasn't working. Though some of the Smith Miners learned to use gas masks and self-contained breathing apparatuses, and listened to lectures on detecting mine gases and avoiding explosions during a week of mine rescue classes that summer, the company was still taking needless chances with their lives. And Davies was finally calling them on it. He conducted an inspection of the Smith's Number 2 seam that fall and found they were still shooting down coal with men on shift and still lacked permanent stoppings, as required by law.

"One thing was evident: the volume of air specified in our mining law was not being conducted to the working faces," Davies wrote in a letter to Freeman. "This could be remedied without much difficulty, but the tendency is to delay and delay until it becomes a major problem."

Besides defending Davies, Freeman was involved in other backroom machinations. Most of them remain mysterious. In a September telegram to Boyle, he announced that Arnold would be leaving the Bureau of Mines and that "without Arnold interference believe Dalrymple [head of the governor's committee] will consent to our request." There is no mention of what that request was, though it probably involved editing the report of the governor's committee. Freeman also met with some Bureau of Mines men in Washington DC and presented affidavits and additional evidence to prove that the stoppings Arnold had allegedly demanded had caused the disaster. After the meeting, he sent a telegram to C. R. Smith, the president of the mine. "Bureau now convinced we got a raw deal," it read.

Whether or not that was true, none of the reports were amended to Freeman's satisfaction and nothing was investigated further. He personally ensured that there was no opportunity to reexamine the scene. After keeping the pumps running in the mine for four or five months, Montana Coal and Iron shut them down. The mine flooded and caved, obliterating any overlooked evidence.

While the men in suits battled through the mail about who was at fault, the families began reaching their own conclusions. Many blamed the company, but wouldn't say so out loud. As long as Montana Coal and Iron still ran salary-paying mines in Bearcreek, some people saw no benefit in offending its leaders. But there was certainly some hostility directed at the Freeman family. Wayne Freeman, who was six when the mine exploded, remembers being called names and getting bullied because of his family's connection to the disaster. His mother wrote in a remembrance, "Since the Freeman men were directors of the mine, their families had to bear the brunt of hearings, remarks, and the actions by some people. We were all strong and survived well."

Regardless of public opinion, Montana Coal and Iron didn't suffer much after the disaster. In a letter he wrote to the president of the company right after the April inquest, James Freeman outlined plans to start harvesting coal from the Number 2 seam: "We should be dumping coal from this new operation within 60 days. In the meantime we will get all of the coal we need from the Foster-Creek mine, from which we expect to produce 1,600 tons per day within 30 days. As we do not get a large demand for coal until August, I am sure we will be ready by that time to produce as much coal as we mined at any time last winter."

Further, he added, the coal from the Number 2 seam would be of better quality than the stuff they'd been getting from the Number 3 seam before the tragedy. "The outlook for next year is better than it has been for many years," he wrote. And even though he had to spend more money than usual that spring "from the disaster and the new improvements" he wasn't worried about funds. "We have sufficient cash on hand to take care of these as well as retire all of our outstanding bonds," he claimed.

Though Freeman might have been painting an extra sunny picture for his boss in order to protect his position, records would show that Montana Coal and Iron did indeed flourish after the disaster. The company produced 477,080 tons of coal in 1943, 150,000 of it going to Army and Navy installations. In 1944 it produced 576,000 tons, and in 1945, with military needs tapering off as the war ended, it still managed to sell 499,810 tons, more than during the year of the disaster. The firm's accounting ledgers would also show that the company took in more income in December 1943 than it had in December 1942, proving that it had recovered quickly.

So it's curious that Freeman would cry poverty. Eight months after the disaster, he received the following letter from the widow of Elmer Price, the dead foreman. She'd handwritten it on small sheets of her own stationery.

Dear Mr. Freeman,

Don't you think the 27 years of faithfull service which Elmer gave to the M.C. & I. Co. warrents some kind of a pension now to help me educate our youngest daughter, she has three years to finish college and it was Elmer's greatest ambition to give the family the best education we could. Tharen had entered College here and is working three hours at night, but I don't see how I can keep her in school with what she is making and the $15.00 per week I get from the State Compensation.

As you know, Elmer was doing the work of two men, that of mine foreman and mining engineer, without any extra compensation except what coal we used during the winter months. When I would get after Elmer about working on the map late at night, sometimes he would say, "maby this will mean a pension for us someday."

I was working in the alterations dept. at I Magnin's store but had a bad spell and the Dr. said I was crowding my heart being stooped over so much sewing so I had to quit.

If you think the work Elmer did for your Co. before he was so cruelly snatched from us is deserving even a small pension I can assure you it will be appreciated. I like California as well I could like any place without Elmer. Having family here helps a lot but outside of Elmer's working hours we were always together so I get very lonely for him.

Please let me hear from you.

Sincerely,
Mrs. Margaret Price

Freeman dictated a response a week later.

Dear Mrs. Price:

I received your letter of October 1st, and notice that you think that payment of some kind should be made to the Estate left by Elmer in appreciation of his long services for the Company.

Mrs. Murray and others have made a similar request and these applications will be considered at the next Directors' meeting of the Company, which will be held on December 15th.

The explosion just about put the Company out of business financially and it has been quite a struggle to raise money enough to open up the new Smith Mine. In view of the financial condition of the company it will not be in a position to help the widows to any great extent. Your letter, however, will be acted upon at the Meeting and I will let you know what the Directors of the Company decide to do shortly after the meeting is held.

I am glad that you like California. I have always liked to be there myself during the winter months.

> *With best wishes, I am,*
> Sincerely yours,
> JAMES Freeman
> Vice President.

None of the women widowed by the Smith Mine disaster ever received compensation from the company.

20 The Crash

This wasn't the graduation ceremony Melvin Anderson had envisioned. Yes, he'd survived all those tedious days of school. And, yes, he would walk away with a diploma in his hand. But the rest of the event lacked the glitter that should have made the day indelible. Instead, the late-May ritual was a blunt reminder of all that had changed since he'd started his senior year. Back in September, his biggest problem seemed to be getting busted for cutting class, and his biggest headache was negotiating his on-again, off-again relationship with his girlfriend. Now, life itself was a challenge for all the bereft, though at least the ordinary days offered the emotional shelter of routine. On special occasions like this, when everyone was supposed to be happy, their wounds were unduly exposed. There was so much missing. The applause when the principal called the graduates' names was muted because so many of the hands clapping belonged to women and children and so few to men. The crowd was sparse, with seats that should have been filled with uncles and grandfathers and cousins remaining empty. And after Melvin and his friends had been declared high school graduates, there were not nearly enough proud fathers kissing their daughters' cheeks or patting their sons' shoulders.

One of the lawyers who represented Montana Coal and Iron during the inquest gave the graduation speech. No record remains of what he said to inspire the graduates. Eight students should have gotten diplomas from Bearcreek High that year, but one of them had dropped out when she moved to Billings to live with her older brother. Of the remaining seven graduates of the class of 1943, five had lost their fathers to the Smith Mine. These included Frankie Mourich, who came back from his new role as a Naval Aviation Cadet to graduate as salutatorian; Betty Hunter, who'd lost her father and stepfather-to-be in the Smith Mine; and, of course, Melvin, whose father had so wanted his children to get a good education. Without that expectation and without that man to please, Melvin had decided to work construction until he figured out what else to do.

More than half the junior class was fatherless, too, but for some reason *The Bear Facts* staff overlooked this fact when naming the upcoming class "The Lucky Seven." They dedicated an entire page of the school year's last issue to the class of 1944, whose motto would be "We Stand Prepared." The page featured a drawing of a large die showing seven dots. It was surrounded by sketches of each junior and a description of their "lucky" attribute. Jane Laird had a Lucky Voice. Each of the other girls had either a Lucky Smile, Lucky Ambition, or a Lucky Figure. One of the two boys in the class was deemed to have Lucky Good Looks, and the other was Lucky in Love. Thelma Mourich had Lucky Hair.

Thelma had already lost the first man in her life. She wasn't about to lose the second. So, on the June day when her steady boyfriend, Eli, was scheduled to leave town to go to war, she married him. He was packed and ready to board the bus at the Red Lodge depot. They left his bags in the car and climbed the steps of the county courthouse. Eli knew the city clerk and had brought enough money with him to keep seventeen-year-old Thelma out of trouble. *Take this*, he said to the clerk as he handed him some cash, *and promise you won't post our marriage in the newspaper or tell anyone about it*. The man agreed, though they needn't have worried much about the newspa-.

per notice. Soon after the disaster, the *Billings Gazette* had stopped running a Bearcreek column in the women's section of the paper, as if the town and its social happenings were already nonexistent. With their privacy secure, Eli only needed to find two souls to witness the ceremony. But whom could he trust? He ran outside and found two drunks, dragged them into the courthouse, and relaxed in the knowledge that they wouldn't remember enough to tattle.

Immediately after becoming man and wife, Eli and Thelma rushed to catch his bus. Eli was one of about forty young men heading to Butte for his medical examination before being inducted into the military. By August he would be stationed at an Army Air Force basic training center in Utah. Thelma didn't know when she'd see him again. They stood around with the other overwrought young couples and weary families, everyone trying to be brave and cheerful, but many certainly failing. Thelma kissed her husband good-bye and watched him go, alone, on what should have been their honeymoon.

Either the bribe had been too meager or the witnesses not drunk enough, but somehow Thelma's mother found out she was sharing her home with another married woman. The next thing Thelma knew, they were sitting on a train headed for California. In San Francisco, where her mother's sister had settled, her mother would get a job with a baking company and Thelma would enroll in a big city high school for her senior year. Frankie Jr. was on his way to a naval detachment in Butte before heading overseas.

But the move hardly cured Thelma of her flirtatious ways. She met a sailor at a hotel bar who said he wanted to marry her. She accepted the proposal and even sent him letters for a while before dropping him. Her mother, once again homesick for Montana, moved them back to Bearcreek after six months. This time they rode the bus. But even getting back to her grandparents and high school friends didn't settle Thelma. She began dating a Red Lodge boy without ever mentioning she was married to Eli. Eventually, of course, someone told him.

"I heard I was going out with a married woman," he said to Thelma.

"Well," she replied, "believe him or believe me."

She eventually realized how selfishly she'd been acting. But at the time, she honestly didn't think she was doing anything wrong as she cheated on her husband. Who knows whether she had been bolstering herself against further grief or whether post-traumatic stress was distorting her judgment. Maybe, after burying so many loved ones, she'd become fatalistic: if death could come at any moment, why not just live? Whatever the cause, her hair might have been lucky after all. Because of a bad knee, Eli was discharged before ever engaging in combat. He eventually learned about some of Thelma's shenanigans, but forgave her anyway.

Fannie Wakenshaw was a far more faithful war bride. She lived with Mary and Bobby in Billings while her husband fought the war. She welcomed him back at the end, but her loyalty didn't fortify the union; the couple divorced six years later. Another Bearcreek pair who'd married shortly before the mine disaster didn't even make it that long. Melvin's brother, Elmer, and his wife split up long before their second anniversary.

Margaret Meiklejohn's marriage would endure, but maybe that was because she didn't rush into it. With her wedding already delayed by the disaster, she took some time to heal herself. She stayed in Washington state for almost a month before returning to her fiancée in Bearcreek. On June 27, exactly four months after she'd stood by the window waiting for her father to come home, she and John drove to Billings, applied for a marriage license, and got married. She had no parents or siblings to witness the event.

As the foothills turned brown from the dry summer heat, some things returned to normal. Cowboys, bull riders, calf ropers, and a double-jointed clown came to town for the annual Fourth of July rodeo in Red Lodge. The multi-day event was shorter due to the war—so many cowboys had traded their wide brims for bullet-resistant helmets—but one of the largest crowds ever showed up to cheer for the competitors. The local band played the usual patriotic songs, but they didn't sound the same without Emil Anderson on the trumpet.

His wife and daughter weren't around to miss his music. In early June, Agnes and Doris went to live in Washington state. Thirty friends and relatives gave them a handkerchief shower the day before they left. Elmer stayed in Carbon County. He'd already left his Bureau of Mines job and gone to work in one of the Montana Coal and Iron mines. His family couldn't believe he would trade his office job for the assignment that had killed his father, but they couldn't talk him out of it. He seemed compelled, his sister thought. Agnes had planned to start over in her new home state, but like so many others, she grew homesick and moved back to Montana before the summer ended. She rented an apartment above a doctor's office on the main drag in Red Lodge and looked for work. One of her best friends, a woman who'd already found a job at JC Penney, dragged her into the drugstore across the street. The owner hired Agnes to operate the soda fountain. Later, she would land a more glamorous gig in a local dress shop.

Doris began her freshman year at Red Lodge High. Despite being one of the new girls, the school year started well for her. She was elected freshman class vice-president, played her father's trumpet in the school band, and was on her way to making first honors for her schoolwork. Melvin's construction career had ended when he broke an ankle on the job, but after recovering he applied for work at the new Smith Mine. He started in September.

Fall was relatively uneventful until Thanksgiving approached. This would involve two more tough firsts: the first traditional family gathering without the head of the household there; the first turkey carved by someone besides Dad. The Saturday night before the holiday, Doris Anderson went with a friend to a shindig at the Catholic church. At the end of the night, she used her last quarter to buy a raffle ticket. The church was giving away a turkey. Doris won it. By the time she got it home, her mother was already in bed.

"Mom," she yelled. "I won a turkey!"

"Put it in the fridge," Agnes said.

"It's alive!"

Wouldn't Melvin be shocked when he came home! But he'd surely be quite late. He was carousing around Red Lodge with his friends. Maybe they'd gone to see *Dead Man's Gulch* at the movies, though Melvin probably would have preferred to wait until Sunday night when the theater would start running *Northern Exposure* with Errol Flynn, one of his favorite actors. Or maybe they had gotten some dinner at the Busy Bee or Natali's. But one activity was certain: Melvin and his friends had spent a good part of the night drinking.

Shortly after two in the morning, they offered a couple of girls a ride back to Bearcreek. The girls were about to hop into Melvin's car when one girl's older brother overheard their conversation. He forbade them from joining the boys because they were too drunk.

Melvin drove, and his best friend Leo Hodnik sat in the passenger's seat. Two other buddies rode in the car behind them. They drove away from the bars and hotels and headed up the big hill that would take them to Bearcreek. It was the same road the rescuers rushed down the day of the disaster, the same road the ambulance and laundry truck drivers took in the opposite direction as they brought the dead miners to the mausoleum.

Melvin was speeding, the gravel under his tires grumbling. He hit the washboards that had rippled the country lane and started bouncing. The car jumped right off the road and into a ditch. It flipped over. Melvin's neck snapped.

The guys in the car behind his saw it all. They stopped short and jumped out. Leo had hurt his head and his knee. His friends helped him up, then all three of them lifted Melvin's limp, lanky body and carried him to the second car. They didn't know that they shouldn't have moved him; they only knew they needed to get him to a doctor. They drove back over the hill to the hospital in Red Lodge. The doctors bandaged Leo and treated him for shock. There was nothing they could do for Melvin.

People rarely take "Class Wills and Prophecies" seriously. But the goofy predictions printed in the year-end issue of *The Bear Facts* would be among the last official records of Melvin Anderson's life. He willed his "ways with women" to a friend in the upcoming class.

"Remember one of Melvin's famous sayings," the paper editors wrote, "and that is never say nothing is impossible."

In the class prophecy, the author imagined running into Melvin decades later, "still as spry as ever" as he "promptly invited me into his beautiful home and introduced me to the family."

They buried him the day before Thanksgiving. His body was laid in an open casket, blue eyes closed, brown curls still soft. A woman sang "Someday We'll Understand." The same minister who'd led the church service before Melvin's graduation now said prayers for him. The friends who'd lived their entire lives with him at their sides carried his coffin out of the chapel. The mourners followed it to the gravesite. They passed Connie's grave with its little stone shoes, skirted the newly settled plots of some forty Smith Mine disaster victims, and slowed down near the fresh stone that marked Emil Anderson's death. Then they lowered his boy into the ground, wept and prayed and wept some more, and tried to go on living.

21 The Survivors

If life worked out the way it's supposed to, everyone who lived through the Smith Mine disaster would have been spared any more heartache for the rest of their lives. The tragedy would have acted like a vaccine against future grief. Instead, it seemed to make many of them more susceptible to bad luck. A disproportionate number of the survivors continued to get bashed by the world.

About a year after the disaster, Mary Wakenshaw found herself attracted to a cowboy whose size and strength reminded her of Bud. Years earlier, through friends, she'd met a range rider who oversaw a government grazing district. One day, he popped up in the Billings store where she worked and asked her to see a show with him. Though he was virtually a stranger, she agreed. Seven months later, still not really knowing the man because he didn't talk much, she married him. She packed herself and Bobby up, rented out her house, and moved to her new husband's rural home in Worden, Montana. For four years, she worked as a postal clerk and telephone operator on top of doing constant farm chores, which included cleaning the milking separator, churning butter, and lugging water to the house. But she didn't want that life forever, so when her husband proposed moving to a big horse ranch where she could work as a cook, Mary opted for divorce instead. She returned to Billings and found a job as a pricer for the Gambles department store. She was soon promoted to the billing department, where she worked until retiring twenty-two years later.

Mary admitted in a written memoir that she should have "left well enuf alone" when it came to men, but then she met another one in 1957 at an Eagles Lodge dance. They married shortly after meeting. Her third husband was a wonderful man, a hard worker, and, unfortunately, an alcoholic. They divorced five years later. Again, Mary kept pushing through her trials. She traveled widely and dedicated herself to volunteer work. When Hollywood came to Montana in the 1970s, she signed up to be an extra in *The Missouri Breaks*. She shared the celluloid with Jack Nicholson and Marlon Brando, appearing onscreen before they did. She sits in a covered buggy with a group of frightened witnesses, all of them shouting and gasping in shock as a thieving cowboy is hanged.

Mary died at age ninety-six, in 2001, in the house she bought with her father's life insurance money. Her ashes are buried in Bud's grave.

Mag Wakenshaw, Bud's mother, married a maintenance engineer she'd met at the hospital where she worked as a cook. She died at age ninety-five, in 1976.

Fannie Wakenshaw divorced Howard Thom in February 1949 and married another man later that year. They had a son and a daughter and stayed together for more than thirty years before separating. She worked as a secretary in various companies for decades and spent her later years taking care of Mary. Fannie died in 2005, a few days after celebrating her eightieth birthday.

Bobby Wakenshaw met the love of his life, Jeanne, in high school. They've been married for close to sixty years and have three grown children and five grandchildren. Bob served four years in the Navy, graduated from Montana State University, and spent most of his career working for the Social Security Administration. He lives in Spokane, Washington. For years he saved the Walnettos he had promised his father.

Thelma Mourich graduated from Bearcreek High School in 1944. The next year, she and Eli welcomed the first of their three children, and Eli started coaching the Bearcreek High School basketball team. Thelma's mother remarried and had her house towed to Red Lodge, breaking up the pair of homes Grandpa Mourich had built for his two sons. After the war, Thelma's brother Frankie graduated from college and spent his life as a chemical engineer.

Thelma's life was relatively uneventful until 1969 when Eli suffered a freak accident. He'd gone into the propane business and had driven to a ranch to make a delivery. He left his truck running and stepped out to close a gate behind him. Before he could make it back to the truck, it ran him over. When Thelma got to the hospital, she could still see tire tracks on Eli's chest. He was in excruciating pain, but he was alert enough to write notes to her.

"I'll never make it," he wrote in one of them. He died after five days in the hospital, at age forty-five. Thelma remarried a colleague of her brother's. Even in middle age, her charm hadn't worn off. Her second husband asked her to marry him the first night they met. They were married for ten years before he died of cancer. Both of her sons also died young: one at age forty-two of cancer and the other at age fifty-four of heart attack. She has a daughter and five grandchildren and lives in Red Lodge.

For a long time after her baby died, Virginia Sommerville would breathe in the strong scent of flowers, like the ones that had filled the funeral parlor, even if there wasn't a petal in sight. Though she couldn't explain the odor, Virginia welcomed it because it made her think Connie was nearby. Virginia spent many nights dreaming about dressing the baby and fixing her hair. Then she had a dream in which she was talking to Jesus.

"Where is Connie?" she asked.

"God's got her," he answered.

That made her feel better, and all the dreams stopped.

But she never stopped breaking into tears when talking about her little girl.

Gil was also brokenhearted about the baby's death. He and Virginia leaned on each other through their grief until he entered the military, where he contracted spinal meningitis. Virginia remembers that he started drinking heavily after his illness. She gave birth to Gil Jr. in 1946—she'd prayed for a boy because she didn't want anyone taking Connie's place—and spent his childhood coddling him. She made sure he ate abundantly and forbade him from going into swimming pools during the polio epidemic. But she didn't take care of herself nearly as well. Gil Sr. started hitting her after their son was born.

He split her lip once, and she ended up in the hospital another time because she wanted to leave a veterans club before Gil was ready. She waited for him in the lounge. When he found her there, he knocked her unconscious. Then, like so many abusive men, he lay under her bed all night apologizing. She put up with the abuse because he was "a prince of a person" when he wasn't drunk. She eventually befriended her mailman, a man who gave her the courage to leave Gil after nearly twenty years of marriage. She married the mailman a couple of years later, and the union lasted until he died thirty years after that. Gil Sr. spent the last ten years of his life sober. He once told his son that he always knew what he did while he was drunk was wrong, but that he couldn't stop himself.

Gil Jr., who lives with his wife in Bearcreek, was a firefighter for thirty-three years.

"I always wanted to help people," he said.

He has three grown children and lives across the street from Virginia, who, after decades of moving around Wyoming and Montana, returned to Bearcreek in 2000. On the frame of her front door she nailed a mezuzah, a decorative holder for a tiny copy of the Ten Commandments that traditionally marks Jewish homes. Virginia isn't Jewish and didn't know the history of her ornament when she bought it. She put it up, she said, "to keep evil spirits away."

Ann Sudar, whose husband, John, had been one of Emil's companions in the barricaded air pocket, died of carbon monoxide poisoning in her home years later. John's baby girl, now a grandmother, still has the helmet on which he wrote his good-bye message.

Two of the killed miners' sons died in World War II. James Laird, brother of Jane and son of Ned, died in January 1945 when his ship was torpedoed. His mother received his Purple Heart. According to available records, only forty-seven men in all of Carbon County died in the war.

After Margaret Meiklejohn married John Cameron, they lived in the house she had shared with her dad. She had some trouble getting on with her life. In the mornings, "I'd start to go make his breakfast and look to see if he was coming." She had difficulty sleeping. A doctor advised John to move her from the house because her "nerves" were getting to her. They moved to Red Lodge, where they ran a candy store for many years. Margaret has one son and still lives in Red Lodge.

During a panel discussion commemorating the sixtieth anniversary of the disaster, she admitted that she'd lost faith in God afterward. "I was very bitter," she said. "It took me a long time to get my faith back."

Eight years after the disaster, Loren Newman, with whom Margaret had battled during the inquest, became a state mine inspector.

Elmer Price's daughter, Tharen, eventually received an associate's degree in Los Angeles. Montana Coal and Iron never helped with tuition costs, so Tharen, her mother, and her sister worked to pay the bulk of them. Elmer's wife, Margaret, never remarried. She remained angry that the company never acknowledged that Elmer had warned them about a potential explosion.

For years after the disaster, Doris Anderson had a hard time crying. She would watch people weeping at movies and find herself miffed. Why cry over fiction when there were so many real and important things to cry about, she wondered. But Doris and her mother, Agnes, were among the disaster witnesses who went on to build happy lives. Agnes married another good man in 1946, had a second daughter, and lived to be ninety-five. Doris was married for thirty-three years before becoming a widow. She has four children, two grandchildren, and five great-grandchildren. She lives in a small town close to Bearcreek.

Her older brother, Elmer, would marry three more times after his first divorce and father six children. He drank heavily for many years, but sobered up before dying in his early sixties.

Less than a year after Melvin's death, the road between Red Lodge and Bearcreek was resurfaced with a "nonskid" mixture of oil and rough gravel to ease miners' travels to and from work.

Dr. Oleinik took a job with the Veterans Administration in Helena soon after the disaster, but he didn't stay long. Maybe because his best efforts couldn't save the miners, he sought a different kind of challenge. He moved to an extremely impoverished Mississippi town to practice medicine. There he met and married a social worker more than twenty years his junior. They had a daughter, who lives in Seattle. The doctor eventually returned to Carbon County. He died in 1967 after falling off a ladder while pruning trees. He had broken his neck.

Blast survivor Willard Reid remained in California working at the sugar refinery. The Montana Coal and Iron management repeatedly asked him to come back to work in the mine. Reid's relatives decided the matter for him at a family meeting. His wife, sons, and father-in-law, who'd been a miner himself, voted against his return-ing to mining, so he wrote to the company and declined any further employment.

It took about three years for his physical wounds to heal com-pletely. But the psychic pain lasted much longer. The freight train sound of rushing wind visited him in his sleep, and he'd wake star-tled from the nightmares. He never blamed anyone for the tragedy, according to his son, but would just say, "They hit a pocket of gas and it exploded."

About five years after the disaster, he ran into fellow survivor Eli Houtonen while in Red Lodge on vacation. It was the first time they'd seen each other since the disaster. Eli wasn't doing well. The once easy-going, jolly man had grown despondent. He'd lost some hearing and had been ordered by doctors never to work again.

"Why didn't you leave me there?" he asked Reid. "I would have been better off."

"Would you have left me there?" Reid replied.

"No," Houtonen said, "I guess I wouldn't."

Though Houtonen's son would say his life ended the day of the accident, he actually died in 1964. The third survivor, Alex Haw-thorne, died in 1960. Reid died in 1988, one day after the forty-fifth anniversary of the disaster.

G. O. Arnold suffered personal heartache, too. There are no reports of why he left the Bureau of Mines so abruptly after the disaster, though his records may have been destroyed. A Freedom of Informa-tion Act request yielded nothing on him; despite the extensive docu-ments he composed about the case, the U.S. government officially has no record of his employment.

He spent time as a mining engineer in Denver. According to his grandniece, he also joined his father-in-law's mine in Colorado, pos-sibly working as a bookkeeper. The family sold the mine in the early 1950s, and the only information on Arnold's further work history consists of a line in his obituary stating that he retired as a Denver cab driver.

His only daughter, Jane, grew into a stunning woman, very cultured, ladylike, funny, and intelligent, who worked as a newspaper reporter in California. She also became a raging alcoholic. According to her former sister-in-law, the Arnolds did all they could to save her. She was married twice and had two children. Her second husband kidnapped and gained legal custody of their son because of her drinking. Her daughter and grandson live in New Mexico. The grandson, Nathan Adams, fondly remembers G. O. Arnold, but said all the memorabilia that he left behind burned in a house fire. Jane choked to death in an alcohol-related incident at about forty-three years of age.

Arnold was a "quiet gentleman," his grandniece said. He lived in a retirement community at end of his life and was quite sought after by ladies because of his manners. He outlived two wives and died in 1984.

Early in 1944, Tony Boyle persuaded Montana Coal and Iron to give each family of a deceased miner fifty dollars in vacation pay. In 1947 he gave an inspiring but ironic speech at a ceremony to dedicate a memorial to the mine disaster victims.

Standing before red granite stones carved with each man's name, he referenced the Bible. "Am I my brother's keeper?" he asked. "Ever since the day when the Lord said unto Cain, 'where is Abel, thy brother?' and the first murderer replied, 'I know not. Am I my brother's keeper?' the question of responsibility for the lives of others has rested upon man. The Lord set a mark upon Cain. And we bear the responsibility today. We *are* our brothers' keeper, and as such it is our duty to so shape the affairs of the coal mining industry that never again will it be necessary for men to die in coal mine explosions."

But then something changed in this man who at one time seemed to sincerely want to help miners. In 1948 he moved to Washington DC to serve as assistant to United Mine Workers president John Lewis.

In 1952, according to author Stuart Brown, a union employee filed a suit claiming he'd been fired for refusing to follow Boyle's order to murder two coal operators. And in 1957, Boyle testified *against* a mine safety bill in Montana because the coal mine his brother ran would have been shut down if it had passed, according to author Trevor Armbrister. He took over as president of the union in 1963. His apathy for working miners became clear immediately after the 1968 Farmington, West Virginia, mine disaster, which killed seventy-eight men. Rather than demand an investigation, Boyle made a speech in which he called the coal company that owned the mine "cooperative and safety-conscious," and deemed the deaths part of the "inherent danger" of mining. The following year, a man named Jock Yablonski ran against him for union president. Though Boyle hung onto his job, Yablonski was in the process of challenging the election results when he, his wife, and his daughter were murdered in their home. Boyle was convicted of ordering the murders and sentenced to three consecutive life terms. He died of a heart attack in prison in 1985.

Shortly after the disaster, W. R. Freeman, who had claimed to have quit Montana Coal and Iron, went to work for the company in Washington state. His brother James transferred him to sales at a reduced salary. W.R.'s grandson Wayne Freeman said a genetic predisposition to mental illness kicked in after the disaster. W.R. once told the boy he was building a bridge out of grass. Wayne's parents urged him not to take anything W.R. said seriously because he was crazy. W.R. died in 1945 of heart failure. Wayne's father, a mine employee who had helped with the rescue, also battled mental illness. He began to pull the hair from his head and his eyebrows one strand at a time, and to hide in closets. Wayne supposes that survivor's guilt and grief triggered their breakdowns.

James Freeman hired the man who had accompanied Arnold on the initial mine inspection to replace his brother W.R. as the Smith Mine superintendent in September 1943. In a letter to the president of Montana Coal and Iron, James wrote, "If we can get Mr. Evans to take the job, the fact that he is an employee of the Bureau of Mines will prove to others, our desire to get a Superintendent who is safety-minded."

That same month, James wrote in a letter to the governor of Montana that he was "greatly interested in making the Montana Coal & Iron Company mines the safest in Montana."

But two years after the disaster, federal inspectors found that the company was still shirking on safety. Among the 1945 recommendations: control the coal dust better, set up an organized safety program, improve electrical safety, add fire protection underground, and improve timbering. The inspection report also noted that injuries in the Smith's Number 2 seam had increased during the first nine months of 1944 and that workers still weren't using permissible shot-firing devices when blasting, or testing for methane before and after blasting. The mine's ventilation was better, according to the report, all underground workers had self-rescuers, and smoking in the mine had been prohibited.

The Smith, which had reopened a few months after the disaster, closed for good two years later due to financial strain. But James continued to try to keep the company afloat. Among his failures: strip mining that yielded low-quality coal, and making up for a slack coal deficit by digging out old, poor-quality slack from a storage pit, both actions bringing serious customer complaints; borrowing $100,000 in the early 1950s to open and develop a new Smith Mine, against the advice of his manager and brother; and investing in a cobalt and copper mine that never turned a profit. On James's watch, the company sold six thousand acres of Carbon County coal lands to pay several years of back taxes.

In 1950, Montana Coal and Iron lost the Great Western Sugar Company contract, on which it had depended since the 1910s, to another coal company. The company lost the cement contract, too. And the Montana Power Company and Anaconda Copper Mining

Company dropped their contracts after they both converted to natural gas.

Railroad changes ultimately killed Montana Coal and Iron. First, trains began to run on diesel fuel instead of steam, so they didn't need coal anymore. Then, in 1953, the train line stopped running to Bearcreek. The company would have had to haul the coal to Red Lodge for transport, another expensive proposition. Instead, it closed forever that June.

James eventually moved to California. He died there in 1973.

On the first anniversary of the disaster, 150 people filled the Bearcreek High School gym for a memorial service. Schools were closed for the day, and miners stopped working during the ceremony. On the tenth anniversary, Montana Coal and Iron ordered wreaths for the monument that stands in the cemetery. And on the fiftieth anniversary, a memorial ceremony was held at a local senior center. The names of all the dead miners were read during a candle-lighting ceremony, and the Red Lodge churches tolled their bells at exactly 9:37 a.m., when the explosion presumably occurred.

Bearcreek High, built large in anticipation of the town's continuing growth, closed in 1950. It was dismantled brick by brick. All that remains are the stone wall, an old swing set, and a merry-go-round the elementary school kids played on when their classes shared the building. The whitewashed "B" is still on the hill. No one knows what happened to the basketball championship trophies.

Notes

All italicized statements are paraphrases rather than direct quotes, indicating that the information supplied is either how I remember it or a summary of what the speaker would have said based on written or other confirmed documents. All non-italicized quotes are direct.

Information about the Smith Mine inspection, explosion, and inquest comes from official reports by the Montana Coal Operator's Association, the Montana Governor's Committee, the federal Bureau of Mines, the Montana State Mine Inspectors, and Montana Coal and Iron (see the bibliography). Information on mining law comes from the *Laws of Montana* of 1909, 1911, 1941, and 1945.

INTRODUCTION

xvi **On Election Day in 2005:** Bearcreek's next mayoral election did not occur until 2009.

xvi **A gray-bearded:** Denny Becker is the owner of "A Teton Treehouse" in Wilson, Wyoming.

xvii **The only reason:** Some sources give the length of the Beartooth Highway as 65 or 67 miles, but byways.org, the Web site of the National Scenic Byways Program, states it is 68.7 miles long.

xx **"In a perfect world":** Cecil Roberts, "Mining in a Perfect World," September 7, 2007, www.huffingtonpost.com.

2. THE INSPECTION

20 **It should have been:** Inspections were not required prior to the passage of the Coal Mine Inspection Act of 1941.

21 **His wife called him:** Arnold's great-grandson Nathan Adams supplied the "Gerry" anecdote.

22 **That would be his youngest brother:** James Freeman was usually called "J.M.," but I will refer to him as James throughout the book to avoid confusion with his brother W.R.

22 **On Friday nights:** These anecdotes are from one of Freeman's nephews, Rev. Jim Beadle.

26 **More than fifteen years:** See Deike, "Ten Years of Safety Service with Closed Lights."

28 **"If I thought the mine":** This recollection of the post-inspection meeting comes from Arnold's reports and inquest testimony. James Freeman never made an official statement on what happened during the meeting, though other alleged witnesses would later claim that he offered to shut the mine down, but Arnold refused.

4. THE UNION

40 **He convinced:** All information on bills Boyle introduced or supported comes from inquest testimony.

44 **His brother James:** According to the U.S. Bureau of Labor Statistics Consumer Price Index inflation calculator, the $1,000 per month that James Freeman earned would have had the same buying power as $12,518 in 2008. If that figure is considered equal to monthly earnings, it would add up to a yearly salary of about $150,000. Freeman often earned much more than $1,000 a month.

45 **Years later:** See Lockard, *Coal: A Memoir and Critique*.

46 **Fifty percent:** The carbon monoxide saturation figure is from the United States Mine Rescue Association and the American Lung Association.

46 **Oleinik testified:** Oleinik spoke about the Montana Supreme Court case during his inquest testimony, but no evidence of the case could be found. It might not have actually reached the state supreme court, despite the miner's attempt to bring it there.

6. THE NOTEBOOK

58 **Meiklejohn must have:** All information on Meiklejohn's last week of work comes from inquest testimony.

62 **Meiklejohn met up with:** Jeff McNeish developed this reconstruction of what happened to Meiklejohn based on his reconstruction of the disaster. See McNeish, *Long March toward Tragedy*, 132.

7. THE EXPLOSION

66 **Their eyes would never:** The impossibility of adjusting to complete dark was explained by Bob Oxner, my tour guide through the Bull Mountain coal mine.

10. THE TRAVELERS

98 **The Freemans consulted:** The *Carbon County News* reported that the Freemans didn't arrive in Bearcreek until Wednesday, four days after the explosion. No other reports were found that confirmed or disputed that report.

13. THE BELOVED

119 **Though he'd filed:** This time frame is from a printed response Arnold submitted to the company's post-disaster report.

14. THE GOOD-BYES

128 **Or maybe David:** The report that John Sommerville was found with his head in his father's lap came from a family relative. Other reports had them found lying side by side.

134 **Eventually, Elmer would:** The board bearing Emil Anderson's message is on display at the Montana Museum of Western History in Helena.

16. THE CLUES

Most details about the investigation come from Davies's reports, written after the post-disaster inspection.

148 **As his neighbors:** Owens's letter was published in the *Carbon County News* on February 24, 1993, after Owens's grandson Ty Ransdell sent it in. It was written on March 10, 1943. Though Ransdell refers to Jim Owens as a sergeant in his cover letter, newspaper reports at the time of the disaster list him as still holding the rank of corporal.

154 **James Freeman also continued:** Freeman's letters are located at the Montana Historical Society.

18. THE INQUEST

170 **"Yes, sir," he said:** All inquest quotes come from *The State of Montana,*

County of Carbon, In the Matter of the Inquest over the 74 Bodies of Certain Persons There Lying Dead, April 12, 1943.

170 **A recent development:** See Jack Thomas's anniversary article on the Cocoanut Grove fire, "The Cocoanut Grove Inferno."

173 **The 1911 laws:** See *Laws of Montana*, 1911, Chapter 120.

Bibliography

OFFICIAL REPORTS

Arnold, G. O., F. J. Bailey, and M. C. McCall. *Final Report of Mine Explosion, Smith Mine, Montana Coal & Iron Company, Washoe, Carbon County, Montana, February 27, 1943.* Washington DC: U.S. Department of the Interior, Bureau of Mines, n.d.

Arnold, G. O., and M. R. Evans. *Coal Mine Inspection Report, Smith Mine, Montana Coal & Iron Company, Washoe Montana, November 19 to 30, 1942.* Washington DC: U.S. Department of the Interior, Bureau of Mines, n.d.

Boyle, W. A., Joe Masini, and Joe Yanchisin. United Mine Workers of America. *Report of Mine Explosion Smith Mine, Montana Coal & Iron Company, Washoe, Carbon County, Montana, February 27, 1943.* n.d.

Buckingham, D. F. Montana Coal Operators Ass'n. Letter to Governor's Committee regarding explosion. July 10, 1943.

Dalrymple, R. H., Abe Douglass, and William Redshaw. *Report of the Governor's Committee Appointed to Investigate the Coal Mine Disaster at Bear Creek, Montana.* July 22, 1943.

Davies, Edward, and Henry, Ben. *Report on Explosion by Montana State Mine Inspectors.* Billings, Montana. May 3, 1943.

Freeman, J. M., and W. A. Romek. *Report on a Mine Explosion That Occurred at the Smith Mine, Washoe, Montana on February 27, 1943–Montana Coal and Iron Company.* Billings, Montana. June 10, 1943.

The State of Montana, County of Carbon, In the Matter of the Inquest over the 74 Bodies of Certain Persons There Lying Dead. April 12, 1943.

G. O. Arnold also submitted several supplementary papers: "Abstracts and Excerpts from Report of Company"; "Explanation of Graph Pertaining to Fire Bosses' Records"; "Comments on Report on Explosion by the United Mine Workers of America"; "Comments on Report on Explosion by Montana State Mine Inspectors"; "Preliminary Federal Mine Inspection Report of November 19 to 30, 1942"; and "Conclusions."

UNPUBLISHED SOURCES

Freeman, James. Letters. Montana Historical Society.

Freeman, Thelma "Stub." "Smith Mine Disaster." April 1984.

Heidenreich, Virginia Louise Clark. "Bearcreek, Montana: A Coal Mining Community." PhD diss., George Washington University, 1977.

Joliet Wranglers 4-H Club. "A History of Carbonado and Boyd." N.d.

Kommers, Vernetta Shepard. "Personal Account of Smith Mine and Montana Coal and Iron History." June 1991.

Pelo, Marvin. "This I Remember: The Pelo Childhood 1923–1944." Mid-1970s.

Romek, William. Memoir. October 1984.

Wakenshaw, Mary Sumicek. Personal memoir. N.d.

Wright, Wendy. "The End of a Mining Legacy: The Freeman/McIntosh Families." N.d.

PUBLISHED SOURCES

Act of Vengeance. VHS. Directed by John Mackenzie. Telepictures Productions, 1985.

Against the Darkness: A Tribute to the Montana Coal Miner. VHS. Produced by Montana Department of State Lands and Silvertip Productions, 1988.

Anderson, Paul. "There Is Something Wrong Down Here: The Smith Mine Disaster, Bearcreek, Montana, 1943." *Montana: The Magazine of Western History*, Spring 1988, 2–13.

Armbrister, Trevor. *Act of Vengeance: The Yablonski Murders and Their Solution*. New York: Saturday Review Press, 1975.

Axline, Jon. "Something of a Nuisance Value: The Montana, Wyoming & Southern Railroad, 1905–1953." *Montana: The Magazine of Western History*, Winter 1999, 48–63.

Blast: Brownie's Vigil at Smith Mine. Audio cassette. Directed, written, and produced by Wayne H. Freeman, 1992.

Brown, Stuart. *A Man Named Tony: The True Story of the Yablonski Murders.* New York: Norton, 1976.

Chadwick, Robert A. "Coal: Montana's Prosaic Treasure." *Montana: The Magazine of Western History*, Autumn 1973, 18–31.

Christensen, Bonnie. *Red Lodge and the Mythic West.* Lawrence: University Press of Kansas, 2002.

Deike, George H. "Ten Years of Safety Service with Closed Lights." *Mine Inspectors Institute of America*, May 19, 1925, 156–72.

DeMarchi, Jane. *Historical Mining Disasters.* Beckley WV: National Mine Health and Safety Academy, 1997.

Diamond, Jared. *Collapse: How Societies Choose to Fail or Succeed.* New York: Viking Penguin, 2005.

Doig, Ivan. *This House of Sky: Landscapes of a Western Mind.* New York: Harcourt, 1978.

Dubofsky, Melvyn, and Warren Van Tine. *John L. Lewis: A Biography.* Champaign: University of Illinois Press, 1986.

"Farewell Notes of Entombed Miners to Loved Ones Tell Story of Heroic Men." *United Mine Workers Journal*, April 1943, 9.

Franklin, Ben A. "Case of the Persistent Prosecutor." *New York Times*, September 9, 1973.

Freese, Barbara. *Coal: A Human History.* Cambridge MA: Perseus Books Group, 2003.

Giesen, Carol A. B. *Coal Miners' Wives: Portraits of Endurance.* Lexington: University Press of Kentucky, 1995.

Goodell, Jeff. *Big Coal: The Dirty Secret behind America's Energy Future.* Boston: Houghton Mifflin, 2006.

Greene, Melissa Fay. *Last Man Out: The Story of the Springhill Mine Disaster.* New York: Harcourt, 2003.

Harlan County, USA. VHS. Directed by Barbara Kopple. Cabin Creek Films, 1977.

Hemingway, Ernest. *For Whom the Bell Tolls.* New York: Scribner, 1940.

Hickam, Homer. *The Coalwood Way.* New York: Delacorte Press, 2000.

———. *We Are Not Afraid.* Florida: Health Communications, 2002.

Howard, Joseph Kinsey. *Montana: High, Wide, and Handsome.* 1943. Reprint, Lincoln: University of Nebraska Press, 2003.

Kauffman, Marv. "Geology of the Red Lodge Area." http://www.ybra.org.

Kittredge, William. Foreword. *The WPA Guide to 1930s Montana.* Tucson:
University of Arizona Press, 1994. Originally published as *Montana: A
State Guide Book* by the Department of Agriculture, Labor, and Industry,
State of Montana, 1939.

Kittredge, William, and Annick Smith, eds. *The Last Best Place: A Montana
Anthology.* Helena: Montana Historical Society, 1988.

Kommers, Vernetta Shepard. *Along the Creek . . . A History of Washoe.* N.p.,
1969.

Kuhlman, Fay. *Bearcreek Montana: A Town Unique.* Bearcreek MT: The Bearcreek Banner, n.d.

Kuhlman, Fay, and Gary Robson. *The Darkest Hour: A Comprehensive Account of the Smith Mine Disaster of 1943.* 2nd ed. Montana: Red Lodge
Books, 2003.

LaFlamme, Lon. *Black Lies.* Lincoln NE: Writer's Showcase Presented by
Writer's Digest, 2000.

Laws of Montana. 1909, 1911, 1941, 1945.

Leamer, Laurence. "Tony Boyle, Arnold Miller and the Ghost of John L.
Lewis." *New York Times,* November 26, 1972.

Lesch, John E. *The First Miracle Drugs: How the Sulfa Drugs Transformed
Medicine.* New York: Oxford University Press, 2007.

Lewis, Arthur H. *Murder by Contract: The People v. "Tough Tony" Boyle.* New
York: Macmillan, 1975.

Linderman, Frank B. *Plenty-Coups: Chief of the Crows.* 1930. Reprint, Lincoln: University of Nebraska Press, 2002.

Lockard, Duane. *Coal: A Memoir and Critique.* Charlottesville: University
Press of Virginia, 1998.

Lynch, Martin. *Mining in World History.* London: Reaktion Books, 2002.

Maclean, Norman. *Young Men and Fire.* Chicago: University of Chicago
Press, 1992.

Matewan. DVD. Directed by John Sayles. Cinecom Pictures, 1987.

McCullough, David. *The Johnstown Flood: The Incredible Story Behind One
of the Most Devastating Disasters America Has Ever Known.* New York:
Simon & Schuster, 1968.

McNeish, Jeffrey E., *Smith Mine Disaster Chronicles.* 3 vols. *Sons of America,
Brothers Underground: Remembering the Victims of Montana's Smith Mine
No. 3; Long March toward Tragedy: Events Surrounding Montana's Smith
Mine No. 3; Quiet Courage: Media Accounts of Montana's Smith Mine No. 3
Disaster.* Jeffrey Edward McNeish, 2007.

McPhee, John. *Rising from the Plains*. New York: Farrar, Strauss and Giroux, 1986.

"Mine Union Chief Denounces Foes." *New York Times*, September 3, 1964.

Olsen, Gregg. *The Deep Dark: Disaster and Redemption in America's Richest Silver Mine*. New York: Crown Publishers, 2005.

Podolsky, Scott H. Review of *Pneumonia before Antibiotics: Therapeutic Evolution and Evaluation in Twentieth Century America*, by Daniel M. Musher. *New England Journal of Medicine* 355 (2006): 2051–52.

Punke, Michael. *Fire and Brimstone: The North Butte Mining Disaster of 1917*. New York: Hyperion, 2006.

The Smith Mine Disaster: 60 Years Afterwards. DVD. Carbon County Historical Society, 2003.

Stafford, William. *The Way It Is: New and Selected Poems*. St. Paul: Graywolf Press, 1998.

Stern, Gerald. *The Buffalo Creek Disaster*. New York: Random House, 1976.

Thomas, Jack. "The Cocoanut Grove Inferno." *Boston Globe*, November 22, 1992.

Toole, K. Ross. *Not in Precious Metals Alone*. Helena: Montana Historical Society Press, 1976.

Zupan, Shirley. *History of Red Lodge*. Red Lodge MT: Carbon County Historical Society, 1989.

Zupan, Shirley, and Harry J. Owens. *Red Lodge: Saga of a Western Area*. Red Lodge MT: Carbon County Historical Society, 1979.